APPROXIMATE GESTURES

APPROXIMATE GESTURES
INFINITE SPACES IN THE FICTION OF
PERCIVAL EVERETT

ANTHONY STEWART

Louisiana State University Press
Baton Rouge

Published by Louisiana State University Press
www.lsupress.org

Designer: Barbara Neely Bourgoyne
Typeface: Whitman
Cover image: suteishi/iStockPhoto.com

Library of Congress Cataloging-in-Publication Data
Names: Stewart, Anthony, 1964– author.
Title: Approximate gestures : infinite spaces in the fiction of Percival Everett / Anthony Stewart.
Description: Baton Rouge : Louisiana State University Press, [2020] | Includes bibliographical
    references and index.
Identifiers: LCCN 2019048797 (print) | LCCN 2019048798 (ebook) | ISBN 978-0-8071-7264-3
    (cloth ; alk. paper) | ISBN 978-0-8071-7383-1 (pdf) | ISBN 978-0-8071-7384-8 (epub)
Subjects: LCSH: Everett, Percival—Criticism and interpretation. | Everett, Percival—Characters. |
    Race in literature.
Classification: LCC PS3555.V34 Z87 2020 (print) | LCC PS3555.V34 (ebook) | DDC 813/.54—dc23
LC record available at https://lccn.loc.gov/2019048797
LC ebook record available at https://lccn.loc.gov/2019048798

To Claire and Campbell

CONTENTS

PREFACE

On the Importance of Warning Signs and Inhabiting Our Uncertainty

By definition a cave must have an opening large enough to allow a human to enter. The cavity can be wind- or water-eroded. It can break miles and miles deep. But it must let a person enter. And that is what is scary about caves, that one can enter.

—*Wounded*

The novel is my way of making meaning.

—Percival Everett, interview with Anne-Laure Tissut

While listening to the podcast *The Wilderness*, which discusses how the Democratic Party might find itself out of the political wilderness following the 2016 presidential election, I was faced with one of the age-old problems of criticism and, for that matter, the problem inherent in expressing any informed opinion, evaluation, or observation at all. Rebecca Traister, the author of *Good and Mad: The Revolutionary Power of Women's Anger,* was attempting to explain what initially appeared in the weeks after the election as something of a statistical curiosity. She was trying to explain why 53 percent of white American women might have voted for the current president when their alternative was herself a white woman. Traister's explanation is based on the notion of minority rule. She stated that the only way a minority—straight white men—stays in power is by dividing the interests of the majority, by "offering incentives to portions of the majority, trying to get them to support your rule. And so there are all kinds of incentives on offer to white women, who are connected to white men, who are the people who have the disproportionate share of power in this country." She characterizes white women's power position as one of "proximal advantage via their connections to white men" ("Chapter Fourteen"). Traister's argument, which seems completely sound and persuasive, had me thinking about something I wrote almost ten years ago, on the difference between how gender and race are (or are not, in the case of race) discussed in the public sphere in Canada, and, from there, how white women have benefited most from whatever affirmative action programs might have emerged in Canada over time. I wrote then: "Since white straight men are still in the majority when it comes to decision-making positions, their comfort level has been instrumental in the success of affirmative action programs centering on gender" (*You Must Be a Basketball Player* 114). I go on to say that white women "have always simply been more familiar to white men than people of color have been. Obviously, it is much easier to integrate into your own population a group that is already in some ways familiar to you" (114). What I'm recognizing as the benefits that accrue to a group from being familiar to those who hold positions of power Traister calls "proximal advantage."

My point here is not the obvious one that I agree with Traister's assertion. I am pointing out that she was broadcast in 2018 making an assertion that will be new to some (perhaps many) of the people who heard it, a position that I published in 2009. And, again, my point is not that I published this argument at all. My point is to emphasize the contingency of our knowledge at any given moment. Traister's right, and, I believe, I'm right. Our observations may be applied to different areas of political life at different times and in different national contexts, but they coalesce around a simple point about who benefits from the state of minority rule under which we always find ourselves living as inhabitants of North America. But just as we know what we know at any moment, we do not as a matter of habit (or a matter of criticism) think a lot about what else we still don't know. We will never know everything, even as we amass specialized knowledge about any given subject. I am intensely (now) aware of the obvious fact that someone has said this already, too. In fact, just in recent casual reading while waiting for my plane to board, I stumbled across a short article on David Hume, usefully titled "David Hume: Why You're Probably Wrong about Everything You Know," by a writer named Zat Rana, in which he points out a commitment in Hume to living a decent life and concludes that Hume's "story shows how we may learn to do the same by accepting doubt (by acknowledging our own ignorance) and living well in spite of that fact."[1]

This article, of course, in turn led me to a very cursory consideration of the philosophical lineage from Hume to Gilles Deleuze and Félix Guattari, as well as to Richard Rorty, among other thinkers who might have agreed with Rana's assertion: "We don't ever observe or deduce something causing an effect, but rather, we fall into habits of thoughts that are reinforced into us because they anticipate a probabilistic connection." My knowledge of Deleuze, Guattari, and Rorty probably should have led me to an exploration of Hume before now, and perhaps it still will. But it hadn't before the happenstance of encountering Rana's article. The lesson here, in part, is that we must always keep reading. But it also means that we should be at least a little unassuming before adopting the kinds of inflexible positions that bigotry, for instance, mandates as its entire reason for being. At times it can feel that when we produce criticism, we do it provisionally almost, to keep our own ignorance at bay, to push back the darkness of what we do not know. We hope that our *mastery* of a subject (a very telling metaphor, indeed) will conceal our otherwise limitless ignorance, or at least hide it momentarily from ourselves.

But what if, instead of hiding from our uncertainty, we embrace it? What benefits might accrue to us if we embrace our own uncertainty as part of what we do know? After all, what bigotry does, in any of its forms, is attempt to make the world smaller and, for the bigot, perhaps more knowable, by making things more certain. What the bigot does not know does not count. But I will argue here that there are innumerable benefits (the extent of which, of course, we cannot know) latent in not just accepting our uncertainty but embracing it as part of an attempt to look deeply into and appreciate the complexities of the infinite space between categories rather than merely fixing on the categories themselves. One of these benefits cannot help but be a resistance to bigotry, which can only seem a good in itself.

An example of the humility that can emerge from inhabiting our uncertainty comes from my own work on Everett and the coincidence of my having gotten to know him personally. In 2017, he visited the Bucknell campus to give a reading, speak to a class that was studying one of his novels, and subject himself to a recorded conversation with me in front of approximately one hundred people. It was a great event, and I remain appreciative of his generosity with his time. Before the official events began, in a private conversation as we wandered around the little town in which Bucknell is located and I live, I brought up his now well-known (in specific circles) decision to refuse to continue speaking to the South Carolina legislature in 1989, in protest of the Confederate battle flag's presence on the statehouse in Columbia. The *South Carolina Encyclopedia* describes the event this way: "Despite his long absence from South Carolina, he involved himself in state politics when he unexpectedly spoke out against the presence of the Confederate flag atop the State House while participating in both the Elizabeth O'Neill Verner Awards ceremonies and the Spoleto Festival in 1989." This brief account is amusing in its references to Everett's "long absence from South Carolina," his "involving himself" in state politics, and the characterization of his protest as "unexpected." All three locutions suggest the actions of an ungracious and ungrateful guest, a characterization that I think Everett would welcome.

Nevertheless, during our conversation he told me that he had rethought his earlier stand regarding the flag and said that if he had it to do again he would not protest the flag's presence because it serves as an apt warning sign, in the way that a sign that says "Minefield" warns the unsuspecting of the presence of concealed incendiary devices. Surprised and delighted, I asked him to repeat the story and his rethinking later that night as part of our public conversation, which he dutifully did.

There are primarily two points to my telling this story, each significantly related to what follows in this book overall. First, his willingness to rethink a position to which he had previously been deeply committed—especially one as fraught as the presence of the Confederate battle flag in southern life (and even more specifically in the life of South Carolina, almost thirty years before a white supremacist terrorist named Dylann Roof murdered nine parishioners in the Emanuel AME Church in Charleston, SC)—shows a commitment to an ever-widening experience with the world rather than an inflexible adherence to one's own beliefs. But, second, returning to my point about the inevitability of uncertainty within criticism and the incompleteness of our knowledge more generally is the fact (by which I am trying not to be embarrassed—I did not say that inhabiting our uncertainty was going to be easy, though) that his ostensible rethinking as he told it to me did not in fact mark as new a position as I had thought when I heard it from him in 2017. Instead, this is a position he has held since at least 2005. In an interview with Alice Mills and Jack Lanco, collected by Joe Weixlmann in *Conversations with Percival Everett,* Everett says:

"Having said that, I now believe that flag ought to be there, ought to be flown atop the State Capitol, ought to be in that chamber for the reason it tells you what the United States really is. You know, when you walk into a minefield, it helps to have a sign that warns: 'Minefield.' It's a good thing and that's how I feel about the United States. Now I have been in many places in the country, I sometimes tell myself they ought to keep a Confederate flag in hotel rooms, just as a reminder" (91). In other words, fully twelve years before his visit to our campus, he had expressed this view in print (in a book a copy of which I own!). Leaving aside my own feelings about the provenance of this revelation as I have come to understand it, it is worth recognizing that if it hadn't been this, it would have been (and probably is) something else. While I'm glad I eventually became aware of the asynchrony between his saying this and my seeing it, the event itself is worth remarking upon, since I know a fair bit about Everett's work. Nevertheless, I had missed this statement, or at least forgotten it (to cut myself a little slack) until preparing the final draft of this book. The book is actually improved more by the timing of my discovery than by the statement itself, because of what my recounting of this discovery reminds us about the enterprise of criticism. We can't know everything. We are partial in both of the predominant senses of that word—incomplete and biased. But this partiality does not preclude our accumulating knowledge. We can and must still make decisions, take stands, exercise judgement. But we must take these actions with the attendant humility that there may come a time when we will have to take a different stand, adopt a new position, or embark upon a different set of actions. And if we recognize what we do not know about a subject, even subjects about which we have come to know quite a lot, then perhaps it becomes more possible to mitigate our attitudes of certainty in regard to subjects (objects, really) about which or whom we do not know much at all. I am arguing in what follows that Everett's work encourages this humility and promotes this new habit of mind, a habit of mind that he demonstrates in relation to one of the most provocative and polarizing symbols related to the region of the country in which he was born and grew up.

All of the sources of information to which we now have routine access—audiobooks, podcasts, all manner of print and documentaries from innumerable venues, sites, and organizations, of varying provenance, commitment, ideological bent, and intellectual quality—only conspire to remind us all the more of how partial our knowledge really is. Everything we learn comes at the price of being reminded of the unknowable dimensions of all that we do not yet and probably will never know. But, again, all is not lost, and what might be lost is a loss we can most easily sustain because of the related benefits that we gain. Recognizing that we are not certain and that we do not know may be foundational to a level of generosity to others that the accumulation of information and its concomitant sense of certainty actively discourages. One of the strategies we deploy in the face of growing uncertainty—even about what we do and do not know—is to segregate ourselves in safe havens of like-mindedness, whether through social media or familiar and congenial news sources or academic or intellectual colleagues with shared interests and approaches. We keep at bay our uncertainties and dreads, as David Foster Wallace has written, by staying "so busy and bombarded with stimuli all the time" (*Everything and More* 13).[2] But this bombardment has a lot to do, in turn, with creating an illusion of certainty, which, in turn, again, promises to make our world smaller, safer, and more comforting to us. But this smallness, safety, and comfort is illusory, and we open up a lot of unexpected possibilities if instead we remember, activate, and inhabit our uncertainty.

ACKNOWLEDGMENTS

As anybody who's ever completed one knows, the work involved in producing a book-length project comprises a lot more than the breadth of the book's subject matter. In my own case, an account of the changes that have taken place in my life over the period of time during which I've been working on this project would require a whole other book. The completion of *Approximate Gestures* has enabled me to come to an entirely new place in terms of how I read, how I articulate what I find when I read, and—most important of all—what I will and will not accept in terms of how I interact with others and how others interact with me. Arriving at this place has been freeing, and I doubt I would be where I am now had I not undertaken this project when I did.

With respect to some of the most recent of those changes, I have been fortunate enough to have been supported by the faculty and administration at Bucknell University. This is especially true of my colleagues in the English Department, who have cared for me at a couple of intensely demanding times in my personal life, as well as on a daily basis. I probably cannot thank them enough for this. I am also thankful to the fund of the John P. Crozer Chair of English Literature, a position that I have held for the past three years and which has been invaluable to my work during that time.

This project has been patiently supported by the staff at Louisiana State University Press. I thank John Easterly, who originally accepted my proposal; Margaret Lovecraft, who extended me the additional time I needed during a particularly eventful period of my personal and professional life; and James Long, who saw the project through to completion.

My work on Everett has been aided by the remarkable group of scholars who work on him now. Marc Amfreville, Sylvie Bauer, Michel Feith, Claude Julien, and Keith Mitchell are just a few of the people who have made significant contributions to my understanding of and thinking about Everett's work. Anne-Laure Tissut has been the beating heart of this group, a crucial organizer of conferences on Everett in France, as well as his French translator. Joe Weixlmann, my coeditor for a special issue of *African American Review* on Everett's work, also edited an invaluable collection of interviews with Everett. In addition, he has served, for me, as an example of scholarly professionalism and personal generosity that I do my best to emulate. And, of course, Percival Everett has produced and continues to add to a body of work unlike anything in American literature.

APPROXIMATE GESTURES

INTRODUCTION
Approximate Gestures, Ghostly Echoes, and the Anticonventional

She was being patronizing again, but I let it go. It was obvious she couldn't help herself. I wondered if there was a name for her condition. She wasn't exactly kissing my ass and she wasn't exactly flirting with me, but with a little shove she'd have shit on her nose and I'd have a date. Perhaps she was not precisely doing anything. Perhaps each and every one of her moves and gestures was approximate.

—*I Am Not Sidney Poitier*

A metaphor cannot be paraphrased.

—*Erasure*

Contingency itself, therefore, is necessary, if for no other reason than it allows the notion of necessity to make sense.

—*The Water Cure*

I am a liberal, which, in the American academy, is almost akin to standing up at a meeting and admitting that one drinks. Conservatives, whether academics or otherwise, have been acclimated to see liberals as some sort of enemy hell-bent on ruining what is best about *their* country, primarily through measures of "political correctness" (an expression they get from Communists, whether they know this or not). They have explicitly announced the United States as *their* country since about November 5, 2008, when a black man had the temerity to get himself elected president of the United States, and they started declaring that they wanted their country back immediately after this event. The election of November 9, 2016, appears to have gone some distance in retrieving their country for them, but this retrieval has not attenuated the rancor over own-ership. I sometimes wonder how they might have behaved had their guy lost. But people on the left, many of whom are actually liberals at best but claim a much more revolutionary bent, scorn liberals who self-identify as such for be-ing wishy-washy ideological sellouts, who are as bad as conservatives, possibly worse for their unwillingness to join the revolution.

When I identify myself as a liberal, then, I need to define my terms. When I identify myself as a member of this beleaguered tribe, I mean what Richard Rorty means in *Contingency, Irony, and Solidarity*. Rorty is in turn borrowing his definition of "liberal" from Judith Shklar, whom Rorty quotes as saying that liberals are the people "who think that cruelty is the worst thing we do" (xv). Rorty is not writing about the "neoliberal," another caste entirely, and he does not propose his book as a treatise in social, economic, or political policy or moral philosophy. The notion of avoiding cruelty carries with it the prospect of wishy-washy relativism, in which we are paralyzed in our attempts to do any-thing because of considerations of how any individual action might negatively affect someone else. In some senses, this outcome might not be a terrible thing, since it would mitigate the certainty that seems to underpin the willingness and ability to be cruel to others. Because I am right, the thinking (or perhaps nonthinking) goes, my actions are justified, irrespective of their extremity or their effects on others. Pretty much any oppression may be understood in these terms and may help explain why so many historical oppressions have relied, at least in part, on some claim to divine authority. "Liberal" in the sense that I am using the term, through Rorty and Shklar, then, does not signify in the ways that we have become used to in the first decades of the twenty-first century. But it is worthwhile to consider as a political and social outlook, nonetheless.

Rorty says something else that holds up well since he first published his book in 1989: "This book tries to show how things look if we drop the demand for a theory which unifies the public and private, and are content to treat the demands of self-creation and of human solidarity as equally valid, yet forever incommensurable" (xv). I think Rorty would have agreed with the statement that we have all the theory, statistics, revolutionary pronouncements, white papers, and other evaluative accoutrements that we need to understand that oppression is a bad thing, that fostering inequality is immoral, and that bigotry in whatever form is an act of cruelty. What we need in order to improve how we interact with others is nothing more and nothing less than the will to do so. This will is inevitably interfered with by self-interest in one form or another, but it is will that might (although does not necessarily) improve things.

His modest introductory declaration of what his book is and is not intended to accomplish is an admirable scholarly model and one I modestly hope to emulate here. What I have said so far enables me to articulate why I am approaching the work of Percival Everett as I am. I am not making an argument for or against liberalism as such, but I begin with this gesture of self-acknowledgment of my own personal and political predisposition and how it manifests itself according to existing political taxonomy in order to characterize where I'm going, in terms that will, I hope, overarch everything else that follows. In other words, I need you to remember what I've said as part of my introduction to this book about the commitment to avoiding cruelty and to remember why I've said it.

And even if we believe that cruelty is the worst thing we do, and we would therefore like that cruelty to stop, it can nevertheless be confidently inferred from human history that at least some of us are willing to authorize cruelty to others, or at least look the other way, at least some of the time. We can reasonably assume, then, that those who are willing to be cruel toward certain people commit or tolerate these acts of cruelty while simultaneously, when they see it as necessary, proscribing acts of cruelty toward those whom they care about, love, or otherwise identify with. The psychological mechanism that enables us to see cruelty as evil when done to us and ours but perhaps acceptable or even necessary when applied to others is called "moral exclusion." In her book *The Sociopath Next Door,* Martha Stout makes the following important point about how this psychological mechanism works, how we are sometimes willing to turn people into what she calls *its*:

Sometimes people appear to deserve our moral exclusion of them, as terrorists appear to do. Other examples of *its* are war criminals, child abductors, and serial killers, and in each of these cases, a considered argument can be (and has been) made, rightly or wrongly, that certain rights to compassionate treatment have been forfeited. But in most cases, our tendency to reduce people to nonbeings is neither considered nor conscious, and throughout history our proclivity to dehumanize has too often been turned against the essentially innocent. The list of out groups that some portion of humankind has at one time or another

3

demoted to the status of hardly even human is extremely long and, ironically, includes categories for nearly every one of us: blacks, Communists, capitalists, gays, Native Americans, Jews, foreigners, "witches," women, Muslims, Christians, the Palestinians, the Israelis, the poor, the rich, the Irish, the English, the Americans, the Sinhalese, Tamils, Albanians, Croats, Serbs, Hutus, Tutsis, and Iraqis, to name but a few. (57–58; emphasis in original)

Stout's point about the commonly nonconsidered or unconscious nature of our reduction of people to nonbeings emphasizes just how toxic our habits of mind can be. Maybe we learn when we are young to dislike or dehumanize members of Group X or Y from our family members, fellow members of our congregation, teachers, coaches, or other people we admire and trust, not to mention what we might learn from individual experiences with members of Group X or Y, or from representatives of them in some form of media. But we eventually forget that we learned these preferences at all. They become habits, unconsidered or unconscious. I am making an argument for keeping as much as is practicable in our thinking at the level of the considered and the conscious. But such a reorientation of our habits of mind takes practice and comes with risks. Encountering examples of this practice can only help us approach it, though. Everett's fiction, in its various expressions, provides such practice.

It is worth keeping in mind the notion of moral exclusion as one of the habits of mind that determine how we interact with our others. I refer to them as "our others" because those who might be "other" to me are not necessarily so to someone else. We all designate our others differently and reserve for them treatment that we would not ever tolerate for members of groups to which we belong. One need not be a sociopath to make such designations, and one need not be a liberal to disapprove of such designations when they disadvantage ourselves and our groups. The extensive list that Stout provides also draws attention to those groups that someone has excluded, whether they be members of particular nationalities, ethnicities, professional positions or strata, sexual identities, or whatever additional criterion we may use to differentiate and then exclude.

The habits of mind that enable moral exclusion are expressions of our reliance upon categories, stereotypes, and conventions. At the same time, categories, stereotypes, and conventions do serve a function, as they help us remember what we have learned. This is partly why rethinking and retraining our habits of mind are such complicated and difficult enterprises. We need generalizations, and generalizations provide us with some sense of certainty, paradoxically. We do not have to reacquire the concept of "dog" with the beginning of each new day, for instance. We remember that category and recognize different kinds of dog when we encounter them. We build up a generalizable dog database. Of course, the associations we build or inherit based on conventions or stereotypes can also be quite malignant. For instance, because of my negative experience with one or two members of Group X, I may now feel completely justified in morally excluding all members of Group X. (I will begin chapter 1 with more discussion of the necessary evil that is the category. For now, the self-serving manipulation of categories through moral exclusion is what is important.) What we need to be able to see is that, while these categories are real to us, they are also metaphors, generalizations, abstractions that inhabit our minds within a language that we construct, a language that helps us make sense of our world. But this metaphorical language also facilitates a distancing from our others, a distancing that makes it all the easier to morally exclude them.

Convention, after all, is just a habit shared by a group of people. While conventions are persistent, though, the habits they encourage need not be per- manent. We hear and read from time to time about white supremacists who leave their organizations and renounce their former beliefs, for instance. If such a transformation is possible for people who appear so committed to their hatreds that they derive a sense of identity from them, those of us with more run-of-the-mill biases stand only a better chance of retraining our own habits of mind. We need the will to change these habits of mind, some impetus to make these changes, and preferably, some examples of how these changes might look or work. I am arguing that Everett's work provides such examples. In fact, I am willing to go as far as to argue that Everett's work is "about" retraining our habits of mind, which is not to say that they are "intended" to effect such a change in us. Everett has said in interviews that he is writing "one big book," but he refuses—understandably—to say what that one big book is about. It is the critic's job to come up with some version of what that one big book might be about. This is mine, and I am hopeful that there will be others.

I can make this assertion that his work is about retraining our habits of mind while accepting the obvious fact that my reading of Everett's work does not suggest that we will be kinder to our others as a result of having read *Walk Me to the Distance,* for instance. That would be nice, but that is a lot to place at the feet of any fiction writer, or any writer at all.[1] But I can suggest the prospect of how we *might* unlearn those habits of mind if provided with enough models of people doing so, and some of his characters provide such examples. That said, as I will return to later, the opening up of the prospect of retraining ourselves does not come with any guarantees. We could produce worse versions of ourselves, after all. What Everett's work models—what it is about—is what it looks like to see the world not in unconventional terms but in *anticonventional* ways. The unconventional can occur accidentally or incidentally. We can appear unconventional, for instance, for no other reason than we do not know what a given convention is and as a result may contravene it without intending to do so. The "anticonventional" must be deliberate, knowing the convention already and then actively opposing it.[2] Opposition to convention is not a simple binary, though, since the anticonventional can take an infinite number of forms, not the least of which is a form that we might usually characterize as negative in one way or another. Ishmael Kidder in *The Water Cure* and Ogden Walker in *Assumption* may be read as examples of such expressions of the anticonventional.

By drawing our attention to the opposition of convention, Everett's texts encourage us to consider where these expectations may have come from in the first place, as well as what they might mean. After all, it must mean something that we expect African American characters to play certain roles, work in certain occupations (and not in others), even speak in certain ways in the literature we read, the films we watch, and the music we listen to. To expect these roles, occupations, and speech patterns is to put our habits of mind fully on display. To see such characters embody unexpected roles invokes the simple questions: Why did I expect something else from this character? What do my expectations say about me as a reader? How else might I be doing all of this? How is this process affecting my perceptions, beliefs, and actions in other aspects of my life?

A lot of what happens in Everett's fiction may be characterized in terms similar to those implied in the first epigraph to this introduction, which is taken from *I Am Not Sidney Poitier.* The emphasis on what this character is *not* doing and the repetition of what is *perhaps* happening create tension by refusing the easy solution of stating what *is* happening. Oftentimes, what we see in Everett's work is a constant approach to something without ever actually reaching that object or ostensible destination. This asymptotic approach (in at least two senses of the word "approach") gestures toward the infinitude that exists between categories, if only we would look for them. The asymptote is, after all, the value that can be calculated and infinitely approached but never reached. As a result, his work constantly puts us in the uncomfortable position of trying to make sense of something that isn't actually happening or even intended to happen, in the way that the instructively named Not Sidney attempts to resolve someone else's intentions in the above quotation. What Everett's work does, though, is instruct us—if we are willing to be so instructed—in the lesson that it may be the approach itself that is of greatest significance. This lesson may then be applied to the world beyond his writing, to the world in which we live, work, and make decisions that affect other people, where the lesson holds the promise of doing us the most good. This approach conveys scope, potential, fluidity, an infinity of possibilities.

This infinity of possibilities is especially important to understanding a writer whose work exposes the innumerable limitations of the labels imposed upon it by critics, reviewers, and any other reader who might discover it. And while it is reasonable to respond to this observation by saying that it might be made about the work of any artist whose work is worth taking seriously, as indeed it might, Everett's work poses a particular case because of how the demands, constraints, frustrations, and potential devastations of convention are so central to so much of the prose fiction that he has produced in the approximately thirty-five years since the publication of *Suder* in 1983. In addition to the by now somewhat standard tensions between the inventions of the artist and the attempts at comprehension by the audience (in whatever role members of that audience might play) is the further complication introduced by Everett's being black. As an African American artist who negotiates the strictures of being an African American artist in ways that create further interference for audience members (much more on this to follow throughout, but especially in chapter 4), Everett issues yet another challenge to the reader who has imbibed the sorts of convention-bound ways of thinking that his work challenges and exposes. No subject in American life is more beholden to the ways of convention-bound thinking than is race. Similarly, few groups within the American population are so subject to the constraints of convention as is the group with which Everett is ethnoracially identified, irrespective of whether he is also identified as an artist or not. So the tension between convention as represented within the work, conventions as imposed upon the work and deployed in attempts to understand the work, and conventions as imposed upon the artist producing the work creates a dynamic and at times bewildering matrix whose innate complexity Everett's work thematizes and explores and skillfully exploits in an attempt to hold at bay the impulse to *explain* the life of African Americans to the white American reading mainstream. Instead of explaining what it's like to be black, Everett's work encourages the perception of both the signals and the noise of information transmission. The recognition of both at the same time goes against all of our acculturation, in which we learn to block out the noise in favor of our exclusive focus on a particular signal. But once we learn to do this, infinite new possibilities open up to us.

This book is an attempt to suggest why the nature of Everett's challenge to his readers is not only valuable, and crucial, to understanding his work, but also to appreciating a potentially salutary model of more broadly beneficial social interaction that his work implies. This model of social interaction, as I am vauntingly calling it here, opposes the sorts of restrictions that convention in all of its forms poses, nowhere more so within American culture than in the sphere of race. In addition to all that I've said so far, the critic who attempts to "explain" any aspect of Everett's work—let alone to attempt some version of an Everett aesthetic—is best advised to accept that a precondition of this objective is necessarily to find oneself occasionally the butt of at least some of Everett's jokes, a precondition to which I have resigned myself as the cost of persisting with this undertaking.[3]

By approaching Everett's work as an array of challenges to be taken on by the reader in a dynamic relationship premised not on solution, resolution, explication, or explanation—all of which presuppose some sort of definitive endpoint—and focusing instead on the dynamic nature of the challenge itself, I hope to model more effectively that not being able to understand Everett's work conclusively is not a pass to be lamented but instead an instructive outcome from which much may be learned. While much that I've said so far may appear to be prefatory, or even cautionary, in nature, neither is my intention. Yes, the journey of a thousand miles really does begin with a single step, as the Tao and any number of bumper stickers and T-shirts tell us. But it is necessary to lay out as clearly as I can from the outset just how central this idea of the approximate gesture—not working toward a conventional, definitive conclusion—is in and to Everett's work before embarking upon the journey itself.

One particularly productive avenue into the notion of the anticonventional is the work of Gilles Deleuze and Félix Guattari, principally because of the intriguing and entrancing ways with which they set out the challenge of comprehending the anticonventional, a part of whose challenge is accepting the inability to find definitive resolution and the potentially infinite possibilities available to our cognition once this acceptance has been arrived at. They begin *A Thousand Plateaus,* the second volume of *Capitalism and Schizophrenia,* by referring to their collaboration on the first volume, *Anti-Oedipus,* in the following completely characteristic passage:

> The two of us wrote *Anti-Oedipus* together. Since each of us was several, there was already quite a crowd. Here we have made use of everything that came within range, what was closest as well as farthest away. We have assigned clever pseudonyms to prevent recognition. Why have we kept our own names? *Out of habit, purely out of habit.* To make ourselves unrecognizable in turn. To render imperceptible, not ourselves, but what makes us act, feel, and think. Also because it's nice to talk like everybody else, to say the sun rises, when everybody knows it's only a matter of speaking. To reach, not the point where one no longer says I, but the point where it is no longer of any importance whether one says I. (3; emphasis added)

Much that Deleuze and Guattari have to say works the way a magic trick does, getting the observer to look in one direction so that the essence of the illusion that happens in another direction will not be noticed. In fact, the magic trick analogy is not quite adequate. Their work is more like a magic trick that enables the audience to know how the trick works while still simultaneously being able to be entertained and amazed by the trick. This implication of their work expresses itself in the distinction between "the point where one no longer says I" and the point where "it is no longer of any importance whether one says I." Our perceptions change when no one says I any longer, but they change within recognizable parameters, like when we go from being quite good to being exceptionally good at a skill. But when it is no longer of any importance whether we say I is a whole unimaginable other order of magnitude of change, like when we give up that skill at which we used to excel and stumble into a whole new consciousness in which we enjoy just being ourselves so much that we no longer need ever to have been proficient at that former skill in the first place. Deleuze and Guattari do not render their actions, feelings, and thoughts more perceptible to their readers. Instead, they attempt to render the processes through which they arrive at these processes more perceptible to their readers. The sometimes distracting syntax militates against immediately recognizing this at-at-least-one-remove process, but that distraction is itself part of their point.[4]

Deleuze and Guattari draw our attention to the sorts of perceptual trade-offs that we make every moment of every day, whether we consciously realize we are doing so or not, perhaps even because we do not realize we are doing so. Every conscious moment we are shutting out far more sensory, intellectual, and emotional, as well as myriad other inputs than we are actually taking in. We do this, in part, as they say, "out of habit, purely out of habit." But we also do it "because it's nice to talk like everybody else," gesturing again at the ubiquity of convention. And it *is* nice to talk like everybody else, or at least like those around us. But we also engage in this continual conscious and unconscious perceptual triage because one fears that to try to take in and to remember consciously everything, to react to everything, to engage with everything we encounter, even just over the course of a single day, is the way toward madness. We cut out inputs to preserve our sanity.

All this is put another way, a more haunting way, by David Foster Wallace, in his book *Everything and More: A Compact History of Infinity.*[5] Wallace helpfully and cannily takes us through the nature of the problem we invariably encounter when negotiating all that amounts to our daily lives. His observations may be applied to the challenges of how we read, as well as how we live. Wallace proposes the following thought experiment as a way into considering the implications of what he calls abstract thinking: "The dreads and dangers of abstract thinking are a big reason why we now all like to stay so busy and bombarded with stimuli all the time. Abstract thinking tends most often to strike during moments of quiet repose. As in for example the early morning, especially if you wake up slightly before your alarm goes off, when it can suddenly and for no reason occur to you that you've been getting out of bed every morning without the slightest doubt that the floor would support you" (13).[6] After acknowledging the necessity for this previously unconscious reliance upon the integrity of our bedroom floor, bringing up the terrifying prospect that "without this confidence based on past experience we'd all go insane, or at least we'd be unable to function because we'd have to stop and deliberate about every last little thing" (13), Wallace destabilizes even this small concession, asking us to consider the status of the confidence we derive from our surrounding world, based on the principle of induction, which he calls the P.I.:

> The P.I. states that if something *x* has happened in certain particular circumstances *n* times in the past, we are justified in believing that the same circumstances will produce *x* on the (*n* + 1)th occasion. The P.I. is wholly respectable and authoritative, and it seems like a well-lit exit out of the whole problem. Until, that is, it happens to strike you (as can occur only in very abstract moods or when there's an unusual amount of time before the alarm goes off) that the P.I. is *itself* merely an abstraction from experience . . . and so now what exactly is it that justifies our confidence in the P.I.? (13; emphasis in original)

And so on. Wallace here gestures at the limit toward which the asymptote approaches infinitely without ever reaching it. What enables our confidence in the P.I.? From there, what enables our confidence in evaluating our confidence in the P.I.? What else might stand in as a resolution to this evaluation? And so on. The question about our confidence in the principle of induction initiates the kind of chain of signification that prompts some to criticize post-structuralism as nihilism. It probably prompts others to find refuge in forms of religious or political inflexibility. It may encourage still others to seek refuge in post-structuralism. Who's to say? Wallace's question about where our confidence in the principle of induction comes from is, for him, an instruction to look for some provisional exit from our abstract musings. It is also a signal to remember, at the same time, that this exit is, in fact, provisional. Characteristically, Wallace does not allow us even that provisional exit. "The ability to halt a line of abstract thinking once you see it has no end," he writes, "is part of what usually distinguishes sane, functional people—people who when the alarm finally goes off can hit the floor without trepidation and plunge into the concrete business of the real workaday world—from the unhinged" (13–14). So now our very sanity relies on our ability to remain unconscious of at least some of what happens to us over the course of a day. We can't think about what Wallace has to say about the nature and the potential costs of abstract thinking without reflecting upon his eventual decision to end his own life. But we must also consider the prospect that the halting of a line of abstract thinking may also be mere convention, even if a respectable and authoritative, not to mention a self-preservative, one. Effectively, Wallace is asking us, in his way, as Deleuze and Guattari are asking us in theirs, and as Everett's work does as well, to consider resistance to this halting and instead to follow these lines of abstract thinking past the point at which we might believe that we control them, if we ever could, and see where they lead.

But the ability to talk like everybody else in order to halt an uncomfortable line of abstract thinking invariably comes at a cost, again, whether we are aware of that cost (really, those many unaccountable costs) or not. For instance, what if what I customarily shut out is precisely what is most important to you? What if my shutting out of that thing actually and actively offends you or threatens to discount your experience of the world around you? We engage in these negotiations constantly whenever we are not alone, but we also train ourselves to shut out conscious awareness of those negotiations and then to shut out that shutting out. And so on.

Percival Everett's work is an object lesson in what is at stake, for better and for worse, if we try to hold at bay that habit that we develop of unconsciously shutting certain things out of our perceptual fields, whether in the interest of abstract thinking, of talking like everyone else, or of preserving our sanity. I say we "try" to hold these inputs at bay because this is obviously an impossible task, a concession one can intuit without a doctorate in cognitive psychology. The above passage from Deleuze and Guattari's introduction to *A Thousand Plateaus* could, in fact, have been voiced by any number of Everett's characters, figures who are perpetually struggling in their different ways with their own ability to get out of bed in the morning and rely on the floor to support their weight, with their sanity, with their ability to operate in the world, to talk like everybody else, intact. The following rumination from Ishmael Kidder, the narrator of Everett's 2007 novel *The Water Cure,* is only one example of what such struggles can look like:

What is between you and your first reflection? Space? The glass of the mirror? That which makes the glass a mirror? You know, you never ever touch or even face the thing that stands in opposition to you, only that which is between you and that thing. You only have experience with the between. But if the between is the thing to which you attend, then what is between you and the between? And what is the between between the betweens? Zeno, Zeno, Zeno. The number of points between here and the moon is infinite. The number of points between you and the door is infinite. Infinity equals infinity, and so the door is as far away as the moon. Still, if we both started walking right now, together, at the same time, I'd make it to the moon before you made it to that door. (46)[7]

We don't attend to the spaces between the betweens, because to do so might render us incapable of taking a single step toward the moon or the door without bumping into something or falling over. Kidder's observations are at the same time right and wrong, right in theory, wrong in practice, as are Zeno's paradoxes to which he refers, figures to which Everett returns almost compulsively in his fiction. And yet it's the simultaneous rightness and wrongness that makes what Kidder says so compelling. The question we are hypnotized into at least momentarily considering is: What if I tried to attend to the betweens, and then to the betweens between any given betweens? And so on. Kidder here, and Deleuze and Guattari, as well as Wallace, gesture toward the radical possibilities put in play merely by recalibrating the focal length of our attentions, by attempting to retrain ourselves out of our habits, to look consciously both nearer and farther afield with the hope of seeing something we had—up until now—missed. This refocusing or retraining doesn't necessarily change anything in our physical world—we still get to the door, we still say the sun rises—but if we continue this refocusing, if we make refocusing a conscious, ongoing commitment, we open up possibilities that we will not have been able to ponder before. These potentially infinite possibilities become apparent to us even as nothing physically changes.

But these infinite possibilities do not come with any guarantees of success, or even of progress. This lack of guarantees, or still worse, the prospect that what we discover through refocusing may run counter to our own interests, is probably one of the many disincentives to such refocusing for many, even if these disincentives are not as dire as those laid out by Wallace. This is all the more the case for those for whom things have always tended to work out favorably. And herein lies a major problem for this idea of refocusing, rethinking, relearning. Why rethink a structure that is working well for me? Sure, it's possible that my success comes at someone else's expense, but provided I and mine (however "we" are defined) continue to prosper, this is a cost that I (not at my most magnanimous, but that too is acceptable to me under certain circumstances) am willing to bear. Yes, we can argue for this refocusing in the interest of some larger good or intellectual stimulation or enlightened altruism or, dare I say, as an academic exercise, but in the end, there will be many who will not take on this challenge for reasons such as these or others for which I am not accounting. But this, too, is part of the paradox in making a case for such rethinking or retraining. I know all of these disincentives exist but am willing to continue making the argument, nevertheless. And I try not to simply put aside the fact that I know of these disincentives as I make my argument. I have to do both of these things at the same time—make the argument and remember the disincentives against it—or else I am suggesting to you that perhaps I do not really believe in what I am saying here, at which point you are completely within your rights to stop reading right now.

◆ ◆ ◆

Everett's short story "The Fix," from his 2004 collection *Damned If I Do,* provides a useful introductory example of the implications of the larger argument that follows, one way into how the challenge of reading Everett's work looks in practice. "The Fix" presents a somewhat unprepossessing character, Sherman Olney, who first appears while being "beaten to near extinction one night by a couple of silky-looking men who seemed to know Sherman and wanted something in particular from him" (3). Sherman is rescued by Douglas Langley, who owns the little sandwich shop next to the alley in which this beating is taking place. Douglas takes the beaten stranger inside his shop and makes him a sandwich. It's at this point that Sherman notices a loud noise being produced by the compressor in Douglas's refrigerator. In response to the noise, he says, "I can fix it" (5).

The one thing Sherman knows how to do is fix things. But his locution here is notable. Before saying what he asks next, "You want me to fix it?" he first asserts that he *can* fix it. This positive assertion does not come across like arrogance from Sherman, in part because of how he was introduced to us, being beaten up in an alley. But the assertion does appear at least out of sequence.

Conventionally, wouldn't he first ask if he might take a look at the fridge, or ask if he can give fixing it a try, before asserting that he can fix it?

As the story proceeds, it is difficult not to begin recognizing allusions to other stories. Sherman's introduction might put us in mind of the beginning of Márquez's "A Very Old Man with Enormous Wings," which finds another everyday couple confronted with another unprepossessing stranger, although this one's unusual characteristic is physical and immediately apparent, whereas Sherman's special talent is revealed over the course of the story: "The light was so weak at noon that when Pelayo was coming back to the house after throwing away the crabs, it was hard for him to see what it was that was moving and groaning in the rear of the courtyard. He had to go very close to see that it was an old man, a very old man, lying face down in the mud, who, in spite of his tremendous efforts, couldn't get up, impeded by his enormous wings" ("A Very Old Man" 203). Like Márquez's very old man, Sherman is a stranger in physical distress who appears out of nowhere as the story begins. Sherman doesn't have wings, but his arrival in the lives of Douglas and his wife, Sheila, carries the sort of conventional promise of which countless stories are made. As Sherman's special talent becomes more obvious, his list of successful repairs extends beyond the walls of the little sandwich shop. Douglas even begins to wonder if Sherman might be a fugitive from the law, since "his presence was disconcerting as he never spoke of his past or family or friends and he never went out, not even to the store" (13).

Douglas doesn't exploit the stranger, though, a temptation to which Pelayo and Elisenda succumb in Márquez's story. Instead, the two men agree on a reasonable exchange. Sherman fixes things in Douglas's shop; Douglas pays Sherman minimum wage, feeds him, and lets him live in the room above the shop. But when Sherman begins fixing things for other people and the nature of his repairs begins to change, moving from the material to the metaphysical, the story's resonances multiply upon themselves as well. Sherman fixes people's relationship problems, tax problems, and parking tickets. Ultimately, he brings a woman back from death, after which Douglas cannot help but ask the questions that the story now requires, "Who are you? Who are you? Are you from outer space or something?" (21). The "or something" part of Douglas's questioning does a lot of work here, since we cannot help but think of stories of other miracles of which we might be aware. For instance, Sherman's humility and lack of interest in material things, not to mention his ability to revive the dead—someone else here, as opposed to himself—puts us in mind of Jesus.

Does this latter reading supersede the earlier Márquez reading? Of course not. But even in our still post-structurally inflected moment, there remains nevertheless a lot of pressure on the literary critic to somehow reconcile conflicting, or even complementary, readings, if only to put our own stamp upon what it is that we have found in a text. Recently, Rita Felski has signaled an increasing sense among critics that part of our work is to scrutinize our own work, as she writes at the beginning of *The Limits of Critique:* "The task of the social critic is now to expose hidden truths and draw out unflattering and counterintuitive meanings that others fail to see. The modern era ushers in a new mode of militant reading: what Ricoeur calls a *hermeneutics of suspicion*" (1; emphasis in original). Felski also notes that scholars are presently "casting a more jaundiced eye on their methods" (2), suggesting that now is an apposite time for the kind of reading of Everett's work that I am proposing here. To leave readings unresolved, unassimilated, unanswered, has at times looked like one has not completed the critic's job. But perhaps, as Felski argues, it's worth casting a jaundiced eye on why we have done things certain ways and considering how else we might function as critics at the present time.

Returning to "The Fix": the Christian allegorical resolution is a tempting and familiar resource within the Judeo-Christian intellectual world, especially with Márquez's character being called an "angel," after all. But "The Fix" does not lend itself to such neat resolution and in fact appears deliberately suspicious of such a resort to allegory, even if our training as literary critics screams out for just such an inclusion in our reading of the story. To approach such an inclusion as a way of resolving the story, though, cheats us out of the benefits that accrue to us through the practice of keeping multiple readings alive and in play, maybe even in conflict, at the same time, even if resolution accords with our more conventional lived practice of selectively shutting things out. Sherman's response to Douglas's understandably panicked questioning is burning-bush simple: "I can fix things." So maybe he's not Jesus, but now his father. "I can fix things" is at least as cryptic and symbolically all-encompassing as "I am that I am," both answering and not answering the important question.

In spite of the "I am that I am" quality of Sherman's reply, the fact that the story does not culminate solely and neatly in the revelation of its Christian allusions moves us past that most conventional of literary critical moves.[8] The simplicity of Sherman's response, in fact, just as compellingly draws us to another misunderstood and intransigent male protagonist, as his response may also remind us of Bartleby's equally enigmatic "I would prefer not to." While Melville's character's presence is unnerving to that story's narrator for the nonanswer quality of his response, though, Everett's character embodies opportunity for those who encounter him. Bartleby articulates refusal, while Sherman voices a weirdly subservient willingness. He all but disappears for a while into his ability to fix things. Nevertheless, the tagline simplicity of Sherman's explanation without explanation becomes both more and less familiar to us as we read "The Fix" because of the numerous reminders of other stories that it conjures in the literary critical imagination.

Sherman does, however, answer Douglas's continued questioning, as Douglas begins to add up at least the implications of his visitor's abilities. "This has something to do with why the men were beating you that night, doesn't it?" (23), he asks Sherman. At first, Sherman is again characteristically cryptic, saying that they were from the government "or some businesses" and wanted him "to fix a bunch of things and I said no" (23). Douglas cannot be blamed for finding this answer unsatisfactory, and it is difficult not to feel dissatisfied ourselves, considering that others ask Sherman to fix any number of material, emotional, and in at least one case, metaphysical problems, and he's never refused a request. In light of Sherman's answer, it is completely reasonable to wonder: What could the government or "some businesses" possibly have asked him to fix for him to have refused, considering bringing someone back from the dead was not beyond his willingness to comply with a request? In other words, we cannot be blamed for wanting definitive answers, as Douglas surely does.

Sherman says to Douglas: "You have to be careful about what you fix. If you fix the valves in an engine, but the bearings are shot, you'll get more compression, but the engine will still burn up. . . . If you irrigate a desert, you might empty a sea. It's a complicated business, fixing things" (23). While Sherman's observations about the law of unintended consequences are no doubt true, they do bring up the additional reasonable question: what might be lost or changed in bringing a person back to life? (Everett's *American Desert* provides at least one set of possible answers to that question, in the person of Theodore Street.) Somewhere along the line, then, Sherman has learned the lesson that the old couple eventually learn in W. W. Jacobs's short fiction classic "The Monkey's Paw," a story that teaches the simple lesson that everything comes at a cost and that some costs are simply not worth the paying. That Sherman has already learned this lesson by the time Douglas rescues him from the alley next to his sandwich shop returns "The Fix" to a much more decidedly secular register than do speculations on his possible biblical lineage. But as the allusions within the story evolve and accumulate and the conversation between the allusions becomes ever more complex, requiring that we remember each of them as they go by, the connotations of the word at the heart of the story also change. These connotative changes point to the uses to which we might put the story as well as the challenges of and the opportunities within the paradoxes that "The Fix" presents us.

The repeated use of the word "fix" in the story, and its preference over the word "repair," which appears much less frequently, draws attention to the significance of the word as itself. To fix is obviously to repair, and "repair" appears initially to be what Sherman actually means, certainly as it applies to Douglas's refrigerator and his wife's electric foot massager. But "fix" also signifies to fix in place, or to fix someone with a gaze, among its many connotations. A similarity that many of its meanings share is that the notion of fixing carries with it the necessary condition of rendering something immovable or unchanging, as in "to make firm or stable," the OED's initial definition of "fix." But to make firm or stable is also how we tend to want to make meaning. In order to make meaning, we are often willing to shut out those inputs that might threaten to destabilize a given strived-for meaning. As we reflect on how Sherman has been fixing people through repairing their possessions and then various aspects of their lives, we must also recognize that fixing people (in place, in status, in our understanding of their humanity) is something else we do all the time without thinking about it. It's a habit, a habit that becomes a paradox at the point when we consciously critique that behavior in others even as we continue to indulge in it ourselves, as we do when we engage in moral exclusion.

The relationship between the slightly different resonances of the word "fix" also plays itself out in the story. After he revives the previously dead woman, Sherman "looked lifeless. He seemed drained of all energy. He lifted his sad face up to look at Douglas" (21). The cost of fixing people takes a physical toll on Sherman, and not for the first time, if the beating at the beginning of the story is to be remembered in the way that Sherman initially explains it to Douglas. In addition to this physical cost, though, Sherman is being fixed in place by everyone else around him, as they affix to the meaning of his life nothing more than the value that they might extract from him. He is an object, a commodity within capitalism, as we remember his relationship to the owner of a sandwich shop. All the while that the television crews predictably descend upon Douglas's little sandwich shop, and he is bombarded with questions about Sherman, questions that he can't, of course, answer, Sherman is described as "sitting at the counter waiting, his face long, his eyes red as if from crying" (22). All he can say eventually is "I have to run away. . . . Everyone knows where I am now" (22). No one knows or cares *who* he is. They just know where he is, and they think they know what he is and, more importantly, what he'll be able to do for them. "Everyone" cannot help but include the organizations represented at the beginning of the story by the two "silly-looking men" who were administering the beating to Sherman—the two men from the government or some businesses. The growing mob has fixed him in place in their imaginations based on their understandings and their own desires. But these desires, like his fixing of "so many machines and so many relationships and so many businesses and concerns and even . . . a dead woman" (24), come exclusively at Sherman's expense.

Another way to understand fixing people, particularly in the present context, is in terms of stereotyping. We resent being stereotyped because such an imposition fixes us in place according to the values and evaluation of someone else. Homi Bhabha makes a version of this point when he discusses stereotyping in *The Location of Culture*: "Fixity, as the sign of cultural/historical/racial difference in the discourse of colonialism, is a paradoxical mode of representation: it connotes rigidity and an unchanging order as well as disorder, degeneracy and daemonic repetition. Likewise the stereotype, which is its major discursive strategy, is a form of knowledge and identification that vacillates between what is always 'in place,' already known, and something that must be anxiously repeated; as if the essential duplicity of the Asiatic or the bestial sexual license of the African that needs no proof, can never really, in discourse, be proved" (66). Bhabha's description of fixity is especially pertinent here because of how he also emphasizes the play of paradox. Fixity for Bhabha enacts the necessity of repetition of that which is obvious and shouldn't need repeating at all but nevertheless needs constant repetition. This is the confrontation between the bigot's need for certainty (which needs constant reiteration) and the uncertainty of the larger world (which is uncontrollable and therefore needs—for some—order imposed upon it). Put another way, there is nothing natural or inevitable about the fixity we impose on others, and this unnatural status may explain why we do it. This imposition must be repeated with a compulsive anxiety that only betrays its own unnaturalness. Perhaps what I'm arguing is that we must counteract the paradoxes of fixity through an equal and opposite paradox expressing itself in maintaining the consciousness of how, what, and whom we are fixing even as we continue doing it. Then perhaps there derives power and persuasion from the refusal of fixity. As Sherman moves from being Márquez's old man to Jesus to God to Bartleby to the monkey's paw—not to mention the innumerable allusions that I have no doubt missed—it becomes our responsibility (if we choose to undertake it) to keep *all* of these resonances in play. We are also advised to remain conscious of the generous and humble recognition of the very real probability of resonances to which we remain ignorant or have forgotten, and, in the process, attempt to resist fixing Sherman ourselves. While this resistance runs counter to much of our training as literary critics, as we attempt to make meaning of what we read, it may be better training for our broader roles as citizens. After all, what holds the above allusions together is their shared status as signs to be interpreted, objects whose meaning derives from the subjects who encounter them.

As a desperate Sherman stands on a bridge, anticipating "a long drop that no one could hope to survive" (24), an equally desperate crowd has gathered behind him, screaming, "Don't! . . . Fix us! Fix us!" (24). They do not know what they are asking of this man with the singular ability to be exploited only for their own ostensible benefits. They want a very specific type of fixing and no other, expressing a selfish desire within the much larger and uncontrollable network of possible outcomes. We cannot, after all, dictate and circumscribe how others will fix us.

Anne-Laure Tissut has described the cumulative effects available in reading Everett's work in her discussion of *The Water Cure*: "Reading *The Water Cure* amounts to a progressive discovery, as the reader reaches an increased awareness, without necessarily reaching any certainty. Rather, the context often invites the reader to intuit the ethical dimension of language" (para. 17). Tissut's formulation of infinite approach without arrival is suggestive again of the metaphor of the asymptote and also returns us to Zeno and the paradox of being both right and wrong. As Everett's protagonist, Ishmael Kidder, reflects on Zeno's paradoxes in *The Water Cure,* he says: "Zeno believed that there was a confusing of physical magnitude with mathematical magnitude, that if you considered them the same, then his paradox was a real problem, depending on what one means by real" (136–37). Leaving aside for the moment the prospect that Kidder may be insane or at least headed in that direction as a result of a disfiguring grief, he understands his Zeno. This confusion of different registers of knowledge—of physical and mathematical magnitudes—can lead our habitual understandings to fallacious conclusions that, nevertheless, appear correct to us at the time. Wallace offers the following typically provisional explanation for this problem: "For instance, the set of all integers is potentially infinite in the sense that there is no largest integer ('in the direction of largeness it is always possible to think of a larger number'); but it is not actually infinite because the set doesn't exist as one complete entity. In other words, numbers for Aristotle compose a successive continuum: there are infinitely many but they never coexist ('One thing can be taken after another endlessly.')" (*Everything and More* 67).[9] Even if Wallace's formulation does not resolve Zeno's paradoxes (he assures us in fact that it doesn't), it is generative in what it enables us to think about as we consider our reading of Everett, our reading in general, and our reading of and interactions with the world around us, more generally still. The relationship between what is actual and what is potential suggests how we might resolve our desire to make meaning in our limiting and fixing way, while remaining alive to the more important necessities of recognizing the limitless world beyond our limited human abilities to make sense of that world in its necessarily limited expressions of itself. Put another way, what Tissut says regarding an increased awareness without reaching any certainty is the important point here, if we accept this increased awareness in all of its dynamism and uncertainty as a value in itself. Our reading of Sherman as containing all of the allusions I've mentioned in addition to the ones to which I remain ignorant is a way of freeing him from our own fixing gaze at least.

Every text is endless, in the same way that Zeno's paradoxes work. Every text has a potentially limitless number of readings if only because of the limitless variety among potential readers; however, all of these readings never coexist simultaneously, so no text is actually limitless at one time. "The Fix" thematizes its potential limitlessness, though, the infinitude of its potential readings, as it draws our attention to what it might mean as well as what else it might mean. What we have noticed so far about the story invites us to suggest further significations within its text, leading us to some brief consideration of the names of the two principal characters. Sherman Olney and Douglas Langley both carry in their surnames traces of singularity, with "Olney" having transposed the middle letters of "only" and "Langley" able at least to remind us of "lonely," especially when accompanied by the auditory resonance of the long *o* vowel sound in Sherman's last name. In different ways, both Sherman and Douglas feel isolated over the course of the story, again highlighting their status as having been fixed in place by those around them. Toward the end of the story, Douglas seems unique in his concern for Sherman's well-being, a concern that leaves Douglas similarly alone. Sherman's wholly unique fixing abilities mean he is like no other, leading to the kind of singularity that resulted in his being beaten up at the beginning of the story and then exploited through much of the rest of it and finally considering suicide at the story's end. Douglas, although married, also appears lonely if for no other reason than his determination not to exploit his new tenant/employee. He does, remember, suggest the arrangement with Sherman that consists in some modest exchange of consideration (a great legal/ economic metaphor in this context) between the two men, as opposed to the exploitations Sherman endures to the benefit of others.

Before moving on to some resolution (such as it is) of my reading of "The Fix," it is worth addressing one additional implication of the story and my reading of it. This implication says much about where I'm going with what I will describe as the kaleidoscopic reading of Everett's fiction that follows. All that I've said about the implications of fixity as they pertain to stereotyping suggest the following considerations: Do I read "The Fix" as I do, in part at least, because I know that Everett is black, even though there's no indication in the story whether Sherman, Douglas, or Sheila is? What role does my understanding of my own blackness play? Does my introduction of stereotyping as a resonance of fixing that opens up the story to me run the risk of fixing the story's meaning in a way that is at least as tendentious and limiting as what happens to Sherman over the course of the story? I have to admit that these are real possibilities, and this admission brings me to a provisional conclusion about Everett's story as a way of bringing me to one of the points of my introduction.

What happens in the story is a synecdoche of what happens in a lot of Everett's work. His situation of his work and of himself as an artist requires that we remember that he is African American while holding at bay—to the best of our abilities—whatever habitual associations we bring to the expressions "African American" and "African American artist." No one expects definitive success in the attempt to keep these impulses at bay, to retrain these habits. The attempt, the good faith attempt, holds value in itself, though. But again, this value is difficult to locate or quantify in any meaningful way, in part because it finds us struggling against what we have been taught to interpret as our own self-interest. We find some *x* result in associating the idea of *the* African American artist or *the* African American experience more generally and have often been rewarded—or at least not punished—for resorting to these familiar formulations. After all, we want to talk like everyone else, and sometimes that benefits us. For instance, those who use expressions like *the African American experience*—as if any such a singular entity actually existed—without being at least laughed at, if not worse, may continue to resort to this nonsensical expression without having to rethink its usage or its status as nonsense. As long as such usages can persist, rethinking associations around ideas like *African American* is made all the more difficult.

Deleuze and Guattari explain the implications of the interrelationship between habit and power, providing an instructive precursor to what Wallace has to say about why we distract ourselves from the realities of abstract thinking— that we would drive ourselves mad if we really contemplated all those elements of our day-to-day lives that we otherwise, and perhaps by necessity, take for granted. What if the real reason, or at least another reason, for this unwillingness to really contemplate consciously more of what we take in on a daily basis is that we do not want to give up the benefits that accrue to at least some of us through a continued adherence to and acceptance of convention? Their formulation requires quoting at some length:

> Every unconscious investment mobilizes a delirious interplay of disinvestments, of counterinvestments, of overinvestments. But we have seen in this context that there were two major types of social investment, segregative and nomadic, just as there were two poles of delirium: first, a paranoiac fascisizing (*fascisant*) type or pole that invests the formation of central sovereignty; overinvests it

by making it the final eternal cause for all the other social forms of history; counterinvests the enclaves or the periphery; and disinvests every free "figure" of desire—yes, I am your kind, and I belong to the superior race and class. And second, a schizorevolutionary type or pole that follows the *lines of escape* of desire; breaches the wall and causes flows to move; assembles its machines and its groups-in-fusion in the enclaves or at the periphery—proceeding in an inverse fashion from that of the other pole: I am not your kind, I belong eternally to the inferior race, I am a beast, a black. Good people say that we must not flee, that to escape is not good, that it isn't effective, and that one must work for reforms. But the revolutionary knows that escape is revolutionary—*withdrawal, freaks*—provided one sweeps away the social cover on leaving, or causes a piece of the system to get lost in the shuffle. What matters is to break through the wall, even if one has to become black like John Brown, George Jackson. "I may take flight, but all the while I am fleeing, I will be looking for a weapon!" (*Anti-Oedipus* 277; emphases in original)

The vertiginous effect of their prose is by design, since a style like this is at least one way to introduce into the static medium of text the dynamic, unpredictable, uncontrollable, and therefore truly revolutionary social, political, and ethical potential that Deleuze and Guattari propose in their notion of the schizorevolutionary. The schizorevolutionary is the figure that Deleuze and Guattari imagine as potentially standing against the paranoia-inducing constraints of "the Oedipus," whether capitalism, the nuclear family, the Oedipal complex itself, or any other constraining expression of convention that so centrally imposes itself on so much of our conscious and unconscious lives as to render almost impossible the imagining of another mode of living, imagining, or desiring. This figure's investment expresses itself in the possibility that resistance may only express itself in withdrawal, since to Deleuze and Guattari's way of thinking, working for reforms within the system or convention is merely another subordination to the workings of that system or convention. At least the schizorevolutionary might sweep away the social covering on leaving or cause a piece of the system to get lost in the shuffle. The schizorevolutionary may be able to change the stakes of the investments within the preexisting system. What we need to take from all of this is that the status of the insider—which includes being an insider with respect to our own habits, which, of course, in the first instance we've learned from someone else—is to be resisted and suspected as a matter of course. After all, the insider who continues to submit to the workings of convention does so because of some benefit, because no other alternative has presented itself, or because of the sheer oppressive power of the convention itself. The characterizations of inferiority and superiority in their description suggests these benefits, as does the metaphor of investment. It is telling, in terms of Deleuze and Guattari and in terms of understanding Everett's work, that the archetype of inferiority that they seize upon is an image of blackness, and the specific exponents of blackness are a member of the Black Panther Party and a revolutionary abolitionist, whose actual whiteness makes clear that Deleuze and Guattari cite blackness here as a symbolic rather than literal state. The nomadic social investment carries with it a potential freedom that the segregative habit of mind steals from us, again, as I keep saying, whether we realize it or not. The nomadic investment does not, of course, guarantee anything (we will return to this idea in discussing *Suder* and, later, *Assumption,* among other texts), but it does at least open up possibilities to imagine real resistance, rejection, or at a minimum, simple refusal and rethinking.

The notion of the schizorevolutionary is invaluable to a consideration of Everett's work, because of how it helps us think about the anticonventional stance that I am arguing is central to his work. The schizorevolutionary's investment is dynamic in ways that do not purport to supply definitive conclusions but in ways that demonstrate the worth of this dynamism as a good in itself. The figure of the schizorevolutionary does not say that we should work toward some dynamic understanding of the world around us in order to get to this place or that, this programmatic, ideological, philosophical, ethical end point or that one. It attempts instead to demonstrate, convince us, really, that the dynamic has its own worth in and of itself. The schizorevolutionary says, like Brown or Jackson, I will have my say on my own terms, and not on the terms of those in power, whatever the cost. Everett's work, I will argue here, does the same thing. It is not about conclusion or conclusiveness, impulses expressed by the desire to "fix" in the ways expressed in Everett's story and in the insidious tendencies of stereotyping, to return to only two of the many available examples of this impulse.

His work issues challenges that, if taken up by his readers, promise to destabilize the habitual practices of reading themselves in ways that may actually translate into how we read (or at least interact with) the world in which we carry on our daily lives and our conventional, habitual, practiced ways of interacting with it. This challenge to our reading practices can, as I will argue explicitly in chapter 4, have genuine implications for how we view that most convention-bound way of interacting with those around us—at least in the United States—the question of race. I will repeat this later but will say it here first. I am not saying that Everett's fiction is *about* race or that understanding what these texts represent about race is some sort of key to unlocking either Everett's texts or the problems of race in the United States (an argumentative concession so obvious as to be embarrassing even to utter). I am saying that the implications of what he's written over more than thirty-five years may help illuminate the problematics of race in American society by suggesting avenues rarely if ever traveled. These avenues encourage the rethinking of questions of race by focusing our attention on the infinite spaces between categories instead of upon the categories themselves.

Deleuze and Guattari eventually work toward a definition of a practice that they envision as far superior to Freudian psychoanalysis, which they call schizo-analysis, and which articulates, again, the potentially revolutionary force implicit in rejecting the Oedipus, the oppressive conventions that govern our lives: "Schizoanalysis is the variable analysis of the n sexes in a subject, beyond the anthropomorphic representation that society imposes on this subject, and with which it represents its own sexuality. The schizoanalytic slogan of the desiring-revolution will be first of all: to each its own sexes" (*Anti-Oedipus* 296). So, Deleuze and Guattari, writing in the late 1960s and early 1970s, demonstrate the revolutionary potential of the schizoanalytic investment, as they do away with gender binaries at a time when feminism is only beginning to register upon most people the oppressive power of patriarchy within capitalism and the developed world. Even as oppressive as our desires and genders can be, then, schizoanalysis suggests a freeing from such constraints, and this freeing, in turn, opens up possibilities that are unavailable to us if we persist in our acceptance of those binaries. What I am doing here is not to attempt a schizoanalytical reading of Everett's work as such, since something so systematic would actually undermine itself as an argument for the value of the anticonventional. I am instead drawing out the implications of such a framework for reading the multifarious body of his work and, perhaps more importantly, attempting to assert a sense of meaning that this multifariousness can convey if we can become more open to the meanings available to us in multifariousness as such. Looking at the infinite space between the poles of any binary may enable this openness, and Everett's fiction provides practice in and encouragement to look at this infinite intermediary space.

Deleuze and Guattari are not suggesting—as I hope is clear—that we get a simple binary choice between the paranoiac and the schizorevolutionary. Their formulations instead suggest the continuum between poles, even those as ostensibly fixed as gender or race have long appeared to be. In other words, their thinking does not presume toward some definitiveness or perfection. An acceptance of imperfection is uncomfortable and humbling. As critics, we usually at least implicitly suggest that our readings have resolved something, but that is not the case in the intellectual world that these two theorists attempt to bring into being. But freeing us from our habitual investments in the value of definitiveness, a fetish really, is not easily accomplished. In the meantime, these suggestions can seem disturbing or at least disorienting. I am arguing that possibilities available in Everett's work create similar discomforts and disorientations but promise similar potential benefits.

So the sense of disorientation that Deleuze and Guattari authorize (since the value of disorientation will probably always require some authorization) stands Sherman on a literal precipice as "The Fix" comes to its conclusion. He has appeared as the nomadic figure throughout the story—nomadic in the conventional sense of the wanderer, and in the Deleuzoguattarian sense in opposition to the segregative, which is hierarchical and conventional (a distinction about which more later). In the conventional sense, for now, Sherman ostensibly comes from nowhere, lives nowhere, and has no history. As he stands on a bridge, contemplating his own conclusion, the segregative crowd gathers near where he stands. They do not express concern for his well-being but instead demand of him the action that has come to signify his entire meaning to them in the story. "'Fix us!' they shouted. 'Fix us! Fix us!'" (24). It is clear that this fixing remains their priority as well as the bane of Sherman's existence. And as it has become the bane of Sherman's existence, so it should become ours, although the crowd do not know this: "Sherman stepped over the railing and stood on the brink, the toes of his shoes pushed well over the edge" (24). It is only at the point when he looks sure to jump that the crowd momentarily sound a call for his life. "'Don't!' they all screamed" (24). Lest we think, though, that they have come to their senses as moral agents, their final words, the final words of the story, reiterate their own priorities: "Fix us! Fix us!" (24).

The way the story concludes, then (I hesitate to say "ends" since the conclusion of this story, as with most of Everett's fiction, is more suggestive than conclusive), argues strongly against a resorting to the comforting convention of closure—another expression of fixity, after all. As he stands on the brink, Sherman promises to do Deleuze and Guattari one better. Yes, he may withdraw—either from the edge or from the conventions that beset him. He may, George Jackson– or John Brown–like, be looking for a weapon. But in any event, he puts us in a quintessentially anticonventional position. This is one final paradox, for now (although hardly *the* final paradox). Even though we have been rightly trained to value human life—even as represented in fictional characters—we should probably be hoping that Sherman jumps. This desire is not the same as the absurdist wish we might find in Ionesco, though. Sherman's most meaningful act is not suicide under all circumstances. But as things stand, in his present situation, his suicide appears his most freeing alternative. It is in this desire for Sherman to end his own life and for us to go against that most basic of our own conditionings that we take a leap into Everett's world and the challenges that he issues to his readers.

◆ ◆ ◆

The cumulative readings of "The Fix," the ways they build to create something constructive but also liminal, and the ways that these readings argue against fixity and the conventions of criticism and mean-making encourage further consideration of the meaning of this liminality as it pertains to the reading of fiction in general and the reading of fiction by an African American writer (as opposed to "African American fiction," another definitive-sounding and limiting categorization) in particular.[10] Based on what I've said so far, it should not come as a surprise that there are limitless possibilities for how to organize what follows, in part because Everett, already prolific, continues to produce. And while it is obvious that this qualification could be made in the introduction of any written text (which is, like Zeno's paradoxes, infinite at the beginning [in theory] but not over the course of its actual trajectory [in practice]), it continues to be crucial that I reiterate this point because of how it helps illuminate Everett's work. So any reading of his work is necessarily, but also constructively, provisional. Everett's work presents itself as a subject of conscious and unavoidable reflection on the sensation in the reader that we only approach the meaning of his work by infinite degrees, in the way that a curve approaches the value of an asymptote infinitely, without ever reaching the value itself. More important is that the approach by infinite degrees has a value (here, in both the mathematical and aesthetic senses of the word) and that the approach itself is instructive.

With these organizational considerations now foregrounded, I will describe my argument as something of a kaleidoscope. After all, asserting the importance of the provisional, the anticonventional, and the infinitely between by way of a linear structure would suggest my lack of commitment to my premise, or worse, my lack of understanding of it. While the latter may still come to pass, the former is not in any doubt. But the combination of the volume, the complexity, and the interconnectedness of this body of work means that returning to the same ground in different ways cannot be avoided, and these returns are also illuminating. I will repeatedly circle back to certain of the novels while adding new ones along the way, just as a kaleidoscope in motion will reveal new patterns through juxtaposition with what we've already seen. In his 2006 interview with me, Everett in fact drew attention to this kaleidoscopic interconnectedness, becoming momentarily as explicit but also characteristically elliptical as he ever is about his work, when he said that he is writing "one big novel" ("Uncategorizable" 121). He added that if he were to tell me (or anyone else, I am assuming; no need to take his admission personally) what that one book was about would mean he would have to kill me. In another interview, he said, "I find it interesting to have what I consider ghostly echoes of characters popping up throughout my work. I never really wanted to say this but I will. I don't consider any work singularly. I think I am writing an entire body of work, as diverse as its pieces are. I see it as one very long work that will finally make sense together" ("An Interview" 83). This appraisal sounds like the kind of logical and hermeneutic trap laid by Deleuze and Guattari in their authors' note to *A Thousand Plateaus*, when they suggest that their plateaus may be read in any order, but that the conclusion is to be read last. Since we cannot know at this moment which of Everett's works will be his last, this body of work's ability to finally make sense together is as provisional as the potential and actual trajectories that it traces for itself over time. As a critic, I may be right at this moment in my reading but wrong (or at least rethinking) in the long run, like Zeno's paradoxes. In fact, it's possible that I might rethink my reading of Everett's work at any point in my own development as a critic, irrespective of which work is his last. Forewarned is forearmed.

The following argument is arranged in two parts, each comprising two chapters. Part I is "Creating Infinite Spaces and the Role of the Schizorevolutionary." The first chapter, "Productive Frustration, Anomalous Agents of Chaos, and Anti–Double Consciousness," will discuss the aspects of Everett's fiction that come closest to what might be called a didactic impulse in this writer's work. Obviously, *didactic* is a term we can only use as a placeholder for what we really mean when examining this body of work, since to characterize Everett's work as didactic would be to risk appearing not only to be the butt of the joke but also to appearing to miss entirely the point of what I have been saying so far. But some instances in his fiction do lend themselves to being read as having some kind of teaching impulse, instances that imply "there is something to be learned here," among the literary, theoretical, allusive, and narrative pyrotechnics that can sometimes make up Everett's work.

For now, one instance of the didactic can stand in for those to follow. Among all of the chaotic poignancy constituting Everett's 1999 novel, *Glyph*, is an accusation that Ralph makes about the reader early in the novel: "Have you to this point assumed that I am white? In my reading, I discovered that if a character was black, then he at some point was required to comb his Afro hairdo, speak on the street using an obvious, ethnically identifiable idiom, live in a certain part of a town, or be called a nigger by someone. White characters, I assumed they were white (often, because of the ways they spoke of other kinds of people), did not seem to need that kind of introduction, or perhaps legitimization, to exist on the page" (54). On the one hand, this moment can remind us of those moments when the narrator appears to look directly into the imagined reader's eyes and say something like, "Reader, I married him." Gestures like Jane Eyre's have come to be identifiable with nineteenth-century literary realism. However, while this kind of gesture may appear familiar, if not completely conventional, the substance of the gesture cannot be similarly characterized. Drawing the reader's attention to his or her own readerly assumptions is risky, especially when imputing to that reader the kind of assumption that a reader is probably most likely to deny. When the subject is race and the many, usually fraught and often negative assumptions that accompany the subject of race—especially when the subject of the discussion is African Americans and others' attitudes toward this subsection of the American population—drawing the reader's attention to their own less-than-progressive assumptions will not necessarily ingratiate a fictional speaker to the accused or exposed reader. Add to this observation the us-versus-them aspect of Ralph's statement, when he points out that a white character need not be legitimized to exist on the page as an African American character always does and adds further that the reader of *Glyph* will probably be white (based on the ethnocultural demographics of the twenty-first-century American reading public) and this finger-pointing takes on an unavoidably admonitory quality. This is what the didactic moment in Everett's fiction can look like. It is not a matter of merely rejecting whatever conventions have preceded this textual moment but of deploying the familiar, if submerged, recognition of how readerly expectation works in a way that draws attention to itself while making the didactic point. The character of the gesture itself must also be reflected upon in the fictional world Everett presents.

The second chapter, "The Persistently Gnawing and Troubling Effort Not to Let Our Guards Down," enables a more extrapolating approach to Everett's work than in chapter 1. If the first chapter is of the Ralph-speaking-directly-to-the-reader-about-race variety, then it's worth stepping back and taking a wider view of some of the broader implications in Everett's fiction. For instance, what role does the ideological state apparatus known as the family play in how we habitually make meaning and, from there, how do Everett's novels both draw our attention to and encourage us to think differently about these attempts at mean-making? For now, we need not look any further than *Cutting Lisa* for an example of what this broadened perspective enables us to think about. A novel in which the main character, John Livesey, feels compelled to conduct an abortion on Lisa, his daughter-in-law, on the kitchen table of her own home revolves around what Livesey feels he is within his rights to do in order to save his family, according to his rather specific interpretations of the words "save" and, more importantly, "family." (In another of Everett's suggestive endings, Livesey is not actually shown performing the abortion. The novel's conclusion leads to this as a completely reasonable inference for the reader to draw, though.) Livesey's willingness to go beyond what we might habitually see as the bounds of family interaction also makes clear that the anticonventional attitudes on display in many of Everett's protagonists do not come with guarantees of our approval or of obvious social progress or benefit.

John Livesey's decision to terminate his daughter-in-law's pregnancy is complicated greatly (although, it would appear, simplified for Livesey) by the fact that the fetus is not related to Livesey by blood. It is the result of an affair that Lisa has had with a man named Greg Yount, a close friend of her husband, Elgin, who is Livesey's son. Elgin, and his daughter, Katy, whom John adores, are related to him by blood. But John's only dominion over the unborn baby exists in John's imagination, and through his idea (ideal, really) of the notion of family. From there, he confers upon himself the right of life and death over the unborn child.

Characteristically, Everett's creation of John Livesey leaves very little room for comfortable resolution, irrespective of whatever our preexisting feelings about abortion may be. In any case, it is safe to assume that we will hold some position on abortion, and that appears to be at least part of the point of the conundrum in which the reader is left as the novel ends. And it has to be said that producing a story that concludes with the suggestion of an abortion and that nevertheless leaves the reader contemplating anything beyond that abortion cannot be an easy feat to have accomplished. This, too, suggests the terrain made available in Everett's fictional world. Eerily, we might even find ourselves put in the horrifying position of thinking that the abortion itself is beside the main point, since the novel sets itself up as something of a referendum on the convention of "family." While there are no overt statements about family here as there is about race in *Glyph,* for instance, *Cutting Lisa* is at least one degree removed from such explicit statement. This extra degree of remove, though, is necessary in our continued nuancing of our reading of Everett's fiction.

Part II is "Religion, Art, and Race in Everett." Chapter 3, "Plateaus of Intensity in a World between Categories," takes the broader implications discussed in chapter 2 and applies them to two important subjects that recur in Everett's work—religion and art. Religion is reliably set up for ridicule in Everett's fictional world, and prayers, as they appear in *Suder, Watershed, American Desert,* and *Percival Everett by Virgil Russell,* leave little doubt about the role that might be imputed to religion as it negatively affects our ability to rethink or to see the spaces in between categories. But while this is the case most of the time in Everett's work, it is also instructive to make sense of what happens when religion is accorded some degree of respect, as happens in *The Body of Martin Aguilera*, in which an unrepresentative religious group does not stand in for organized religion as a whole but appears to represent another expression of infinite possibilities. And if Everett's body of work is one long novel, as he suggests, then its treatment of the role of art helps hold it together. Art is a source of anxiety, struggle, and disagreement but also hope, meaning, and, at times, intimacy, as is apparent in *Percival Everett by Virgil Russell* and *So Much Blue*.

Finally, with the rest of the discussion in place, it will be worth extrapolating in our reading of Everett's fiction to talk about what his novels make available in thinking about questions of race as a convention. This will be the task of chapter 4, "The Trace of Race and Difficult Likenesses." While Everett's fiction complicates questions of race, it does not negate or ignore them. How these complex works encourage the crossing or at least blurring of the conventional lines that we draw in our considerations of race suggests a further reconsideration of lines in general. The life of Theodore Street in *American Desert* emphasizes the point about lines, as he introduces his own story:

> That Theodore Street was dead was not a matter open to debate. The irony of his accidental death went unobserved as no one knew that Theodore was on his way to commit suicide when he was, shall we say, interrupted. Now the irony is lost amid the confusion created by Ted's death, departure, demise, dissolution and further by the fact that Ted chooses to relate his own story in third person, an unusual (the occasional politician and athlete aside), but acceptable device, given that, in a most profound way, he stood—or stands even—outside himself, not so much on the parapet of consciousness but on life itself, it being perhaps the case that neither entails, necessarily, the other. (3)

Convention dictates that the line between life and death is largely unbreachable, at least to those of us not trained as physicians or theologians. But *American Desert* begins with exactly such a breach, as well as a quite elaborate drawing of attention to the breach. An additional breach of convention is just as important to understanding Everett's work, though, and that is the breaching of narrative convention. While a deceased narrator is not without precedent, Everett's deployment of this trope as an introductory salvo (combined with the macabre irony that the narrator was on his way to commit suicide when he is killed in an accident) sets a tone of narrative rule breaking that expands in its significance throughout what follows in *American Desert*. Ted's "death, departure, demise, dissolution," in other words, not only does not impede the telling of a good story but adds significantly to the challenges that Everett's fiction poses.

◆ ◆ ◆

I've already affirmed here my awareness that the critic doesn't "solve" anything. We can, however, contribute to an overall picture of something, contribute to the making of meaning, but this making of meaning is, by its nature, incomplete. This recognition brings with it another question, peculiar to studying the work of Percival Everett and to any attempt to make some sort of argument that encompasses even some of the broad sweep of his work. All of his readers must recognize the possibility that we are at times the butt of some of his jokes. I particularly acknowledge myself in this role in my discussion of word play in *Glyph* in chapter 1. Nevertheless, as there is value in understanding without resolution, it is worth making the attempt of understanding even in the face of having the joke turn on ourselves.

A related matter arises from the outset, then, and that is the matter of scope. Not only because of the volume of Everett's production but more importantly because of the density of his fiction, it would probably be the very essence of falling into a trap even to attempt to address all of Everett's work in one book. I will admit that that was my initial intention, but the pointlessness of that endeavor became apparent to me as I kept returning to certain of his novels in order to elaborate upon points I was making about others. Hence the notion of the kaleidoscope. Once we start opening up the prospects of allusions in Everett's work that gesture toward books written by other people, the matrix at work becomes unwieldy, to say the least. I think Rone Shavers has put this best, in an interview with Everett from 2004: "In almost every one of his works, you peel away one layer of references and meaning only to find another, only to then discover another, only to come upon another, until—well, you get the idea. Welcome, then, to an interview about everything, because in many ways, the meaning of everything is the only subject Everett really writes about" ("Percival Everett" 58). I would only modify Shavers's point by saying that *everything* in

Everett's work includes, and maybe even relies upon, everything else in Everett's work. Of course, again, all art poses such problems, and the more we know, the more we realize we do not know.[11] As a result of these very real limitations of world and time, I have concentrated on a number of Everett's works, which will stand in as synecdoches for the rest. To say that they are representative of his work is to miss yet another point. So I don't call them that, but I will return to some novels to make different but related points.

A few years ago I published an article that, with time, has become the premise for this book: "What I'll suggest, here, is that Everett's fiction is not fiction at all, or at least, not just fiction, but that it is an attempt to hew out and work in the spaces in between conventional literary categories, not in order to provide answers—as critics conventionally attempt to do—but to provoke further questions that might be asked about his work and by extension the works of other writers, as well" ("Setting One's House in Order" 217–18). But stating things this way still sounds like I am making a concession where none needs be made. The great challenge of criticism is, has always been, and will always be the challenge of incompleteness. We cannot know everything. And even when some rare individual emerges who appears to know everything at that moment (apparently, there was a time when Sir Isaac Newton was said to know all there was to know about physics), it does not take long to realize that what appeared at the time to be everything was only that—the appearance of everything.

Alberto Toscano expresses suspicion about the critic's task in his preface to Eric Alliez's *The Signature of the World*, a book on Deleuze and Guattari's philosophy, with the following salvo: "The strictures of quality assessment and the self-reinforcing imperatives of the market have consigned philosophers, as of late, to a regime of publication—of *poubéllication,* to adopt Lacan's portmanteau quip—dominated by the exhaustive introduction, the definitive treatment of the comparative exercise in ecumenical interdisciplinarity" (ix). Toscano's remarks are not intended to be glib, but, like Rita Felski's on the hermeneutics of suspicion, to situate the task of the critic within the broader function of criticism more generally. Felski's and Toscano's arguments share some anxiety, or perhaps more accurately self-consciousness, about the state and task of the critic. I am no different. But Everett's work in particular provides an apposite occasion for making sense of what this self-consciousness can teach the critic, the reader, and perhaps the citizen more generally about how each of us interacts with the culture in which we find ourselves. Deleuze and Guattari, similarly, are instructive in making sense of this precarious position by making this precariousness legible and possibly generative.

In fact, Everett makes a point similar to this in his interviews, as he describes his experience writing in an interview with Barbara DeMarco-Barrett and Marrie Stone: "The fascinating thing about writing novels or making any art is I think I know something when I start, and what I'm taught by the time I reach the end is that I didn't know *that*. It's a way of exposing my own ignorance and teaching me that knowing less is better" ("Interview with Percival Everett" 149–50). This relationship between the state of thinking we know something and discovering—through learning—all that we don't know is a profoundly instructive process for Everett, one that he appears to have harnessed for his own benefit as an artist, or at least one that he has come to embrace and from which he continues to learn. There is a great deal of potential value in this lesson, I am arguing. But this kind of learning flies directly in the face of the model of mastery, of expertise, that still persists for the critic. But critics are always provisional in what we argue, since we can very easily stumble upon something after we've published our work that at least sheds a different light on that about which we were formerly so certain or simply inspires us to rethink something we formerly believed and asserted quite confidently.

And this is the challenge that Everett's work issues to his readers. What matters, then, is working within this constraint, recognizing it less as a constraint and more as an active producer of meaning. It draws our attention to the provisional nature of meaning, the contingency of our relationships with the conventions that enable us to forget about this contingency and to move along—for better and for worse—as if this contingency does not exist and make or find meaning in spite of provisionality, contingency, and convention. In other words, we proceed with the unexamined certainty that the bedroom floor will continue to support our weight this morning, too.

One example makes the larger point here. I have recently (over the last three or so years) had an almost complete change of heart regarding my views about Ralph Ellison.[12] The details of the change of heart are not really the point here. What is the point is that I have spoken to who knows how many students about Ellison over the course of my career, based on what I used to believe about him and his work. I've published a couple of articles and delivered many more conference papers on his work and cited him as an example of something specific about how African Americans might see themselves and other issues like that. Now, I am just as sure about how I feel about Ellison as I was before. As his narrator in *Invisible Man* says,

> What and how much had I lost by trying to do only what was expected of me instead of what I myself had wished to do? What a waste, what a senseless waste! But what of those things which you actually didn't like, not because you were not supposed to like them, not because to dislike them was considered a mark of refinement and education—but because you actually found them distasteful? *The very idea annoyed me. How could you know?* It involved a problem of choice. I would have to weigh many things carefully before deciding and there would be some things that would cause quite a bit of trouble, simply because I had never formed a personal attitude toward so much. *I had accepted the accepted attitudes and it had made life seem simple.* (266–67; emphases added)

This is what the experience of the kind of provisional existence typical of an Everett character sounds like when described by an Ellison character, the character who firmly believes that identity is something *true* and definitive, an investment toward which one aspires. The narrator's annoyance with the uncertainty of not being able to know what actually motivates him suggests something essential that he desires from his sense of understanding in the world. His acceptance of the accepted attitudes that had made his life simple (which is always at least one attraction of such attitudes) is a source of intense frustration at the point when it no longer works for him or provides the answers upon which he has previously relied. This view contradicts the more provisional notion of identity that we see in Everett's protagonists, whereby they present an identity to which they are committed and which, in many cases, changes into another identity, to which they are equally committed. This is how the provisional works and what the anticonventional investment of many of his protagonists makes possible. At each stage, the sense of identity, the ability to adopt a point of view, the willingness to take a stand, is available, even within the possibility that circumstances may change, leading to a new sense of identity, point of view, or stance. The provisional attitude leaves one open to prospects that perhaps we might not otherwise have seen.

APPROXIMATE GESTURES

Everett's fiction has been understood in a remarkable variety of ways when we consider how relatively few people read and study his work. His fiction has been discussed as postmodernist; for its contribution to the development of the genre of the western; for its relationship to, explication of, and parody of post-structuralism; for its philosophical underpinnings; for its humor; and, of course, for its role as a possible new expression of African American literature; as well as, of course, its failings as African American literature.[13] And while all of this critical interrogation is essential, it leaves unexamined the meaning of this variety as a subject of discussion in and of itself. If we approach Everett's work as a corpus that issues a number of challenges to the reader, then we cannot help but meditate on the meaning of that challenge itself. This meditation is what is intended in what follows.

The contrast between the article and the book-length study is quite manifest when approaching Everett's fiction. The article can be, obviously, quite focused in its attention and penetrate to the heart of a specific text, idea, theme, approach, etc. The book must take on something broader, more expansive. So I will approach Everett's work here, in part, as an opportunity to introduce his work to readers who may not be familiar with it. Since I have in the past referred to the group of critics who work on Everett as a coterie, picking up on that usage as presented in one of his novels, I know that the group of readers unfamiliar with his work is substantial. But I will not approach the book as an introduction in the way that I might provide a catalog of his work, perhaps a chronology, and a summative review of the criticism on his writing, in part because I have been spared that task by others who have done it admirably and thoroughly.[14] I will, instead, approach Everett's work as a dynamic, roiling, intra-allusive kaleidoscope that looks outward at the world as well as inward at itself to create the kinds of contingent meanings that we can then deploy to make meaning in the world however we find it and wherever we are in it. In fact, approaching his work this way is consonant with the lessons, opportunities, and challenges his work provides and models. I am working here less toward mastery of Everett's work and more toward the case for a dynamic resistance to mastery, a constructive frustration that is itself difficult to get at but also profoundly instructive. In fact, it is just as pertinent to this study to imagine an entirely different kaleidoscopic approach to these texts being equally illuminating and instructive, quite possibly in ways similar to this study and different in others. Such a conclusion would be entirely appropriate to Everett's work and to my approach to it here.

In other words, as many of Everett's main characters transit in between established categories, opening possibilities that are not readily apparent to us most of the time, it's worth considering his novels as similarly carving out spaces in between categories and opening up to us opportunities for perceptions that were previously hidden or rendered less apparent because of the weight of convention on our perceptions of the world. This approach necessitates that some texts will receive more attention than others, but this is not to suggest that the texts that receive more attention here are more "important" than others that do not. Another approach might find different texts gaining prominence. That, too, must be part of the prospect in the approach I am taking here. I look forward to reading and learning from these other approaches.

◆ ◆ ◆

I will conclude by making two points as a signal to what follows. First, part of what lies at the center of this book is the understanding, perhaps the acceptance, that this reading of Everett implies its own provisionality. What looks right now cannot help but be subject to revision later. This does not mean that everything goes, that nihilism is ascendant. It's more hopeful than that, because we are brought to a place where we can see the value in making meaning even as we recognize that the meaning we make now will by necessity change because of what else we learn later. There is a vitality in this discovery. Second, this is not a literary critical book masquerading as a philosophical treatise. I am a literary critic, and this is an attempt to read Everett's work. But it is a reading of Everett's work that points to something that literary criticism *as literary criticism* can do, which is to point to improved habits of mind and help us think more deeply about how we position ourselves in and engage with the world around us.

I

CREATING INFINITE SPACES AND THE ROLE OF THE SCHIZOREVOLUTIONARY

1

PRODUCTIVE FRUSTRATION, ANOMALOUS AGENTS OF CHAOS, AND ANTI–DOUBLE CONSCIOUSNESS

This is why Said means so much to me, he said. You see, Said was young when he heard that statement made by Golda Meir, that there are no Palestinian people, and when he heard this, he became involved in the Palestinian question. He knew then that difference is never accepted. You are different, okay, but that difference is never seen as containing its own value. Difference as orientalist entertainment is allowed, but difference with its own intrinsic value, no. You can wait forever, and no one will give you that value.

—Teju Cole, *Open City*

I will begin with infinity.

—*Glyph*

The broad scope, dizzying variety, almost limitless breadth, and sheer volume of Everett's work means that attempting to impose any sort of even provisional order upon it is a fool's errand from the beginning. And yet, in spite of ourselves, we can still always find meaning, in one form or another. As Thelonious "Monk" Ellison, the narrator of *Erasure*, muses on the subject of meaning in language, so we can take some comfort in the critical enterprise:

> It's incredible that a sentence is ever understood. Mere sounds strung together by some agent attempting to mean some thing, but the meaning need not and does not confine itself to that intention. Those sounds, strung as they are in

their peculiar and particular order, never change, but do nothing but change. Even if grammatical recognitions are crude, meaning is present. Even if the words are utterly confusing, there is meaning. Even if the semantic relationships are only general or categorical. Even if the language is unknown. Meaning is internal, external, orbital, but still there is no such thing as propositional content. Language never really effaces its own presence, but creates the illusion that it does in cases where meaning presumes a first priority. (44)

The ambition to impose some order, in some form, is the role of the critic, after all. So the immediate disjunction between theory and practice where Everett's fiction is concerned sets the critic up for failure, or at least disappointment. But this disappointment can itself be instructive in teaching what else might be derived from the practice of criticism. All of this is especially the case if the argument under construction is an attempt to demonstrate the significance of not working toward some definitive solution and deriving instead some intelligible sense of the latently limitless meanings available in the spaces in between recognizable categories.

Daniel W. Smith brings together these points about the discernment of meaning and the role of the critic in his discussion of ethics in the work of Gilles Deleuze. Smith writes:

In a sense, morality is not unlike aesthetics: much aesthetic theory is written, not from the viewpoint of the artist who creates, but rather from the viewpoint of a spectator who is making judgements about works of art they did not create, and perhaps could not create. Similarly, morality has tended to be developed, not from the viewpoint of those who act, but rather from the viewpoint of those who feel the effects of the actions of others. Both are driven by a mania to judge; this is why philosophers are obsessed with analyzing "aesthetic judgments" and "moral judgments." (181)

This "mania to judge" encourages, perhaps even requires, from the critic—like the spectator or those who feel the effects of others' actions, as Smith formulates above—a desire for completeness, for definitiveness, that stands in for and as meaning. When we see this mania in the moral context in which Smith situates it, we see more clearly, perhaps, what is at stake for the critic, why the work of the critic becomes so important, at least for the critic. There is something moral, something metaphysical, in deriving meaning from art. This meaning, then—the implication goes—must have a moral component as part of its importance; otherwise, it is merely, in the very meanest sense of this expression, an academic exercise. My argument that the retrained habits of mind that may be made available to us through a reading of Everett's work may translate to our relationship to and judgments of the larger world around us derives from suggestions like Smith's, as well as Deleuze and Guattari's, of the moral character of aesthetic judgment.

Of course, following from this discussion is some consideration of who is making the judgments—making meaning—where one stands when meaning is being made, and perhaps an imperative to consider our positioning when we (and others) make meaning. The passage in the epigraph from Teju Cole's *Open City* poses the relatively obvious but easily taken for granted point that the version of meaning that prevails under any circumstances will, in the first instance at least, be that version of meaning underwritten by some dominant interest. In the passage, a young man named Farouq argues that difference within the orientalist framework that he is critiquing only has value in its potential to be exchanged for something of value as determined by the interests of the dominant group. But if difference never contains its own intrinsic value, as he says, then what options are open to members of marginalized, disenfranchised, *different* groups? One option is to give oneself up to the status quo, giving oneself up to the whims of others, possibly gaining the whole world but losing one's own soul. Another option is to oppose perpetually, in the hope that opposition will eventually lead to incremental improvements or even revolution, however either term might be understood. Alternatively still, one might attempt to ignore these ideological, racial, social, and political realities altogether, working not in ignorance of the reality of one's surroundings but as if these realities did not persist. To refuse to play the game, as the game theorists would have it regarding the prisoner's dilemma. bell hooks makes a similar observation about the importance of point of view, or more simply still of *interest*, when considerations of identity are at stake: "When the dominant culture demands that the Other be offered as sign that progressive political change is taking place, that the American Dream can indeed be inclusive of difference, it invites a resurgence of essentialist cultural nationalism. The acknowledged Other must assume recognizable forms" (26). In other words, cultural expression need not solely be translated into a culturally recognizable form, but the disenfranchised must be aware of this aspect of cultural transaction. Any of these options, of course, brings with it risk. While it becomes clear to the narrator of *Open City* that Farouq is a proponent for the more revolutionary option, and the same may be said of hooks's position, Everett may be approached as a member of this latter, schizorevolutionary group, in which the outcome is much less certain, while the resistance is nevertheless enacted.

If I am right in locating Everett within this third option, I hope I will not be misunderstood as equating him with the unnamed artist that Langston Hughes famously describes in "The Negro Artist and the Racial Mountain," the black artist who does not wish to be identified as a black artist but only as an artist, as some imaginarily universal avatar who just happens to be black. That artist wants to downplay his or her race and the role race may play in the evaluation of his or her work. Everett's practice may best be understood as much more complex and demanding on the evaluator of his art than a mere denial of the reality of being raced in America, occupied as it is instead with producing art that actively issues challenges to its readers also to resist this simple denial and then allowing those challenges to be worked out by readers themselves. In this model, the art becomes an impetus for reflection and discussion but gives little in the way of positive instruction, as a more conventional revolutionary might. These challenges, then, shift the onus from the producer of the work of art in question to the consumer, whether reader, critic, reviewer, or whoever, and not to be resolved by the artist at all. In other words, the artist absents himself not only (in Everett's case) from the *arguments* about race in the country but also from race as it relates to aesthetics, as well as the judgments on either subject. The artist has, of course, already taken on these stakes at least implicitly as a matter of course in producing art within the culture as we find it. Everett's work makes sure that his readers must also be aware of these stakes and struggle with whatever possible answers they come up with. His work might be understood as adopting an anti–double consciousness posture, where instead of seeing oneself through the eyes of others, as Du Bois's famous formulation has it, the black subject attempts to see himself or herself as if the eyes of that other do not matter to the black subject's self-perception. When I say *anti–double consciousness,* I am not suggesting some kind of unity, some unified consciousness that lives in harmony with itself, irrespective of what happens around, to, or within it. I am suggesting something closer to a multiple consciousness, which engages with itself and the world in many different ways, sometimes in sequence, sometimes simultaneously. I suppose that I am positing a form of consciousness for black people that approximates what I imagine (for that's all I can do) is the experience that white people have with their consciousnesses most of the time and without having to think about it or claim it in any way. While I recognize the possibly utopian nature of this idea, it is nevertheless worth considering, if only because of the prospects that it opens up. In this attitude, the black subject is less determined by the eyes of the white observer and less seduced into an attempt to explain blackness to that observer. When we remember that, for Du Bois, the observer looks at the black subject with contempt, any relief from that gaze must be at least considered, even if only in the imagination. And as with my distinction between unconventional and anticonventional, the distinction between being unaware of this gaze as opposed to actively resisting it holds here. The challenges issued by Everett's work, then, carry with them broader implications as well, which extend beyond the bounds of literary criticism, enacting among other significances the moral realm that Smith discusses in examining Deleuze's considerations regarding ethics.

One way that the challenge issued by Everett's work may be understood— and only one way, for now, since the nature of my argument asserts that there are infinite ways as well as infinite challenges—is the requirement of a vigilant, persistent, and critical self-awareness of one's own practices and the assumptions and premises upon which those practices are based.[1] These practices and assumptions are based, in part, on the ability to believe in and rely upon the principle of induction that Wallace discusses. These inductions (of the nature that because the floor has supported my weight each morning when I have awakened up until now, I can reasonably infer that the floor will again support my weight on any particular morning) in turn rely, again in part, upon recognizable categories. These may be categories we recognize as preexisting, categories that we synthesize from the world around us, categories we inherit from others, and miscellaneous categories that may hold higher or lower stakes for us in terms of our belief in them.

While categories are cognitively essential to our ability to make meaning and make sense of the world around us, they can also lead, just as necessarily, into traps of perception that can become difficult to escape. One of those traps can be categories that we inherit, the belief that all members of Group X are invariably endowed with Negative Trait Y. As David Schneider begins *The Psychology of Stereotyping*, "Stereotypes wear the black hats in social science" (1). Schneider's opening gambit itself relies upon his reader recognizing, if not subscribing to, conventionalized negative associations with the color black, with the *good* guys wearing the white hats and the *bad* guys wearing the black in that heavily conventionalized genre, the western. (The reliance of the western upon convention may help explain Everett's returning to that mode of fiction again and again.)² The good/bad dichotomy as represented in associations with headwear also again highlights the point Daniel W. Smith makes about the moral resonances of aesthetic judgments. Schneider adds that "stereotypes are the common cold of social interaction—ubiquitous, infectious, irritating, and hard to get rid of" (1). But he gets to the heart of the matter when he writes, "To give up our capacity to form stereotypes, we would probably have to give up our capacity to generalize, and that is a trade none of us should be willing to make. The ability to generalize is a central, primitive, hard-wired cognitive activity" (8). He amplifies this crucial point as follows:

> Categorization itself is ubiquitous. Our whole language of nouns (as well as adjectives and adverbs) is built around the fact that we group animals, plants, things, events, and people into categories. Those who argue that people have limited cognitive resources with which to tame a complex environment suggest that categories are helpful in simplifying the world. . . . To say that an animal is a dog is to encourage its dog qualities, to shellac its Rover individuality—a necessary process in a world with too many unique Rovers. However, others . . . have argued that the essential cognitive problem we humans face is not too much but rather too little information, and that categories help us infer information not directly given by our senses. We know that Rover can bite and bark, even if we do not catch her in the act. Both perspectives are helpful. We group things into categories because we expect that the things within a given category will be similar in some ways and different in others from things alien to the category. This gives us predictive control over the environment, a leg up in deciding on appropriate behavior. (64)

According to either school of thought, though, categories are necessary. Whether our world provides us with too little information or too much, this *predictive control* serves as a collection of metaphysical bookmarks in our lives' experience, enabling us to pick where we left off the day before, enabling us to make assumptions about any given Rover we might meet on Tuesday based on the Rovers we might have met on Monday and every day previous, without having to relearn each day that "dog" is a category in the world and that it probably comes with certain attributes—barking and biting—shared by those members even loosely associated with this category. But you'll notice that the function of the category frees us from the burden of relearning, which is precisely the challenge in favor of which I am arguing here. That's where this starts to get complicated.

As useful as Schneider's discussion is, though, we might be wise to think back to Wallace's observations about the principle of induction one more time. If I can accurately remember that the last golden-colored dog with a wagging tail, floppy ears, and a happy-looking face didn't bite me, then I can safely assume that the next one won't either and act accordingly when confronted by one. I would then be completely understandable in my negative and bewildered reaction if the next golden-colored dog that looked like the last number of golden-colored dogs nevertheless bit my hand when I tried to pat it on the head. Categories provide us predictive control, it's true, but these predictions are not foolproof, whether with golden-colored dogs or differently colored people, and must still exist in a world of our evaluations. In other words, generalizing would appear to be necessary, but each generalization need not be unassailable or unexamined.

Kurt Vonnegut provides a memorable example of one such possible set of implications in his 1973 novel, *Breakfast of Champions*. The passage is quite long, but it contributes significantly to this point about categories and the assumptions that we reasonably base upon them:

> Teachers of children in the United States of America wrote this date on blackboards again and again, and asked the children to memorize it with pride and joy:
>
> 1492

The teachers told the children that this was when their continent was discovered by human beings. Actually, millions of human beings were already
living full and imaginative lives on the continent in 1492. That was simply the
year in which sea pirates began to cheat and rob and kill them.

Here was another piece of evil nonsense which children were taught: that
the sea pirates eventually created a government which became a beacon of
freedom to human beings everywhere else. There were pictures and statues of
this supposed imaginary beacon for children to see. It was sort of an ice cream
cone on fire. It looked like this: [Here the novel includes a crude sketch of the
Statue of Liberty's torch]

Actually, the sea pirates who had the most to do with the creation of the
new government owned human slaves. They used human beings for machinery,
and, even after slavery was eliminated, because it was so embarrassing, they and
their descendants continued to think of ordinary human beings as machines.

• • •

The sea pirates were white. The people who were already on the continent
when the pirates arrived were copper-colored. When slavery was introduced
onto the continent, the slaves were black.

Color was everything.

• • •

Here is how the pirates were able to take whatever they wanted from anybody
else: they had the best boats in the world, and they were meaner than anybody
else, and they had gunpowder, which was a mixture of potassium nitrate, char-
coal, and sulphur. They touched this seemingly listless powder with fire, and it
turned violently into gas. This gas blew projectiles out of metal tubes at terrific
velocities. The projectiles cut through meat and bone very easily; so the pirates
could wreck the wiring or the bellows or the plumbing of a stubborn human
being, even when he was far, far away.

The chief weapon of the sea pirates, however, was their capacity to astonish.
Nobody else could believe, until it was much too late, how heartless and greedy
they were. (10–12)[3]

Vonnegut's remarkable passage does a great deal of work here. If the alternate version of history provided in *Breakfast of Champions* were the conventional version that schoolchildren received—substituting "sea pirates" for "pilgrims," "cheat, rob, and kill" for "discover," and "heartlessness and cruelty" for "spirit of adventure and the rejection of tyranny"—one has to wonder how much pride and joy people would take in proclaiming their families came to the "New World" on the Mayflower. But perhaps just as important is the point that this is the association that is taught to schoolchildren, usually without the encouragement to see it as a conventional narrative with an ideological purpose or as one interpretation among other possibilities. There is nothing innate about the association of "pilgrims" with "spirit of adventure" as opposed to "heartlessness." So not only is who tells the story important to how conventions and the categories based on them come into being and function, but just as important is whom the storytellers tell, especially if they can pass on these associations to the next generation through the ubiquity of one of the ideological state apparatuses, as Louis Althusser famously calls the system of education.

Another crucial point about categories is that we are best advised to learn as much from what they do not teach us as from what they are intended to teach us. For instance, if the next golden retriever we meet does bite us, we can choose to dismiss that individual dog's behavior as an exception that proves the ongoing comforting rule about golden retrievers more generally, as we have come to know them, or think we know them. Alternatively, we can rethink what we thought we knew about the set of assumptions that led us to believe all golden retrievers are lovable, gentle creatures in the first place. At this stage of things, the challenge we face is not one or the other but to become aware of the limitless space available along a continuum of possibilities. For all kinds of reasons that we couldn't possibly know, there are all kinds of behaviors open to golden retrievers. Categories offer the same kind of paradoxes that Zeno theorizes, then. They're useful in potential but can be malign in any given actuality. Of course, we might also question our reliance upon categories altogether and examine what this questioning yields us, which is an opportunity that much of Everett's work has to offer us.

◆ ◆ ◆

What Ralph seems most concerned about over the course of his thinking that eventually makes up the text of *Glyph* is the value, but also the constraints, of categories. It is the continuum, then, and not any individual point along the continuum to which Ralph's attention is drawn and to which he draws ours. As he thinks about Zeno's paradoxes and about his parents' thinking about him, as the novel begins, he comes to the following conclusion, which does stand to reason: "But while they stewed, I watched and contemplated potential and actual infinities and interestingly I found that there is no space between the two, that the arrow may indeed halve the distance to its target until the cows come home, but the target and the arrow situated together in my field of vision were therefore in the same place and so the arrow was there and not there, making Zeno both right and wrong" (5). Ralph has clearly read his Aristotle, or at least his David Foster Wallace (and knowing Ralph, it is probably both), as he works through Aristotle's distinction between the set of actual instances of something and the set of potential instances of something as a way provisionally to resolve the problems Zeno proposes. As Wallace puts this, "Counterarguments about sequential time or subintervals or even actual human movements will always end up impoverishing the Dichotomy and failing to state the real difficulties involved" (*Everything and More* 64). The real difficulties exist in this form: "If '∞' really means 'without end,' then an infinite sequence is one where, however many terms are taken, there are still others that remain to be taken. Meaning forget street-crossing or nose-touching: Zeno can run the whole cruncher in terms of abstract sequences and the fact that there is something inherently contradictory or paradoxical in the idea of an infinite sequence ever being completed" (64). Ralph's potential versus actual infinities solution in the specific case of Zeno's paradoxes seizes upon what so much of Everett's work does more generally. It draws our attention to how *else* we might think about something. Wallace makes this particular case (relatively) simpler when he differentiates between the potentially infinite set of integers and the actual set of integers, as I discuss in my introduction.

So, finally, here, the infinite is always in play in all of its infinite variations, and this infinitude, as it pertains to our reading, is actually generative rather than prohibitive or daunting, making our understanding cumulative and complex rather than a zero-sum game, in which one reading supersedes another. We can always start thinking about what else might be available within a set of terms. When he silently (always silently) listens to an argument between his parents, Ralph again returns to this well-known paradox. His mother says to his father, "But yet you put your name on your few articles and your perpetually near-completed book" (12), and Ralph seizes upon the formulation of perpetual near completion, thinking to himself, "Zing! Zeno could have had no quarrel with that arrow" (12). If we can set aside the squeamish familiarity and characteristic anxiety induced by the image of the perpetually unfinished manuscript, what Ralph's early reflections on Zeno, his parents, and his place in the world do is make clear the priority of his storytelling. He is not working toward anything so much as always working something out. It is in this working out that the fun of *Glyph* resides for the reader as well.

This infinitude of potential and actual readings available in Everett's work, readings that exist in all art, but which his work actively highlights and keeps in play, registers itself in the ways that several of Everett's characters embody multiple positions at the same time, rendering themselves something new at every point in their stories. For instance, Ralph is not a baby or a genius, nor even a baby and a genius. Either resolution to the conundrum posed by his character implies some satisfaction with, or acceptance of, the categories *baby* and *genius*. This satisfaction, in turn, suggests the comfort of appealing to and relying upon the ways that either *baby* or *genius* already resonates with us. *Glyph* works at its best, though, when each category is destabilized in the creation of something new, a baby who is still a baby, even though he has an IQ measured at 475.

As he and his parents sit in a waiting room before having his IQ tested, after he has revealed to them that at the age of two and a half years he can read and write at a level of discernment that would be the envy of his academic father, Ralph provides one of the moments that register his state as neither merely *baby* nor merely *genius* but something wholly beyond our conventional ability to describe him: "My parents watched me read and take notes, sitting on the sofa, pretending to read themselves, but studying me all the while. During those gaps in time when my eyes were not on a book and my hand not set to writing (i.e. when I was thinking), they would sit up straight as if feeling the initial trembling of an earthquake. I did not like the effect I had on them and I regretted having allowed them knowledge of my capacities" (31–32). His parents' edginess around him is attributable to their inability to make sense of what he is. They just know that he isn't what they've come to expect a baby—their baby—to be. He is able to resolve the weirdness of his own status by explaining it from his perspective, which is all any of us ever has. His resolution completely demystifies his own status as a genius but reminds us that he is a baby: "They thought I was a genius and this I found laughable. I reserved that designation for someone who could drive a car or at least hold his shit" (32).[4] But this is *his* resolution of himself as conundrum. His answer does not release us from having to make sense of him.

Strictly speaking, the terms "baby" and "genius" are not necessarily a mutual exclusion. In fact, as Malcolm Gladwell has put it, "Genius, in the popular conception, is inextricably tied up with precocity—doing something truly creative, we're inclined to think, requires the freshness and exuberance and energy of youth." But this conventionalized view, whether constructive, accurate, or otherwise, is usually accompanied by some sense of a trade-off—the precocious reader who is bad at sports, the musical genius who lacks even the most basic of social graces. What matters in Everett's portrayal of Ralph is Ralph's self-consciousness and his insistence that we are required to be aware of his status as a baby in equal measure to his status as a genius. It is this simultaneous awareness that characterizes the challenge of Ralph in *Glyph*.

His liminality is emphasized by the text as it returns to his anticonventional nature more than once, and usually with the juxtaposition described above. After having been kidnapped by a psychology researcher who sees in Ralph a possible Nobel Prize for herself, Ralph says, "I read that night about the Devonian Period and the Eocene, Oligocene, and Miocene epochs, and learned more about the evolution of the horse than anyone needs to know," but makes sure to convey, in a note to one of his captors, what else is on his mind,

I need some type of hard crackers.
I'm teething and I'm getting cranky. (64)

A constant awareness of these conventionally disparate elements to the character is rendered inescapable to *Glyph*.

While the juxtaposition of *Glyph* and Everett's first novel, *Suder,* appears counterintuitive initially, because of the theoretical pyrotechnics of the former and the ostensible aesthetic modesty of the latter, and while this juxtaposition might also appear almost completely arbitrary to anyone unaware that they were written by the same author, the juxtaposition is justified and illuminated by an argument highlighting the priorities and challenges of Everett's work. Similar to how crucial it is that we remember both Ralph's IQ and his status as a baby in *Glyph,* this simultaneous focus on the space in between categories characterizes Craig in *Suder.* Craig's crisis focuses on his difficulty in reconciling himself to the categories into which others attempt to fit him. He is haunted by his double consciousness, in other words, and only frees himself when he adopts the anti–double consciousness that enables his decisions at the novel's end.

Suder worries about his own sanity as he faces his crisis and is brought back to his childhood, during which his mother acts crazy for long periods. Both as a child and as an adult, Craig worries that he's inherited insanity from his mother: "And again I was scared to death that whatever sickness was loose in my mother was also loose in me" (82). He is beset on all sides by the pressures of being categorized by others, a condition that confounds his ability to understand himself. As he searches for answers to his crisis, then, he tries to resist what others keep telling him that he is: "As I'm walking down I start to think that maybe I'm asking too much for anyone to listen to my problems. I mean, maybe people can't listen and understand if they're busy expecting things of me. This matter of expectations is really getting to me and I begin to have an identity crisis of sorts. I don't know if I'm Craig Suder the ballplayer, or Craig Suder the husband, or Craig Suder the fellow talking to the fat Germans in the elevator" (43). Craig's "identity crisis of sorts" is similar to those many adults have at some point in their lives and certainly many literary creations have. And many think quite profoundly about these crises as they endure them. Craig's crisis, though, is distinctive in how eventually generative it is for all that he does over the course of the novel, as he tries to come to some resolution, which, as both he and we realize, is not about resolving the crisis as such, but about moving on in some way that enables the subject to continue to exist along with the crisis.

The pressure of the expectations of others is less the issue in *Suder,* though, than are the absurd ways in which they manifest themselves. Sid Willis, the manager of the Seattle Mariners during Craig's time with them, admits to Craig that he "wasn't ever happy playing baseball," acknowledging that he "resented the reason they let me into the majors" (83). When Craig asks Sid what the reason was, the ridiculous nature of these expectations is put on full display: "Well, when I started there wasn't but four or five blacks playing in the big leagues and they were all excellent—Jackie Robinson, Satchel Paige, and like that. And they brought me in because they was looking for a darky that wasn't so good. . . . I guess they figured they had to show that dark folks could be bad, too. I mean, every black playing was great and then came Sid Willis, Mr. Below Average" (83). The humor of the sequence resides in how completely believable Willis's interpretation of others' reasoning actually is. Categories, after all, are predictive and simplifying, and they help us make sense of the world around us. In addition, a category like "excellent black ballplayer" might come into obvious conflict with a desire for the continued dominance of white supremacy. One way to inscribe white supremacy under this new athletic dispensation is to display a black ballplayer who is "below average." Of course, the two-stage punch line of this episode leaves no doubt that the role of categories is vital. Stage one is when Sid reveals that he is not black at all but "a Narragansett Indian" (83). He says, "Those damn white boys on the team would call me nigger and I'd tell them I was an Indian, and they'd just laugh" (83). Stage two of the punch line is delivered when Sid says, "Then one season things just fell into place and I was hitting like three-fifty and they let me go" (83). Craig, still unclear of the point of the story, asks, "Why'd they do that?" and Sid explains, "Because all of a sudden I was another excellent dark-skinned ballplayer, that's why" (83). As the Native American and the African American commiserate over their labeling by others, Sid finally states, definitively, "That's white folks" (83).[5] Obviously, Sid's "That's white folks" peroration is also the imposition of a category, but as I mentioned earlier, who tells the story is as important as the story itself being told. Sid and Craig both end up being determined by the inaccurate categorizing by those around them, many of whom are white. That Sid is miscategorized but loses his job anyway stresses the point about the power of who tells the story.

Craig's resolution, which looks completely reasonable within the world Everett creates, is to make himself into a man who flies as a bird. This is a wholly different state from being a man who wants to be a bird, since a man who wants to be a bird is willing to give up being a man in some way, just as a baby who is a genius conventionally would require of us that we see him as less baby and more genius. A choice is usually required. The indefinite nature of this resolution is given voice by the jazz pianist Bud Powell, who is a friend of Craig's father's and stays with the family for a little while during Craig's childhood. It is Powell who proposes that Craig's mother's behavior, which has been by turns emotionally and even sexually abusive toward her two sons, may have its own explanation. His first explanation comprises Powell's introduction of jazz to a young Craig, through the Charlie Parker recording "Ornithology."

> We were silent for a time while he struck a series of chords that filled the room. Then Ma came running through in her coat and went out the front door. Mr. Powell stopped playing.
> "My mother's crazy," I said. My eyes fell to my lap.
> "Maybe not crazy," said Mr. Powell. "Maybe just different." (77)

When this trope of "difference" recurs a few pages later, it is a concept for Craig to mull over: "I could hear Bud playing the piano downstairs. I kept hearing his words. He said that maybe Ma was just different. I was searching for 'just different' in the woman dashing back and forth, back and forth, but all I saw was crazy" (82).

This "just different" formulation looks like a test for the reader as well as the characters in *Suder*, especially as Kathy Suder's behavior gets more extreme. When she appears running behind a pickup truck with her Svengali, white supremacist dentist Dr. McCoy, sitting on the tailgate, Craig's father encourages his two sons (and Bud Powell joins in) to throw rocks at the truck: "We pelted the truck with gravel. Daddy picked up Ma over his shoulder and carried her into the house" (106). Even after this episode, Powell returns to his formulation: "'Maybe just different,' Bud said" (106).

Bud Powell intuits about Kathy something that will later become apparent in her son. She has determined a problem and has figured her own way of addressing it. Her perverse-looking decision to run around her town in a heavy fur coat appears more than "just different" at first, but it makes sense when she eventually states why she's doing it. She tells her son, "Running . . . to lose weight . . . Lou Ann . . . Narramore . . . skinny . . . lose weight" (22). Her "just different" reason makes sense to her. She is afraid that her husband is having an affair with Lou Ann Narramore, a woman in town, and wants to lose weight so she will be more attractive to him. This explanation works typically for an Everett character. It explains this one character's one decision and suggests the prospect that other unusual-looking decisions or actions in the text might also have comprehensible, if bizarrely applied, answers. Of course, those other explanations are not provided, but their prospective existence suggests what else might lie beyond the frame of the narrative and of the reader's cognition. Just because we don't see something, after all, does not mean it doesn't exist. Kathy Suder's provisional resolution suggests resolutions in others that are similarly indefinite but strangely satisfying for being indefinite. In a moving gesture of compassion and empathy toward the end of the novel, Craig's father decides to join his wife in running around their town. Craig asks why his father is doing this, since this decision only exacerbates Craig's anxiety that insanity may run in his family. His father's answer, "Let's say I don't want her to run alone" (146), is telling in its provisional nature, punctuated by his "Let's say," as well as its answer without really answering.

But this provisional answer characterizes how and why Craig decides he wants to jump off Willet Rock and fly like a bird over Ezra Pond. Jincy, the little girl he unofficially adopts and/or rescues and/or abducts, expresses her completely reasonable anxiety about Craig's desire to fly, but in response to her question "Why?" regarding his motivation, all he says, simply, is "I want to be free" (146). This answer is a lot like his mother's halting answer about Lou Ann Narramore and his father's about why he starts running with his wife. It is also comprehensible in the context of Ralph's determination that a genius is someone who can drive a car and/or hold his shit. They are all answers that do not resolve anything for anyone else, but this lack of resolution is significant for the person providing the answer alone.

Craig's desire to fly like a bird involves making several preparations that look like his mother's decision to run around their town. He says, "I plan to raise my body temperature and loosen up my neck and eat worms" (142) in response to his being told by a zoologist, Richard Beckwith, about these three attributes of avian physiology that distinguish birds from human beings. Beckwith is an almost purely symbolic figure in the novel, whose function expresses itself entirely in term of his compulsive bent toward taxonomy. Every animal mentioned in Beckwith's presence is reflexively fixed by him according to its Latin typology. This typing is most symbolic of what Suder is trying to escape, a point that is made unrelentingly clear in the text's final scene. Beckwith serves as little more than an embodiment of Suder's problems with being categorized in particular and the problem of categorizing more generally.

In order to be free of categorizing, then, Suder will make himself into something that he—and only he—is, something that completely defies category because of its inhabitation of a position between recognizable categories. The compelling nature of his decision compares tellingly to his father's understanding of Kathy's compulsion to run. As his father says he does not want Kathy to run alone, so Jincy, upon being told that Craig wants to fly, starts digging worms for him to eat. At first, this comes across from her as something of a dare: "For you to eat. You want to be free, don't you?" (146), since Jincy does not want him to fly because it's so obviously dangerous. But once she hands him a worm and says, "Eat it" (147), she grasps the depth of his conviction: "I take it and tilt my head back and let it slide down my throat and it wiggles as it goes down" (147). The seriousness of the situation finally hits her at this moment: "Jincy is smiling and crying at the same time. I pull her to me and hug her and she cries harder" (147).

The novel's resolution, such as it is, draws together as much as can be drawn together by the end. At the moment of truth, Jincy raises the kind of objection raised in another text about the meaning available in a lack of conventional resolution, *Waiting for Godot*. She says, regarding his garbage-bag wings, "What if they don't work? What if you fall? You could die. I'll be left alone" (164). As with Vladimir and Estragon as they contemplate suicide at two different points in the play, the major fear is not death but being left alone.

The novel's resolution is triumphant within the parameters it has set for itself:

> Now I'm making big circles and I'm pretty much in charge and I'm slowly going down. I can see Jincy and Renoir by the lake and Jincy's waving.
>
> I'm feeling the wind on my face and listening to it roaring past my ears and I've got an erection. And I'm flying, goddamnit, I'm flying. Then I see Beckwith on a ridge with the hunters and he's pointing up at me. I imagine him to say, "Homo sapiens."
>
> And I says, "Craig Suder." (171)

In "Giving the People What They Want," I wrote this about the novel's final scene: "This terminal flourish defines Suder on his own terms, as it's fair to say that he is the only man—black or not—in the world living in a cabin in the woods with a nine-year-old white girl whom he has rescued from her abusive mother, who owns an elephant as a pet, and is, at this moment, flying" (124). While I maintain that this evaluation is true, as far as it goes, it is the voice of a critic looking for resolution from his own reading. I can stand by this reading, but it does need amplification. My amplification of my former reading does not negate that reading but adds to it and marks again the prospect of additional readings that I am not producing here, but which also exist within the text for the reading of others. Potential readings as opposed to actual readings.

It is difficult now not to see the crucial role played by Richard Beckwith at the end of *Suder,* as he is cast in the role of categorizing Craig Suder yet again. But Craig can't hear Beckwith, of course, flying in the air, with the wind roaring past his ears. He has, however, so completely internalized others' views of him that he doesn't have to hear him. Beckwith is an agent of the double consciousness that has determined so much of Suder's life. He stands in for all the reasons why the black subject sees himself through the eyes of someone else. In order to hold this dynamic at bay, if only for a moment, Craig has taken steps that appear suicidal to Jincy and Beckwith, although they have completely different stakes in Suder's actions. The move from the reflexive imagining of Beckwith typing him as "homo sapiens" to his own final calling out of his own name as "Craig Suder" is characteristic of the categorizing, since Suder must go from the general categorizing name others impose upon him through to the specific individual name of who he provisionally knows himself to be. This identity is provisional if only because he can't stay in the air forever. Not even a bird can. He cannot assume this name but must instead announce it, even as he flies naked and under his own power. Under these conditions, it doesn't matter, for instance, whether or not he lands successfully or is killed as a result of plummeting into Ezra Pond.[6] The nature of his identity relies upon it being both definitive ("Craig Suder") and provisional (suspended in midair). Removing either would make him entirely something else. He exists, at this moment, somewhere along the continuum between the man named *Craig Suder* and the *homo sapiens* flying through the air. At any point, it is impossible to say where along the continuum he may conclusively be found.

In "A Bird of a Different Feather," Uzzie Cannon argues that "when characters in Everett's novels happen to be racially identified as African American, one could argue that they perform a 'postmodern' blackness in which their experiences as *human beings* transcend race" (94). And while this notion of transcendence is tempting, and helps us understand just how transformative Everett's contributions to thinking about race are, it needs to be pushed quite a bit further. The suggestion of "the author's seemingly easy ability to move beyond race in his novels" (94), like transcendence, works best if we forget what has come before where race is concerned. But when we remember the history of oppression and injustice, as well as triumph over and struggle against these formative elements of American history, it is very difficult ever to talk convincingly about the transcendence of race. Think of just how far Craig Suder must go in order to individuate himself, and how unusual Everett has to make Suder before we do not concentrate exclusively on his being a black character. This last point again draws out Everett's aesthetic and what it means to strive toward some notion of the infinite. The story's lack of a clear resolution in the conventional sense regarding the protagonist's decision to fly announces clearly that the resolution of the text is not the issue here. His ability to identify himself provisionally through his unusual actions suggests something much more important than what he is called or how his story ends. His culminating action suggests additional possibilities that go beyond merely acceding to or opposing the categories that he may represent, inhabit, or have imposed upon him. No one transcends race, least of all in America. Race is always more like the return of the repressed, like a trace—always present in some form or other. The more generative and revolutionary challenge has been to confront it with an anti–double consciousness, which is not to be confused with some sort of single consciousness (whatever that might look like), or transcendence, but to assert oneself—to the best of one's abilities—on one's own terms.

◆ ◆ ◆

If *Glyph* might productively be read as a challenge to keep the competing aspects of a character in mind at the same time and engaging with this new subject position to be created from this simultaneity, and *Suder* is about the space that can be navigated between categories imposed on an individual black subject who attempts to navigate his (in this case) subjectivity on his (again) own terms, then *The Water Cure* (2007) can be read as a case study in navigating between categories a character imposes upon himself. In fact, *The Water Cure* presents almost too many oppositions of categories to keep straight without the critic running the risk of feeling his or her own sanity being imperiled. Male/female, black/white, legal/illegal, individual/structural, sane/insane, chaos/order, just/ unjust, good/evil are all negotiated and implicated in what Ishmael Kidder is trying to resolve in the world that he inhabits after the kidnap, rape, and murder of his eleven-year-old daughter, Lane. There are invariably more of these oppositions that I am not accounting for here, and the point of this argument is not to work toward some resolution of them—a point I feel I need to reiterate, perhaps even compulsively—but to point them out as sites of what might be called a *productive frustration* because of how they are not resolved over the course of the novel.

The idea of productive frustration is another way of circling back to the significance of the lack of resolution in much if not all of Everett's fiction. Embracing this frustration as significant in and of itself is not an easy sell, but I will continue to make the case. While I characterize the novels in this phase of my argument as approaching more explicit and more direct demonstrations of this value, *The Water Cure* pairs the directness of tone displayed in much of *Suder* with the technical virtuosity of *Glyph*, making it potentially even more frustrating as a reading exercise than *Glyph* can be. *The Water Cure* may be read as an argument for the value of productive frustration over destructive certainty.

The Water Cure is harrowing at times, and this quality of the narrative explains much about the friction Ishmael Kidder creates within the many binaries in conflict in the text. To oversimplify for a moment: he is an ostensibly good man tempted to act like a very bad man because of the horrible circumstances into which he has been immersed. His description early in the novel of the pressure he and his ex-wife, Charlotte, experience during the search for Lane is heartbreaking in its vividness, even as it rehearses the familiar Zen koan: "And so a longstanding philosophical question was answered for me: if your child screams in the forest and there is no one around to hear, does she make a sound? It turns out that she does not" (10). Lest the descriptions of the strain the parents experience descend into the maudlin, however, the narrative modulates its consideration of the emotional devastation at its heart with the sometimes perverse juxtapositions that remind us that, even under these circumstances, nothing is just one thing or the other, that we often inhabit spaces in between the categories that are primarily being experienced at a given moment, even if those categories are horror and grief: "Early the next morning, a detective, a woman, came to Charlotte's door, and we all saw this as a bad sign and in fact it was, as the news she delivered was that a young girl matching Lane's description had been found in a ravine beside a park by two boys and their dog" (11). Initially, this scene creates the almost-too-familiar feeling of a television crime procedural, and the denotative description tempts us to envision a character we already know from television. But the realism of this introduction juxtaposes itself immediately with the surreal moment of what follows: "She had gone into so much detail, it seemed to me, about the park that led to a ditch that fed into a concrete drainage canal, and the boys, aged nine and ten, not brothers, but across-the-street neighbors, that I found myself asking, without knowing why or even that I was asking, 'What kind of dog was it?'"(11–12).

This otherwise irrelevant question serves as something of a leitmotif through the rest of *The Water Cure*, punctuating the futility of trying to make definitive something that cannot be resolved. Among the narrative fragments that make up the novel, the detective reappears to attempt to answer the non sequitur (more about non sequiturs later) but also to move things along, even though such an objective cannot be accomplished: "'I don't know what kind of dog it was,' the detective said, without the least bit of irony or even judgment of my question. 'One of you will have to come down and see the body, to identify the body.' Of course. It was so simple. One of us would have to do that. One of us" (52). Ishmael draws attention to the inadequate but highly conventional nature of the expression *identify the body* as he considers exactly what the detective has asked of him and/or Charlotte.

> That's what I did. I identified my daughter. For the first and last time in my life, I identified my daughter. I had spotted her many times, on playgrounds, across rooms, in crowds of children. Once when she was costumed up like an elf among other elves I had even recognized her, but I had never identified her. And as I stood there in the medical examiner's surprisingly warm room, I realized that I did not recognize her, that the thing I was identifying was no one I knew, and I wondered if there was something to all that talk about spirit and soul. Then I looked again, and there was my daughter, there was Lane, both identified and as recognizable as she had been three days earlier, except that she was now dead. (52)

The reflections here on the perverseness of identifying his daughter cannot help but draw our attention, at least a little, to the idea of identity itself, and the inevitable inadequacy of someone imposing an identity on any of us. In effect, that is what Ishmael is being asked to do—to impose an identity on Lane. Even the dead Lane exists in a state beyond words, beyond certainty, beyond categories, and even as her father expresses his grief, he also expresses that nothing he says or does (including *identifying* her) is adequate in any way to the event in which he finds himself immersed. This juxtaposition of the surreally sad and the intellectually complex is how *The Water Cure* distinguishes itself among Everett's novels. It shares this juxtaposition with *Percival Everett by Virgil Russell*, which I will discuss later, as an example of the more indirect approach to the problem of infinite categories in Everett's novels.

The resonance of *identify* in this enervating passage is emphasized by what immediately precedes it, another passage that ensures that we see the inadequacy in this notion of identifying someone, particularly someone we love, when what has happened to that person—not to their identity—is the important part: "I come back to the question, as I always come back to the question, how is it that I am I, or me, the I or me depending on whether the first I is really I and not merely some word 'I' designating another 'not I'? One thing I am not, as in the consideration of natural kinds, is a conjunctive list of attributes that when taken all together make me an instance of me and perhaps only me" (51). These reflections, which continue a bit longer and iterate the kind of dog again before the passage quoted above, just shading its resonance this time as opposed to full leitmotif, also introduce the association with Lane before that other passage about *identifying* her: "So, there are two things that mark me as distinct, as the individual thing that I am: the death of my daughter and the particular location in space. The notion, the claim, even the reality of my daughter's death is a vapor, cannot be touched, and so the only real identity I have is my spatial orientation to the rest of the world" (51). If identity is one's spatial orientation to the rest of the world—a compelling thought, to say the least—then our language of identity starts to look all the weaker, and so bound up in convention alone that it all ends up looking no more meaningful than the locution to *identify a body* does.

The performance of a writer (Kidder) presented by a writer (Everett) so that both writers can demonstrate the inadequacy of language, in part because of its conventional nature—which is what makes language possible, in part, in the first place—is sobering in its own implications. The passage from *Erasure* with which I began this chapter bears repeating: "It's incredible that a sentence is ever understood. Mere sounds strung together by some agent attempting to mean some thing, but the meaning need not and does not confine itself to that intention." And yet, while we know this about language and its inadequacy, we are nevertheless able to make ourselves understood to one another, for the most part. Ishmael and Charlotte do know, after all, what the detective means when she says that one of them is going to have to *identify* Lane, for all of the inadequacy of that expression. It means because of its conventional nature. It is inadequate, though, for the same reason.

The significance of this leitmotif and its inconclusiveness expresses itself ultimately by serving as the last episode in the narrative. Again, it is introduced first, a page or so earlier, in one of the instances that reaffirms the importance of the inconclusive in Everett's fictional world. This is a recapitulation of the scene in which the detective originally asks the parents to identify their daughter. This time, though, the passage looks like this: "Gnarly the nixt mourning, a defective, a wombman, keyme to Carelot's dour and we call thaw this as a bid sighn and din pact twas, as the mews she deviled was that a jung guirrel match-king Lane's dyscryption had beleaf sound kin a revene bedsighed a parque by twooth bouys and fir daweg" (214).[7] The rest of the earlier passage is delivered in this Jabberwocky-esque translation, making clear, as Carroll's famous poem does, just how much we rely on convention and association among words in order to make meaning. That words like "mourning," "defective," and "womb-man" appear strangely appropriate in their implications in this passage does a great deal of work for any argument about how language and meaning making are inexact and inconclusive arts. However, even while all of this is going on in the passage, it concludes like this: "And the beyes, daged nilne and tend, knot bothers, but hacriss-the-strait gnawhboys, that I found myself asking, without knowing why or even that I was asking, 'What kind of dog was it?'" (214). As this question recurs here, there is a sense being conveyed that under no circumstances are we to miss it. It is all the more noticeable in this passage, after all, appended to the end of a paragraph that would require every ounce of readerly attention to make sense of, but it is also readily identifiable if—as would be understandable in the case of most readers—the reader were to skim over the paragraph. In either case, it is important that we recognize the question.

The leitmotif of repeating the ostensibly irrelevant question identifying the breed of dog modulates the emotional tenor of *The Water Cure*. As we move back and forth between the story of the abducted little girl and the effect of that abduction on the little girl's father, on the one hand, and broader considerations about ethics, sanity, and justice, on the other, one of the nexus points at which these two strata of the novel intersect is this question about the breed of a dog. When this theme makes its final appearance in the novel, its cumulative significance is sounded, in all of its inconclusiveness.

Ishmael Kidder's story concludes with Kidder reflecting upon his own actions over the course of the novel. He states, among other things, "I am a good citizen, patrolling my own borders and keeping my own peace and nailing my own mirrors into place even if they are set to cast no reflections of my own" (215). This reference to mirrors gestures at another leitmotif in a novel of leitmotifs, which is worth addressing before returning to the last mention of the dog.

The Water Cure makes extensive use of the mirror as an icon of the inconclusive, of the unresolvable, in ways that are at the same time haunting and instructive. The mirror is an appropriate vehicle for this novel since so much of the conflict in *The Water Cure* is of the me/not-me variety. Again, though, the variations available even within nominal solutions always resonate just below the surface in *The Water Cure*, as Ishmael thinks to himself, "Let's try the mirrors. Mirrors and metaphors, that's where our answers lie. Answers lie. Isn't language beautiful?" (46). Ishmael's seizing upon this beautiful double entendre within *answers lie* reveals an uncomfortable truth and reminds us of his priority for destabilizing any sense of the definitive as he tries to make sense of who he is in this new world in which Lane's murder is not just the kind of event every parent dreads: "What is between you and the mirror," he asks, "the first mirror, if in fact you can actually see that one in particular, if you can in fact see a mirror at all and not merely your reflection?" (46). I have already cited an extended section of this reflection (for that is the right word here) on mirrors in the introduction to this book and won't repeat it here, but only note this point to signal the length of the passage itself. The salient point here is how the metaphor of the mirror operates in revealing important aspects of Ishmael's consciousness and Everett's aesthetic.

As Ishmael makes the rounds to "the JCPenney in Taos" (106), among other places, to buy what begins to appear like more mirrors than any sane person needs,[8] he becomes intensely aware—appropriately—of how he appears to others, as he makes these purchases. He mentions the Venus effect to one vendor, as he continues making his purchases. The Venus effect, in which "if I can see you in a mirror, then you can see me" (107) becomes very important in his continued torture of the man that he thinks kidnapped, raped, and murdered his daughter. He needs to arrange these mirrors so that the captive man cannot escape seeing his own reflection, but never see Ishmael's. As he explains the Venus effect, his self-consciousness registers itself in his description of the JCPenney clerk to whom he speaks, whose "truckish quality was replaced by one of, not annoyance, or boredom, but of a hushed, tight-lipped, subdued alarm" (107). He continues, nevertheless: "'Mirrors work that way,' I said. 'You can't conceal yourself in a mirror. Did you know that? Your reflection exists in and of itself, is a thing itself. It might depend on your presence, but it is not a part of you. It's a thing in this world, yet you can't touch it and you can't find it and it has no depth, none at all'" (107). The reflection, then, exists in the same dimension as Ralph in *Glyph*, Craig Suder, and Ishmael Kidder in *The Water Cure*, indeed as all fictional creations. It's just that the convention of reading encourages us to forget about the fundamental nonexistence of the characters who nevertheless capture our imaginations as we read. The reflection does not represent an actual being but instead represents an epistemological challenge that the reader must engage with, or must forget in order to make reading possible, let alone enjoyable. The reflection exists in and of itself, not one or the other, like so much in the world that Everett creates. And this in-and-of-itself world is limitless, bounded only by our ability to understand it and free ourselves from the conventions that invariably stand in the way of this broader comprehension.

The status of the reflection takes on a much more immediate and physical quality, though, when Ishmael returns to his "work" (torturing the man in his basement) with a total of eighteen mirrors: "Light splashed and flashed everywhere as I dealt with them. I stood them, nailed them, and taped them around my work in the basement. I arranged them so that my subject could find his face no matter where he looked, and then I removed the hood from his head. He appeared startled by his reflection" (107). The reflection now has a visceral quality, as it startles the man because it reflects him, although this is a version of himself that he has never seen before. Again, the reflection both is and is not him to the extent that it is quite oppressively (for Ishmael's prisoner, at least) something in and of itself. It might also be said that Ishmael's captive experiences a level of disorientation that at times resembles the reader's experience with *The Water Cure*.

The vertiginous effect of being required to focus all at once on many things that are each not just one thing becomes inescapable at the point when Ishmael says to his captive, whom he calls by a variety of empty signifiers, "'When I hurt you, and I will,' I said, my voice smooth chocolate" (107–8), is how he begins his next reflection on reflections. The sense of anticipation in this introduction of the certainty of the pain to follow is then folded into where he has already been, with the significance of mirrors and reflections:

> "I want you to see all these other people and wonder which one of you is feeling the pain, which of you is feeling the pain more, less, which of you is only watching and feeling nothing." Since I had the mirrors configured to offer him reflections of himself and reflections of his reflection I could not see him in any of the mirrors, my understanding of the Venus effect, and therefore it was only faith that allowed me to posit and believe that his reflections actually existed. If I tilted a mirror so that I could see his face, then he would be able to see me and *I didn't want to be there for him.* I wanted him to have the company of infinite incidence and refraction, unending repetition, the forever drip drip drip of his own image. (108; emphasis added)[9]

The logic of the placement of the mirrors, the logic of Ishmael's mind, and the logic of *The Water Cure* more generally all mean that the man being tortured is obviously and multiply present, even though he principally exists only as an infinite recurrence of ephemeral images. His torturer, by contrast, is absent, invisible from the image, but manifestly present as he inflicts real pain that his victim experiences and watches images of himself experience. One is there but not there, the other not there but there. To appreciate each man's simultaneous states requires our ability to free ourselves from conventional ways of thinking and not thinking about categories as nominally essential as presence and absence.

All of this leads us back to the concluding iteration of the question about the breed of the dog at the scene where Lane's body is found. The passage that ends with the dog question also begins with a reflection on reflections. Because of the nature of many of the passages in *The Water Cure* (I hesitate to use the word *paragraph* here), the critic is also required to reflect very carefully upon how much of a given section to excerpt:

> Mirror set by mirror facing mirror showing mirror reflecting mirror etching mirror casting mirror back and forth at one end, but where with his face at one end and mirror upon mirror, taking no energy to work, making reflections that have no end, *just infinite middle,* infinite faces that are not his, for him to see, his rough face made smooth, his head halved in size by distance again and again, gaze and return, and not a single photon his, and his guilty eyes well up and who cares if the tears or the guilt are true? (214–15; emphasis added)

The "infinite middle" is where Everett's work takes place, where most of his main characters live, and where his fiction challenges us to search for meaning. So the tortured character whom Ishmael names variously throughout the novel may not be the right man, a prospect that is both salient and irrelevant to what happens in the novel. The question "Who cares if the tears or the guilt are true?" draws our attention necessarily back to the only place in the text where the culpability of the tortured character (and, of course, *tortured character* could also describe Ishmael, but here I mean the character Ishmael is torturing) is even mentioned. Characteristically, it is mentioned in passing,[10] in a sequence that Ishmael only imagines, in which a state trooper stops him as he drives with the man in the trunk of his car. Call it "driving while kidnapping":

> "What is that noise?" he would ask.
> "That would be the man in my trunk. . . ."
> "Mind telling me why you've got him in there?"
> "He's the man who raped, tortured, and killed my eleven-year-old daughter."
> "What do you plan to do with him?"
> "You don't want to know," I would say.
> The officer would then close the trunk and tip his hat to me. "Watch your speed, okay?"
> "Thank you, officer." (42–43)

Anyone who's ever been stopped by the police will recognize the end of the conversation, with the words of caution about speed by the officer and the ritual thanking of the officer by the stopped motorist. The motorist is not likely to engage the officer further after this point, nor is the officer likely to make further conversation. Normally—and this is not a normal situation—this would be the end of the encounter. But the officer still has—understandably—one more question, and it's an important one.

> "Are you sure you have the right man?"
> "No, I'm not."
> "You have a good day, sir. God bless America." (43)

The trooper's patriotic peroration does help explain why some critics read *The Water Cure* as a critique of George W. Bush's foreign policy.[11] Indeed, that reading is worth keeping in mind as complementary to this one, since political measures are so often based upon notions of categorical (again, in several senses of that word) certainty, which are not always, nevertheless, correct. The imaginary trooper's close-enough acceptance of Ishmael's imagined answers does emerge from Ishmael's imagination, it is true, but it also draws attention to the very real dangers of certainty. Ishmael thinks to himself, as he brings to a close the story that is *The Water Cure,* "While I recall the last breath of the last life that I stole, rightly, righteously, correctly, justifiedly, honorably, sinlessly, done with precision and calm, always calm, a true indicator of the rightness of any action, because someone always has to pay" (215). Rightness, calmness, and sinlessness, among other attributes, contribute the first part of the equation that Ishmael arrives at, the part on the left-hand side of the equal sign. All of this certainty (whether actually right or wrong doesn't matter, ultimately) brings him to his inescapable conclusion, that someone always has to pay. And so the man he keeps in his basement has.

The novel ends with more questions and inconclusive answers: "Will my daughter grow older in my dreams? Why do reasonable people entertain the ontological argument? and What kind of dog was it?" (216). All that has preceded these questions should prepare us for the anticlimax to come, but the anticlimax is still shattering: "And the answers are: No, Because they can, and Some kind of retriever" (216). The novel's ending tells us, in effect, that this is not the ending, any more than what has preceded this ending has really ended anything. What the ending does, in fact, is send us back through the novel to find out what it might actually have been about in the first place, since it clearly isn't about what we were expecting, for if it had been, we would not feel so let down by its ending.

So, what is the novel about, then? Obviously, based on everything I've said so far, I cannot definitively answer that question, and even to attempt to do so would undermine the argument I've been making. More than this, though, is to recognize that the novel draws our attention to the reality that we can never be definitive in our readings of texts. We contribute to a broader understanding, complementing what has gone before based on how our interests differ from those of others who have read the text, the times in which we read it, and our conventionalized instruction on what to look for as we read, among other factors. Overall, the categories we usually rely upon to make meaning actually shut down our ability to see the world in its larger complexities, but we can nevertheless open our minds to the infinite possibilities, if we take on the challenge issued by a text like *The Water Cure*. After all, the novel identifies itself in these terms:

Fragments. Frag-ments. Frags. Fr. m ents. This work is not fragmented;
    it is fragments. (16)

And, of course, even this characterization is qualified by what follows: "So, all sections are fragments, except for this one because it lives here, in this spot, among the fragments, and has a specified job concerning those fragments surrounding it. A fragment? Connective tissue? The story itself? Oh, the story itself, that ever-thickening center" (16–17). The "ever-thickening center" should put us in mind of the *infinite middle* that Kidder also comments on. But what is the "ever-thickening center" of the story? The phrase merely calls to our attention more questions about what the story—any story—actually means or is. Even the notion of "story" is a category that we can identify, define, replicate, and analyze, but it is also a category that changes over time. Categories are based on something, after all. Everett's novels are invariably about something, to be sure. But they are also about something else. *Something* is limited. *Something else* is infinite.

While a little on the nose, Ishmael's declaration to his captive may also apply as a declaration the text makes to its reader:

> I can do what I like at any moment I like in this document or text or however we name it because this is my world, universe, neighborhood, note (though I hate seeing the word note in my notes), and I can do what I damn well please and fuck you if you think I'm ignoring the rules and fuck you if you think that I'm being indulgent and fuck you if you think that references to archaic philosophical notions are mere erudition, which they are not, but fuck you anyway because this is my world and you're welcome to it if you want to enter and if you don't want to enter then fuck you twice anyway and if you do want inside then fuck you trice because you fucking deserve it. (88)

That this is Ishmael's world, universe, neighborhood, etc. is, of course, unimpeachably true, and, again, reminds us of the simple point that the same may be said of Sir Gawain or Hamlet or Clarissa Dalloway or Jane Eyre. These moments are simultaneously reminders and admonitions, but they are also declarations of an aesthetic that draws attention to itself and to its implications, leaving us to decide whether or not we consider it indulgent. But in addition, that aesthetic includes the imperative that we never forget that we are in fact reading. These texts are not for readers to *lose themselves* in but are for active readerly participation and engagement, even at times, destabilization and unsettling. Texts like *The Water Cure* situate the reader in the infinite middle, the ever-thickening center between the conscious reflection that they are reading and the suspension of disbelief so long ago counseled as part of our reading. Again, we can ask ourselves whether we consider this approach indulgent. What we are not allowed to do, though, is forget that we are reading, as is evidenced later, when the above passage is referred back to: "I call the president of my country (here, because I can, because this is my world, and you're welcome to it, if not welcome in it) (and someplace in some other note I said for you to fuck off or fuck yourself) I call him the Marquis Façade" (122). Not that one is probably going to forget having been sworn at as much as happens in the former passage, but still, the overt reference here back to that passage does more than remind. It suggests that the former passage has some additional resonance that perhaps we missed the first time through. Again, *something* is limited; *something else* is infinite.

Part of Ishmael's struggle in *The Water Cure* arises from his attempts to categorize himself accurately, if not definitively. Who knows? Maybe he is trying to identify himself, as he is called upon to identify Lane. His daughter's horrible fate has left him adrift in a moral universe in which he can justify torturing a man. As he considers the prospect of killing a couple of people who break into his house because they mistakenly think he's a drug dealer, he insists, perhaps to convince himself: "I am not a bad man. I don't want to hurt them, to kill them. I don't even want to scare them, really" (194). He has carved out an infinite space that intermittently makes sense to him, on the continuum between the otherwise comforting designations of "good" and "bad."

His obsession with identity, his and that of others, occasionally has to do with some notion of stability, as reflected in these words to his captive: "What is a stable identity? You are not the man you were when we met, not the same man you were before I first tied you up to that plank. You are not the same man who raped and murdered my little girl. Even though you are, you are not. You were the sinner, but now you are the punished, someone new altogether" (126–27). It is this "someone new altogether" that troubles the novel, for Ishmael and for his interlocutor, whether that interlocutor be the man in his basement or his reader. After all, if the man in his basement is the same man even though he is not, then the same evaluation must apply to Ishmael and, we have to at least wonder, perhaps to us, too. This *someone new altogether* identity also helps explain why Ishmael writes under the pseudonym "Estelle Gilliam": "Initially, I adopted a pseudonymous existence both as a means and as an end. A black man wasn't going to sell many romance novels to school middle-aged perm-headed nail-decaled bus drivers, beauticians, and trailer parkers. I also enjoyed my anonymity for its own sake. To some extent. And it served some kind of Zen region of my soul by feeding my lack of ambition or desire for fame and attention, a lack for which I felt great and notably ironic pride" (203). But even this purely pragmatic decision about the marketability of his identity cannot be simple, as Ishmael mulls over his relationship to Estelle more than once: "But of course Estelle Gilliam and I occupy the same space, but not a single statement concerning me can be applied to her. My real and unsettling question is: 'Whose space has been invaded?'" (59). Monk asks a version of this same question in thinking about his relationship to Stagg R. Leigh. It's clear that Ishmael's never completely sure about the answer to this question any more than he knows how much ill a good man can do and still consider himself a good man: "So virtue is knowledge. It is the same thing to know what is good as it is to be good. And I believe with all my heart that I know what is good" (59). That his language breaks down immediately after this assertion to one form of the somewhat phonetic language into which he intermittently descends does not reassure us that he is right or sure or good.

The infinite prospects of readings and meanings are made literal early in *The Water Cure* during a remembered conversation between Ishmael and Lane:

> We can count forever. That is infinity, so to speak. But we do not have names for most of the numbers in the world of infinity. This is one million: 1,000,000.
>
> What is this called? 1,000,000,000,000,000,000,000,000,000,000,000, 000,001.
>
> We do not have infinite words. But we could. If we wanted to we could. If we wanted to. Is there a name for this want? If we want one. We can talk forever.
>
> And we will.
>
> But what is the name of this desire? (17–18)

The desire to name the desire for infinite words brings up the question of infinity in ways that complement where we've been so far. Even if we can come up with such a word—at the end of this sequence, Ishmael names that desire "love," for instance—we are no closer to solving the problem of infinity in any way better than we've already seen attempted by Aristotle, Wallace, and Ralph. The potential set of possible words is infinite, but the actual set at any moment is finite. But, in a way, so what? Lane is still dead, and that's the point.

That Lane is dead is part of the *something else* that resides within the infinite of *The Water Cure,* and that reality challenges us to read in one unconventional way while already being challenged to read in another unconventional way:

> Lastly, imaghost sublimighty.
> Always imessgine the weaves at the breach.
> Now pushking, rearing, constant, undenifable.
> Ever may you may luke at the send and at the soon.
> Imassing a storm.

Severely imagure the surf.

Deadly huge, rollackng, massive, sowell after swell, thundjurious.

Ever still you kinknot terror your eyes aweee.

And you killnow that the wives will newt reach you.

Duely the waves are furightning and though you are not afreud, you fear these waves.

Do you understand me? (186)

The poetic typography combines with the again Carroll-esque language of almost-nonsense words to create the kind of cognitive challenge that is always characteristic of Everett's fiction in one way or another. I emphasize *almost* nonsense words because the transformation from "afraid" to "afreud" would have made the psychoanalyst smile, as might have the interplay between "waves" and "wives" contributing to the stormy lack of resolution that besets Ishmael's life after he and Charlotte divorce and Lane is murdered. But while all of this is happening, Ishmael's underlying meaning is staring us in the face, if we recognize it. The poem is an acrostic, a form for which we have a word, even if we are unused to encountering it in the middle of a father's grief over losing his daughter. The first letters of each line combine to spell out LANE IS DEAD, with the final line, "Do you understand me?" serving both to camouflage the acrostic a little further and to emphasize its presence, by asking the reader to return to look at what may have at first been overlooked, which is also how—one imagines—missing persons are searched for.

This acrostic, in turn, recalls my introductory admission of possibly being the butt of Everett's occasional jokes, but at least in the case of the acrostic there is a payoff to reading for the *something else*. Now we must return to *Glyph* for an example of why we might be forgiven for being a little gun-shy in devoting any extra time to some of the challenges embedded in Everett's work. Ralph proposes the following: "Suppose I made all e's t's and all r's w's and all c's a's and all p's q's and all l's h's and s's n's and all o's k's and all g's d's and all i's u's and vice versa. Then water would now be RCETW. And suppose I made such substitutions throughout the alphabet. Would it still be English?" (131). Having decided on the code himself, he has of course worked out the answer; although he makes us work for it: "Yep. Wchql rkihg neuhh nqtco Tsdhunl" (131). It's very difficult

CREATING INFINITE SPACES AND THE ROLE OF THE SCHIZOREVOLUTIONARY

to resist the temptation to solve this sentence for ourselves. And when we do, "Wchql rkihg neuhh nqtco Tsdhunl," somewhat anticlimactically, translates to: "Ralph would still speak English" (131). As he said.

A similar effect occurs in *Percival Everett by Virgil Russell*—the letters of the alphabet are listed during the telling of one of the innumerable stories in that novel. The entire alphabet is presented, but the list ends like this: "W, X, Y, and so on" (109). It's very difficult not to read the entire alphabetical listing, out of a sense that it must mean something else, that maybe one of the letters will be omitted, and that the omission holds some meaning. As it turns out, the only letter omitted is Z, replaced by *and so on,* but it's very difficult not to read the whole list, just to be sure.

So while we get resolution in these two instances, it is only short lived, since we are not finished. Returning to *Glyph,* the initial neat proposition and solution, "Ralph would still speak English" is followed by more reflection on the pleasures of language and is then, in turn, followed by what appears to be the quod erat demonstrandum toward which this entire exercise in codes and code breaking has been working: "Ysuwu dwu pn ywlbqx lp vlbylnp. Ysu dzynw lx pny audv" (131). Perhaps someone more adept at codes, puzzles, or games than I would have been able to look at this second, longer sentence and immediately see its solution. (Again, it bears repeating that working on Everett's fiction can and probably will lead to the critic being the butt of at least one of the texts' jokes.) But when we work out this second sentence—as I attempted to—we find that it is gibberish. This is the punch line. Check and mate. Game, set, and match.

At the risk of momentarily playing the role of the party bore who explains a joke, it is worth pausing here to consider how this joke works, as it has much to add to a discussion of the significance of the infinite in Everett's work. The way the two coded sentences work together is what is important here. The first, shorter one follows logically from the paragraph in which it is situated. It is also quite satisfying when we work out the sentence using the code provided and find that we have accomplished something germane to the paragraph itself. "Ralph would still speak English" confirms something about Ralph, language, maybe even life itself. The system works. All is right with the world.

But the successful working out of the first coded sentence encourages us to attempt to solve the second. More than this, it encourages the expectation that the second sentence will also work out. After all, it's the same code, and the first sentence worked out. But this is how convention, expectation, and assumption work. Think back to Wallace's discussion of the principle of induction. Why do we expect the second sentence to work out just because the first did? One certain way to draw attention to a pattern is to break it. But first that pattern must be established. One way to draw attention to expectations is to leave them unfulfilled. So when the second coded sentence results in gibberish, we are embarrassed, to be sure, but we are also chastened and instructed in how, why, and that we operate on conventions that do not necessarily deserve our unexamined confidence. We assume the bedroom floor will hold our weight this morning for no other reason than that it has each morning up until now.

Finally, the literal connection between the two coded sentences foregrounds this aspect of confidence that we place in our expectations and the conventions upon which they are based. After the coded confirmation that the code itself works, Ralph writes: "Language was my bed. More, writing was my bed. I felt safe in it. I needed it. I trusted it. I wrote notes to myself and read them. I wondered what they meant. I put notes away and tried to forget them so I could find and read them. I would tear them up and rearrange the words, read them backwards, read every other word" (131). The elements of trust, reliance, and need imbricated in the practice of our reading are conventions of this practice that we lose sight of as we age and become more and more used to being able to read. It is appropriate that it is a child, even if an extremely unusual one, who reminds us of what is at stake in our reading, and in our learning to read. But he also reminds us of what is at stake in the two coded sentences, since the first reinforces our ill-advised trust in the second. When the second does not work, we are within our rights to feel not only disappointed but betrayed. It's no wonder we rely upon convention.

It takes a while to get used to looking into the unaccustomed and infinite space between categories that Everett's fiction inhabits and draws our attention to, but once you get used to it, it's remarkable what we start to find. The rhizomatic ways that earlier novels' implications reemerge in later novels presses home the point about what that infinite space starts to mean and to look like. Ralph's discoveries about how language works reemerge in *The Water Cure* when Ishmael describes himself to Sally, his agent: "I'm what you call local color" and then immediately follows that declaration with this one: "roloc lacol llac uoy tahw m'I" (171).[12] Fortunately, this passage doesn't take as long to decode as the former one in *Glyph*, but it cannot help but remind us of the child-narrator's reveling in the possibilities and unaccustomed plasticity of the written word. The same point may be made about another passage, in which Ishmael does create the kind of passage we saw in *Glyph*. While this one is not based on a code, but on expected word order, it does take some work to decipher: "No I text am contains here in to it torture its this own man context. Context this is man always killed external my to child the and thing dreams said. How can you I are continue to breathe understand while a he text is is never alive there in in the this text world" (198). The text should remind us of Ralph's ruminations of how else he might interact with written language: *I would tear them up and rearrange the words, read them backwards, read every other word.* This passage requires that we read the even-numbered words for one meaning, and the odd-numbered words for another. The above three sentences, then, are actually six, making two completely different statements that capture the something and the something else of the novel. The first statement reads:

> No text contains in it its own context. Context is always external to the thing said. How you are to understand a text is alive in the text.

The second statement reads:

> I am here to torture this man. This man killed my child and dreams. Can I continue breathe while he is never there in this world.

The first one is principally intellectual, reflecting on some of the aesthetic and philosophical content of *The Water Cure*, while the second is prominent in its emotional and ethical dimensions. The emotional nature of the second statement may explain why it appears to break down slightly toward its conclusion, as *breathe* should be *breathing* and *never* makes more sense as *ever*. We might even be tempted to gather up a couple of the words from the parallel sentence, creating *How can I continue to breathe while he is alive in this world.* Even the deciphering of the two propositions is not as simple as taking each odd-numbered word followed by each even-numbered word, since a pattern emerges within the three sentences that reveal themselves as six. For the first proposition to be legible, we must take the even-numbered words in the first sentence, then the odd-numbered words in the second, followed by the even-numbered words in the third. The second proposition requires the opposite pattern (even-odd-even). Instances like these—and there are others—put one in mind of Sylvie Bauer's indispensable observations about Everett's novel *Zulus*. Bauer notices the many occasions of linguistic syncope, "the loss of one or more sounds or letters in the interior of a word" (166) on display in Everett's fiction. Linguistic syncope is "a deviation from the norm, the law of speaking, the introduction of slight disorders challenging the prescriptive order of spelling" (166). Her discussion of moments like this, moments of "fertile chaos in which letters have it their own way" (167), opens countless possibilities for thinking about the uncontrollable potential within language and therefore within reading. (Her observations hold the added gift of forgiving ourselves when, after painstaking proofreading, we still find typos in our finished manuscripts.) From there, the moves to the limitless possibilities for cognition are actually quite daunting. The novels, then, are more and more about expression that does not conclude or define but instead only opens up wider and wider. The ability to make meaning in *The Water Cure* depends principally on any given reader's ability and willingness to engage with it in the anticonventional and sometimes quite physical ways that Ralph describes in *Glyph,* and that Ishmael's typography demonstrates in *The Water Cure.*

Revenge fantasies obviously require revenge. And while imprisoning and torturing the man that you think murdered your daughter qualifies as revenge, we are not being unreasonable in expecting that Ishmael will murder this man by the end of the novel. This would appear to be the most conventional expression of revenge. We may actually even be hoping that he will. But, again, if that might be what the novel is about, the question by the end of *The Water Cure* is—as is always the case with Everett's fiction—what else it's about. In part, perhaps it's about power—the power to render someone else powerless, and the power of the narrator. This novel in particular at least suggests that these two forms of power are much the same thing.

It is most important to Ishmael that this man know that he is completely under his control and that this control will extend over the rest of the man's life. This recognition perhaps makes killing him not only beside the point but counter to Ishmael's interest. As with the question of the breed of the dog, among other things, the novel makes it abundantly clear that nothing will bring Lane back, and this is the anticlimax upon which capital punishment may be based—the notion of "closure" that is supposed to accompany execution, but probably never does. Ishmael, in a remarkable passage that is almost two pages long and one sentence, says, among other things: "I want you to take time and with your mind review, go over, take an inventory of your body, realize that there are no, external anyway, parts missing, you are bleeding from no place, you bear no bruises or other marks, realize, in other words, that I have left no sign, no sign of my presence, no sign of our connection, no sign of my art, my business with you" (212). The narrator and torturer informs his reader and captive that the latter now occupies a position somewhere on a continuum established entirely by Ishmael. He shows no sign of injury, but has been injured. He shows no sign of trauma, but has been traumatized (of course, the same could be said of Ishmael). By making this statement, Ishmael makes sure that the man in his basement cannot get used to and take for granted his new condition. He must take inventory of it, at his captor's insistence.

But, as Ishmael turns his attention to his own role, he becomes his most fearsome. Since the man has not seen Ishmael's face, because of the Venus effect, he can only imagine Ishmael's face. We can imagine that he saw it when they met before Ishmael kidnapped him, but of course who really remembers the face of a passing stranger? Ishmael muses: "You do have a vague recollection, one from long ago, on a cool night, of my face, faint, vague, and ghostly, mere suggestion, like the face of god, except of course that I exist, maybe" (212). This brief joke about belief is particularly salient to Everett's work, as will become clearer in chapter 3, when I discuss the way he represents religion in his work. For now, it sets up the point to be made about why it is not worthwhile to murder this man: "I want you to find a perverse and uneasy satisfaction, a strange comfort, in your state of terror, a state that should approximate joy, but not quite, as I almost want you to find peace in the knowledge of my existence, in the knowledge that if I found you once I will find you again" (212). This is a declaration of complete ontological power over another, one of the few approaches toward something we might see as an absolute in Everett's work. In fact, this declaration by Ishmael, as he prepares surprisingly to release his captive, reads almost like a prayer, with its intonations of a godlike presence in this man's life from now on. As Ishmael tells the man "I will never leave you," his peroration admits little doubt about the finality of the man's release: "Know that I have killed, will kill, and that is only part of what instills fear, that what chills your blood is the fact that I can give life, that it is my gift to give" (213). Ishmael's revenge is in allowing the man to live, in the knowledge that he no longer controls his own life. Ishmael now exists, at least for this one other man, somewhere along the continuum between the categories of man and god.

The ways that the notion of the unresolved, the in between, the contingent, the provisional, recurs rhizomatically throughout Everett's work in characters like Ralph Townsend, Craig Suder, and Ishmael Kidder find an almost literalized representation in the form of Theodore Street, the protagonist and third-person narrator of *American Desert*. To start, Street's name characterizes the intermediate in itself, since the street can be a destination and also a route to a destination, the route being a place but at the same time a conduit to a place,[13] and so occupies a position not unlike Ishmael and his captive, who both are present but invisible to one another, in the mirrors at least, thanks to the Venus effect. Here, there are several layers to the unresolved nature just of this character's name. Also like the narrator of *The Water Cure* does intermittently, Theodore Street capriciously "chooses to relate his own story in third person" (3) from the beginning of the novel, a decision that has a weird effect that is different from the similar narrative decision that Ishmael makes intermittently. Ishmael's decision is a momentary expression of power: "I shook my head. Rather, he shook his head as I now shift to third person (because I can) to convey a sense of distance and at once, ironically (as all things are ironic), to offer this intrusion that makes me and so you even close to the narration and so to the story and so to the pain" (153). Ishmael's alteration on narrative point of view comes across as almost petulant, another way for him to impose his will over this man who he thinks may have murdered his daughter. His deployment of this strategy certainly does carry some of the sense of distancing that is evident in the device's use in *American Desert*, but in *American Desert* the device is all distancing, while also not distancing at all. Of course, this simultaneity requires the taking on of yet another challenge issued by Everett in his construction of this character. The challenge here is that it becomes very easy (conventional, really) to hear the narrator's voice as just that of another third-person speaker. We have to remind ourselves consciously and frequently that we are actually reading a first-person narrator speaking of himself in the third person and not a third-person narrator. It might also be posited that perhaps all third-person narrators are speaking this way, but we never think of them like this because we have gotten so used to thinking of the third-person narrator in the heavily conventionalized ways that we tend to. But for our purposes here, it is crucial that we keep in mind that Theodore Street is speaking of himself in the third person and then proceed from there.

With its in between first- and third-person narrative perspective, the introduction of *American Desert* creates some quite striking resonances, as the novel begins with an almost slapstick irony—the manner in which Theodore finds himself dead in the first place. These introductory sentences also precede the announcement of the narrative perspective to be employed, so they create the first impression of telling a joke at Theodore's expense, rather than what they are, which is a self-deprecating and somewhat alarming account of a man's own interrupted suicide attempt: "That Theodore Street was dead was not a matter open to debate. The irony of his accidental death went unobserved as no one knew that Theodore was on his way to commit suicide when he was, shall we say, interrupted" (3). After some reflection on the nature of his narrative voice, we get down to the nature of the irony he mentions:

He was driving at a respectable clip along Ocean Boulevard when a fat man chased his nails-painted poodle out into the street before a UPS truck, causing the driver of the huge, brown block to swerve and slide into a lane of oncoming traffic, the oncoming traffic in this case being Ted Street in his 1978 Lancia coupe. The truck and the Lancia met violently and whereas his vehicle halted quite abruptly, Ted did not, but continued in the same direction he had been traveling through the already cracked windscreen. Remarkably, Ted's face suffered not a single scratch and neither did his body break about the ribs, clavicles, arms or legs, but his head did become rather cleanly detached from the rest of him. (3–4)

There is an element of the surreal here as well as the slapstick, as Ted's head shows no outward sign of trauma, but for its severance from the rest of his body. But while the head is undamaged, it is nevertheless severed, and so the reactions of those who happen upon the scene are as might be expected: "It was a jagged but complete wound around his neck that left one seasoned police officer vomiting by the accordion front fender of the Lancia while the young rookie on patrol with him stood, mouth agape, staring at the head lying on the asphalt" (4). The details come thick and fast, leaving us a little bewildered, from the outset, as to where to imagine ourselves looking. It becomes difficult to figure out which is the main priority of this opening sequence—the details of Ted's death,[14] the reactions to it, or where his death is supposed to have left him: "Unlike the stories of beheaded Frenchmen stealing one last, pitiful look at their cast-off bodies, Ted had no such perception. He died instantly and, in a manner of speaking, completely. The UPS man was beside himself, so much so that he would later attend Ted Street's funeral and subsequently take a civil service examination in order to change his profession" (4). The representative of the coroner's office, "not the coroner himself" (4), feels he should call his office "to ask whether head and body should be placed in the same or separate bags" (4).

The macabre humor in the mixing up of priorities in this opening sequence rests on the familiar and conventional anxieties most human beings share about death. The frontier between life and death conventionally stands as one of the more seemingly impermeable categorical boundaries. However, in *American Desert* this is not the case. Because of the seemingly categorical way that Ted dies, with his head completely severed from the rest of his body, a linguistic convention, which is revisited in *The Water Cure* three years later and which we've already addressed here, emerges. At the morgue, the already uncomfortable question is made all the more uncomfortable because of how Ted dies: "The matter, however, rang with an air of incompleteness, as it was the case that the body was never identified, only the head and isn't that what is always required? That the body be identified? 'We want you to come down and identify the body,' the cop always says. Never, 'Is that his head?'" (5). Whereas *The Water Cure*'s critique of the inadequacy of this conventional turn of phrase is fraught with emotion and trauma, as it is associated immediately with Lane's violation and murder, and with the resultant cruelty and torment of Ishmael Kidder, in *American Desert* the expression does not carry the same resonance and the stakes appear much lower, even though this narrative, like the other one, is considering the death of one of the characters, here, the narrator.[15]

Of course, the point at which Ted's unconventional relationship with life, with death, and with the position he adopts in proximity to these two familiar states of being reaches its most unsettled point in *American Desert* when he "sat up in his coffin" (11) at his own funeral. As may be reasonably expected, this event causes a stir in the church. Ted, who, we are to remember, is narrating his own story in the third person, is all too aware of how such an action might affect a group of people. "A hush filled the church, as one might expect" (11), he says. The punch line of the sentence, though, is "but it was not long-lived" (11), since the observation of the length of the hush's life obliquely comments on Ted's own. In addition, this understated comment inadequately introduces the chaos that predictably follows, which includes his wife occupying one of these states of being uncomfortably in between categories, as "Gloria Street fainted but remained frozen upright with wide-open eyes" (11). Once this first wave of reaction has crested, the scene shifts back to Ted: "Amid the chanting and screaming and farting, Ted Street climbed out of his box and faced them all. As it turned out, his trousers had been just Mr. Ash's size and so he was naked from the waist down, his tallywacker hanging rather handsomely out in front of him. Ted Street looked at all the faces, studying them one by one and remembering their voices and their turns to and away from him" (12). The decision of Mr. Ash, the undertaker, to steal the trousers off of a corpse in his charge—under all other circumstances a crime that he would be reasonable in assuming would normally go undetected—is exposed for all to see, as is Ted; although it is fair to assume that if there was one thing about Ted's funeral that they would remember it would not be that he was not wearing pants.

As with Ralph, much of the characterization of Ted's breach of categories requires the reader to keep in mind some contradictory aspect of the protagonist that opposes what we are seeing the rest of the time. As I've already said, it is crucial to remember that Ralph is a baby in order for the complex effects of his self-characterizations as well as his descriptions of others and the world around him to carry the resonance that constitutes so much of what is most significant about *Glyph*. He is not just a baby, nor just a genius, but something wholly new, that requires something wholly different from his reader in order to appreciate who Ralph is.

With Ted, his rising from the dead at his own funeral brings with it similar ontological as well as tactical questions for a novelist. Put simply, how dead can Ted be and still be the narrator and an active character in the story being told? At first, he is dead in that he has been prepared for burial by undertakers. Perhaps the decision of one of the undertakers to steal his trousers is evidence of the man's confidence that Ted is dead. The first reminder that Ted is in fact dead occurs when he is trying to calm others down after he rises: "Ted wanted to call out to the people in the church, tell them to calm down and take their seats or, at least, leave in an orderly fashion, but his mouth was sewn shut and so he could only say, 'Mumm, mmmmm, mum'" (16). Ted's resurrection might as well recall that of Jesus; although the search for further parallels is largely fruitless, even as any resurrection tempts anyone raised within the Judeo-Christian universe to look for them, nonetheless. But a search for parallels is not completely without purpose, a point to which I'll return shortly.[16]

The world into which Ted reemerges is not forgotten by the narrative or the narrator, though: "Ted's resurrection caused a stir, a terrible riot which spread from the church and into the streets, resulting later in the arrest of seventeen gang members who saw the shocked, enlightened mass as prime targets for robbery and their general entertainment" (16). This description is important because by 2004, when *American Desert* is published, few American cities are more habitually associated with large-scale civil unrest than is Los Angeles, where the novel is set. And yet, as the narrative's focal length finally settles on the immediate problem of Ted's family attempting to acclimate themselves to this new reality, we get a moment that almost makes sense, within the senselessness of the scene: "Ted and Gloria and the children walked from the altar, down a narrow and dark corridor and out the back into the alley. They would not have known that there was a riot going on except for the screaming and blowing of horns which seemed so far away" (17). This last point makes sense. It is easy—within reason, of course—to see why the family might be largely oblivious to their surroundings, considering what has just happened to one of their members.

After making a second attempt to calm the people around him, "Mummmm, mmmmm," Ted stands in front of Mr. Graves (get it?), one of the undertakers, and says, "Mmmmumf." Graves, realizing what is being asked of him, "took out his Swiss Army pocketknife and with trembling hands slit all but three of the stitches of Ted Street's mouth before fainting" (17). This gesture enables Ted to say to the gathering, "Ehvabuzy cam noun" and "Wuwax" (17). Later, in response to his daughter Emily's question, "Daddy, how can you be alive?" (17), and before his wife cuts the remaining sutures holding his mouth closed, Ted replies to his daughter, "Awn dn nnoh" (17). These utterances bring us back to the earlier point about parallels in the text. Instead of parallels with Jesus, a temptation we have already seen in Everett's work in "The Fix," it's worth remembering how the coded language works in *Glyph* and *The Water Cure*. Here we get a sense of how resilient language is in its ability to communicate meaning, since "Ehvabuzy cam noun" can be relatively easily recognized, especially in light of the context, as "Everybody calm down." Similarly, "Wuwax" looks enough like "Relax" to enable us to see it lurking behind the w's. "Awn dn nnoh" expresses possibly how the reader is feeling as well, by this early point in the text. I don't know.

Emily appeals to the category that may be applied to the circumstances in which her father finds himself, in an understandable attempt to find a potential answer: "Are you a ghost, Daddy?" (19). As Emily is unsure of her family's state, so is her father: "No, I don't think I'm a ghost, honey" (19). Everyone is familiar with the category of *ghost*—that quintessential figure existing between the worlds of the living and the dead—and brings with this idea some associations of what to be ghostlike might entail. But it is something completely different to be confronted with the circumstances in which this familiar category appears at the same time both possible and inadequate.

While the family's struggle with Ted's new state of being is obviously emotional, it manifests itself most often through questions of category, since this is really all we have as mechanisms through which to understand our world. We can resort to some systematized method of organizing our worlds (like familial, religious, political, social affiliation), but even these still rely upon some categorization of what is acceptable or unacceptable, based on the organizing beliefs or principles of the group affiliation. Emily becomes a cipher for this struggle: "'You're a freak,' she snapped. 'How can you be alive?' Then she started to shake all over and call for her mother. 'Mommy! Mommy!'" (25). Emily's search for answers based on what she already knows—be that the conventions of *alive* and *dead* or the succor she finds in an appeal to *Mommy*, which she repeats as if to reassure herself that at least her mother is recognizable and present, not to mention recognizably alive. Her brother Perry seems to attempt a more accepting attitude toward what has happened:

> "I'm glad you're not dead, Daddy," Perry said.
> "Thanks, sport," Ted said. (25)

While his sister wants something definitive by way of solution, Perry accepts what he knows, as far as he can see. He knows his father is *not dead,* and he knows he's happy about that.

The beginning of *American Desert* juxtaposes the metaphysical questions of Ted's state of being with the completely mundane elements of everyday life in ways that disorient and repeatedly issue challenges to the reader to make sense of something unlike what they are used to, and possibly to release themselves from the conventions to which they have grown accustomed. From there, this release can lead to some questioning of what purpose these conventions serve and whether release from them brings with it possibilities that their existence actively forecloses upon. There are predictable moments, for instance, as when the Channel 5 news team reports on Ted's story: "Bill, what we have been able to piece together is that a man who was presumed dead, and was being funeralized at the church you see burning behind me, sat up in his coffin and walked out. Details are terribly sketchy, as you might imagine" (27). As Tracy, the reporter, stands among the rioters, all of whom also need some satisfying, recognizable answer, it is difficult not to reflect upon just how important recognizable answers become to us and how violently we can react when we are denied them. A man breaching the line between life and death is a particular example of such a breach but stands in for others, and the moment when Tracy is speaking is especially important to understanding which answers help and which do not: "'Well, Bill,' Tracy said, 'that's one of the things we and everyone else are trying to figure out. It seems this man's head was completely cut off from his body in a traffic accident just three days ago'" (27). In other words, *American Desert* is telling us that Ted is not a Christ analogy, although Ted did at least wait the customary (if that's the right word) three days before he arose from his death. While the Christ analogy is part of our conventional narrative for such an event, we are challenged to look farther and deeper in order to make meaning within the world this novel presents. It might even be said that the outrageous nature of being asked to believe that this man has risen from his own death after three days casts a critical light on the outrageousness of believing that another man accomplished this feat.

Along with the more surreal and macabre aspects of the novel's depiction of the not-dead Ted Street is its almost necessary attention to the basics of his condition. As Ralph reminds us that he cannot control his own shit because he's a toddler, Ted reminds us that he is not alive in any conventional sense of that word. As he sits in the taxi that is driving him and his family home through the rioting,

> he wondered if his heart was beating at all. He put his hand flat against his chest and searched, but found no pulse. He felt strangely that without the sound of his heart, his ears were even more open to the sounds around him. He could hear the driver's molars pull from then sink again into the gum he was chewing, every crackle of the taxi's radio, the miss of a bad lifter in the engine, gravel crunching under the weight of the driver's heel as he shifted between acceler-ator and brake pedals, the barking of a young dog away from the direction of the rioting. (23)

He can even hear that it's a *young* dog. He notes later, "that in addition to having no pulse, he could stop breathing entirely if he chose and there would be no change in his condition. He did have to inhale and exhale to speak and, in a way, he expected to feel his breath as this icy blast passing up through his sloppily reassembled esophagus, but he felt nothing of the sort, though he could, with his intensified hearing, locate a catch in his throat when making the ah and oh sounds" (25). The weird physiological realities of his state of being are central to and recurrent in *American Desert*. The repetition of his having no pulse but nevertheless functioning as if he were alive emphasizes much about Ted, but also about many of Everett's main characters. Because they are not one thing or another—think again about Craig's suspended state of being at the end of *Suder*—the emphasis is on their being something wholly different and new, and this state of being requires something different and new from the reader who encounters them.

Immediately preceding his reflections on this discrepancy between being alive and his almost complete lack of physiological function, Ted expresses his own burgeoning acceptance of his qualified state of being through his modifica-tions of his state of being: "He felt oddly alive, though he couldn't feel his heart thumping in his chest as he had at other times in the past when he thought he was feeling acutely alive, like the time he had been chased by a bear when camping in the Sierras" (22–23). His comparison of being *oddly* alive (which brings with it a sense of uncertainty and undecidedness, while at the same time sounding exactly appropriate to his condition) with being *acutely* alive (with its assertion of the definitiveness of life that is said to accompany the anticipation of imminent death) says much about Ted's change in his own understanding of being alive. This qualified, revived, and revised sense of life is characteristic of a figure who begins the telling of his own story by describing the irony of the circumstances surrounding his own death, his attempted suicide, and his decision to tell his own story in the third person. All of these narrative decisions enforce on the reader the challenge to engage with this text in ways to which the reader is probably unused, or else find something else to read.

Again, like Ralph, this anticonventional character finds himself coming to the attention of others who desire different answers to the kinds of questions his existence provokes. Ted becomes the object of attention of a cult leader named Big Daddy. The details of what follows are less important here than is the persistence of Ted's self-conscious reflections on his state. For instance, he indulges himself in his narrative with the following observation: "He was tired, dead tired and his imagining that—being dead tired—caused him a laugh he thought he deserved, certainly needed" (238). These moments of self-consciously delivered cheap puns can initially seem almost beneath the level at which Everett's texts work, but they again point instead to another kind of shortcoming to which we are susceptible when we cleave to conventional criteria of aesthetic (and maybe moral) judgment. The *dead tired* moment is striking in the way it appears out of place. And yet it signals how the text draws our attention to what else it is probably about. If we can even question the line between life and death and emerge with some refreshed appreciation for what is available once we forge past the conventional frontiers of our perceptions, what else might be available to us? This is a question worth pondering, and Everett's text provides an opportunity for such reflection, although, again, without succumbing to the temptation of trying to produce some definitive answer, since any would be facile.

Instead of definitive answers, the focus here, for the moment, is the line between high and low comedy, and on the infinite possibilities of the line itself. At the risk of appearing excessive, it is worth returning to a long segment of *Glyph* as a way to demonstrate how Everett's narrator (and Everett, it must be said) plays with and emphasizes the infinite possibilities available through contemplation of a line, suggesting other possibilities of other lines, and so on.

This narrative interlude is one of the most didactic moments on this point in all of Everett's fiction:

> Truth and falsity. Sense and nonsense. Self and nonself. Reason and madness. Centrality and marginality. The only thing standing between any of these properties is a drawn line. But a line has no depth, no depth, and so is no boundary at all. Its ends are merely positions in space and as such mean only something to each other by some orientation that might be a line, straight or curved. And so, I know I occupy some point in space *sane* because I can see and orient myself in relation to another point *insane* and as I observe the line that gives them both meaning, I realize that the line does not separate them, but connects them. And I realize as well, my heart pounding that I can, since I have two points and a line, find other points beyond the point *insane* and that I really cannot tell which point is which since points in space have no dimension. Likewise, it is true as I look behind me at the endpoint *sane* that it is really no endpoint at all. So, the line goes that way behind me and this way in front of me and I can't tell where on the line I am standing and so I bisect that line with another line and I say that *insane* is over there. But how do I know that it has not circled around behind me? How do I know that the point on the line *insane* has not planned it this way? Maybe I should walk forward so that it cannot sneak up behind me. Maybe I should run. Or maybe the point *insane* hasn't moved at all and has planned it that way. Perhaps the point *sane* has abandoned me. Maybe the two points are working together. I am not paranoid. I am not paranoid. I just won't move. That's it. I will stay right where I am, fixed in space. (61)

The way these reflections begin to sound like paranoia, as they consider the prospect that the lines are conspiring against the speaker, contradict the actually schizoid nature of these reflections, as Deleuze and Guattari use that expression. Even the resolution to fix oneself in space is actually all potential, all dynamic resistance to the conventions of space, time, sanity, insanity, paranoia, schizophrenia, not to mention all of the spaces we are invited to imagine connecting any of these or other positions within the imaginative matrix sketched here. These lines, attributed in the novel to the Swiss linguist and philosopher Emil Staiger, in conversation with the American literary theorist and critic J. Hillis Miller, provide the sense of dimension (*depth* is the word Staiger uses) that the line actually has. Even as Staiger asserts that the line has no depth, he contradicts this assertion in the observations that surround it. The dynamism and infinite potential in the line that governs the boundary between any two or more categories are evident here, even as Miller replies, deflating the whole situation: "I used to have a car like that. Sometimes, when it was really cold, it would never start" (61). Staiger's words also bring us back to Wallace's observations about why it's easier to accept preexisting assumptions rather than entertain the prospect that this morning will be the one when the bedroom floor will not bear our weight. But what Staiger says reminds us of just how complex any line can be and perhaps why it can be so reassuring not to look too closely at any of the lines that govern our lives.

Another way of thinking about how these lines of convention draw attention to the space in between categories but also determine how we think about them, connect them in our imaginations, and can end up being controlled by them, as well as how they pose perceptual challenges to thinking about them differently emerges from the work of Leonard Cassuto. Cassuto talks about the grotesque as a way to think about the space—he says the tension—between categories: "My analysis of the grotesque is accordingly founded upon the desire for order and its persistent violation by the grotesque, and not on any assumption that this order is actually possible. Individuals seek order in their own lives, and so repress disturbing childhood fears with varying degrees of partial success. Cultures do the same, banning threats to their own order via taboo. The grotesque always manages to evade these thought police. It is a constant intrusion on order, an anomalous agent of chaos" (9). Cassuto's felicitous expression—"anomalous agent of chaos"—could serve as a description of many of Everett's main characters, but especially those discussed in this chapter. While categories, as Cassuto says, satisfy our "demand for form and order" (9), these characters frustrate this demand, this desire, at practically every turn. What is left is the challenge to figure out the meaning of such characters at all. And this is no mean feat. As Cassuto puts this, "Violating accepted boundaries is a serious business, then. It represents an attack on the entire cultural enterprise. Likewise, it becomes a threat to the entire learning endeavor, for it questions the context of knowledge" (11). Everett's characters question the context of knowledge, and it is no wonder, as a result, that they and their stories can be a little unsettling.

The conclusion (again, using that word because it's nice to talk like everybody else, even if this word may not apply best to Everett's work) of *American Desert* can come across as quite didactic. This sense of releasing oneself from convention that runs as an undercurrent of the novel—or, at least, my reading of it—leads, it would seem, to a couple of moments of clarity for Ted. As he thinks to himself about himself, he realizes what about him has changed for the better and is able to trace these changes back to his rethinking of the ostensibly most elemental division between life and death:

> He used to think that dead was dead, but that notion had been proven wrong. He used to believe that the world was on its faithful spinning course and that was that, but now he knew, *things were the way they were until, simply, they changed.* Now, he was going to change something. In fact, he already had. First death had changed his concept of life. Then, resurrection had changed him as a person, made him so much more than he ever had been in life. And now, living after death had altered him yet again; he had turned a corner in his mind, accepting his remarkable station, coming to understand his immortality, his place. There was a change in his eyes, the way he tilted his head when he observed things in the world, a change in the way he pointed, turned, walked. His voice had become softer, his words fewer and more carefully chosen. (271–72; emphasis added)

This reflective moment suggests what may be available to us at the point that we free ourselves to rethink the conventions that govern so much of our lives. Ted was sure that he understood the difference between life and death, but living after death results in many new and beneficial changes in him, not the least of which is his becoming a better listener and, it would appear, a better person. The experience would appear to have humbled him, leaving him open to discovering new things about himself, the members of his family, and the world around him, a world he was so sure that he understood at the beginning of the novel that he was willing to kill himself in order to escape it.

Perhaps the more surreal aspects of *American Desert* conspire to distract us from these more metaphysical, not to mention hermeneutic, possibilities. If so, Ted brings us back to these more metaphysical considerations one last time, after he has saved—with the help of one of the cult's many Jesuses (someone must have considered the plural as *Jesi*)—the lives of fifty children being held hostage by a cult who have identified him as Satan. He arrives at these observations in a couple of different ways. First, he talks about where he's been:

> I am dead. I died and I am dead and I can tell you no more about the meaning of life than I could when I was alive. But I know everything about the meaning of death. I saw no white light, attractive or otherwise. I felt no sweet feeling of relief or understanding or ease. I felt nothing. Happily, I can also report that I experienced no pain. However, now I am nothing but pain. To myself, my family and to you.
>
> I am no hero. I knew the children were there and so I did the decent thing, the right thing. I am no angel. There is no god for which I might serve as an emissary. I am no savior. I am no messiah. I am, finally, in this life, a decent man. (290)

His peroration is almost moving in its benedictory quality, as he gestures toward releasing those listening to him (and reading his words, it must also be said) because of his having experienced the fate that many of us fear most: "I was dead, when my head was apart from me, I was dead. Death is not a bad thing and one ought to stay dead when death comes. If nothing else, I have learned this. I wish that I had no mouth, so that my silence would mean as much as my words. I wish that my words had no meaning. I wish that you could all feel my death, so that you would cease fearing it" (290–91). His desire to be without a mouth, so that his silence would speak is especially telling, since he suggests that even those most conventional and expected tools of communication—words—do not carry with them all that we tend to endow them with. The novel has really only said this, but this is a lot. If this is where we look, then we can take great satisfaction from its ending, as Ted slowly undoes the undertaker's stitching that has been holding his head to the rest of his body since his funeral, and "grabbed his head between his two hands, removed it and set it in his lap, closed his eyes and stayed dead" (291).

◆ ◆ ◆

Suder, Glyph, The Water Cure, and *American Desert* all manage to convey something important about Everett's aesthetic as well as about how we tend to make meaning. But as Cassuto says, this making of meaning, upon which we tend to rely, is a high-stakes game, as is interfering with how we normally do it. But these four novels, and much of the rest of Everett's body of work, make important inroads into demonstrating how we might think differently about what we've become most used to. In order for these novels to work this magic, though, the reader must take on a great responsibility in accepting the challenge that the novels issue. These four novels are relatively explicit in mounting this challenge and engaging the reader in the question, What else are these texts about? This is why I began with them. In what follows, with these examples in place, it will become apparent how else this writer's work issues its challenges.

2

THE PERSISTENTLY GNAWING AND TROUBLING EFFORT NOT TO LET OUR GUARDS DOWN

Once more. Say you are in the country; in some high land of lakes. Take almost any path you please, and ten to one it carries you down in a dale, and leaves you there by a pool in the stream. There is magic in it. Let the most absent-minded of men be plunged in his deepest reveries—stand that man on his legs, set his feet a-going, and he will infallibly lead you to water, if water there be in all that region. Should you ever be athirst in the great American desert, try this experiment, if your caravan happens to be supplied with a metaphysical professor. Yes, as everyone knows, meditation and water are wedded for ever.

—*Moby-Dick*

You never get the book you wanted, you settle for the book you get. I've always felt that when a book ended there was something I didn't see, and usually when I remark the discovery it's too late to do anything about it.

—James Baldwin, "The Art of Fiction"

Habit is a great deadener.

—*Waiting for Godot*

A focus on the infinite space available to us that exists in between the established and familiar categories that govern our lives does not mean that nothing matters, that we can't understand anything, that we cannot hold beliefs or take positions, or that there's nothing to learn once we accept the existence of this infinite space. We know that Ralph Townsend does love his mother. Irrespective of whatever else we can be sure about in *Glyph,* we know this fact to be true. We know that Craig Suder can fly and that this is really important to him, regardless of whether or not he sticks the landing. We know that Ishmael Kidder decides, for his own reasons, not to murder the man he believes to have kidnapped, raped, and murdered his little girl, and that in not killing the man, Ishmael now owns him. While it is difficult to disentangle this resolution from everything else that happens in *The Water Cure,* we might also have to engage—for a moment, at least—with the prospect that Ishmael is capable of something approaching grace, something that many (perhaps even most of us) under similar circumstances would not be capable of. And we know that Ted Street is a better man after having lived for a while as a dead man. He, too, arrives at a conclusion that outstrips even the bizarre circumstances under which we encounter him. Even as these characters carve out existence in between the categories with which we are more accustomed, we can know these things about them.

Everett's work is full of provisional, suggested resolutions as well as conclusions of which we can be certain, like those listed above. John Livesey, in *Cutting Lisa,* appears to decide that performing an abortion on his daughter-in-law on the kitchen table of the house she shares with his son and granddaughter is the way to reconcile his ideas about family with the reality that the child his daughter-in-law is carrying is not his son's, and by extension, not a member of his family, as he understands the term. The proposed *History of the African-American People* is never published, or even written, unless, of course, we count the text with that title that details the circumstances under which the *History* is not written. Gus is left to kill several neo-Nazis who themselves have committed a murder over the course of *Wounded,* leaving us to puzzle over whether or not we agree with Gus's actions and what our decision says about us. As with John Livesey at the end of *Cutting Lisa,* though, the killing does not take place within the plot of the novel. (A related question is whether Everett poses characters like neo-Nazis, child murderers, and racist US senators more as sacrificial caricatures than as actual characters, because they are easy to morally exclude with little or no compunction.) Thelonious Ellison prepares to accept his Book Award for *Fuck,* the ghetto novel that he writes as Stagg R. Leigh, as a satirical counter—he thinks—to Juanita Mae Jenkins's best seller, *We's Lives in Da Ghetto.*

But in writing his satire, Ellison becomes a victim of forces that he should have known would appropriate and co-opt his original intentions.

In each of these cases, the conclusion can leave the novel's meaning in a provisional state at best, and in a condition of moral ambivalence as well. What I've called this constructive frustration of resolution can appear deliberate, since it happens with so many of Everett's novels, inviting the reader—if so inclined—to entertain possible options concerning the meaning of the lack of resolution in and of itself. As I've already said, I am inclined to see this lack of definitive resolution as meaningful in itself, and, I should add, perhaps even hopeful in terms of the instruction it might provide us in dealing with aspects of the world around us that we do not understand. These aspects can be, for instance, people who are in some way different from ourselves. Instead of imposing our own sense of certainty upon these differences—insisting that *they* become more like *us*—recognizing our own uncertainty as in some way constructive suggests something hopeful about how else we might interact with and come to understand difference.

Each of the novels discussed in my first chapter presents what appears to be a somewhat didactic central character who provides a lesson in an aesthetic and perhaps a philosophy that undergirds Everett's fiction. These characters articulate directly some statement or position with respect to their willingness to make sense of their worlds. Such characters are, however, the exceptions that prove some other rule in the overall fictional world that Everett creates, not to mention the world in which we all live. It is worthwhile, therefore, to delve into more typical presentations, characters who instead imply, sidle up to, hint at, gesture toward what may be at work in Everett's fiction.

The move away from the more direct expositional character means a move toward characters and situations that are even more distracting and cause us to become engrossed in the stories themselves, perhaps even at the expense of being able to extrapolate meaning that goes beyond the *plot* as such. Cathy Caruth, in *Unclaimed Experience*, gestures toward this problem: "I would argue that de Man's allusion to this moment in the history of philosophy suggests that it is a paradigm for a problem that is central to contemporary theory: the recognition that direct or phenomenal reference to the world means, paradoxically, the production of a fiction; or otherwise put, that reference is radically different from physical law" (76). Caruth's observation about the necessary indirectness of our ability to refer to our experiences and how this indirectness in turn requires the creation of fictions is not itself news. In fact, it is reminiscent of Wallace's observation about inductive reasoning, which relies upon—among other things—our not being conscious of it as a process, as a fiction, as a phenomenon that governs our everyday lives.

To further this point, I will rely here upon Ralph Townsend's words, when he says "There is no such thing as digression" (127), and inject, at some length, an observation made by Tom Vanderbilt, in his book *Traffic*, which provides useful insights into the act of driving a car, another habitual practice that we take for granted as adults that is governed almost entirely by unexamined assumptions:

> Habits, psychologists suggest, provide a way to reduce the amount of mental energy that must be expended on routine tasks. Habits also form a mind-set, which gives us cues on how to behave in certain settings. So when we enter a familiar setting, like the streets around our house, habitual behavior takes over. On the one hand, this is efficient: it frees us from having to gather all sorts of new information, from getting sidetracked. Yet on the other hand, because we are expending less energy on analyzing what is around us, we may be letting our mental guard down. If in three years there has never been a car coming out of the Joneses' driveway in the morning, what happens on the first day of the fourth year, when suddenly there is? Will we see it in time? Will we see it at all? Our feeling of safety and control is also a weakness. A study by a group of Israeli researchers found that drivers committed more traffic violations on familiar routes than on unfamiliar routes. (15)

So, sure, we need not expend as much mental energy when negotiating the streets near our home, but this mental economy can mean a lack of vigilance that can be costly if something in this otherwise familiar environment changes unexpectedly. Vanderbilt—like Wallace, Caruth, and Schneider—cautions us how hypnotizing habit can be and how double-edged habit can be when something changes. Everett's work has the salutary effect of jolting us back into consciousness, keeping us from letting our guard down as we negotiate the familiar roads that we travel when reading, especially when reading work that arrives under the habit-forming and -encouraging heading of "African American Literature."

One trope that recurs in Everett's more recent fiction is the appearance of a character named "Percival Everett," who is likely to be a black college English professor who writes novels that are underappreciated by the general reading public. Sometimes, as in *A History of the African-American People[Proposed] by Strom Thurmond, as Told to Percival Everett & James Kincaid* or *I Am Not Sidney Poitier* or *Percival Everett by Virgil Russell,* this Everett character is someone very similar to the author himself. In *Erasure,* though, this character resembles Everett in manner and what appears to be predisposition, if not also in name. In each application, though, it is critical, and probably most constructive in producing our readings, that we not fall into the habit of interpreting the character as some kind of proxy for the author of the same name. That habitual practice can get us into all kinds of trouble, not unlike that of expecting certain specific things—and only those certain specific things—from novels written by African American writers.[1]

Cathy Caruth's warning that "the recognition that direct or phenomenal reference to the world means, paradoxically, the production of a fiction" is crucial to keep in mind. Remember that Caruth calls this a problem that is central to contemporary theory, a category that will safely accommodate literary criticism. In criticism, after all, we are always producing fictions based on the texts we read. We must always be vigilant in our awareness of the fictions we produce, especially when we feel that we are on what we perceive to be the solid foundation built on our habitual (conventional, really) reading practices, expectations, and training.

Here it is also worthwhile to remember how Deleuze and Guattari introduce *A Thousand Plateaus,* with their acknowledgment that they use their own names and conventional expressions like the sun rises "out of habit, purely out of habit," and "because it's nice to talk like everybody else." Deleuze and Guattari draw our attention, again, to the sorts of perceptual trade-offs that we make every moment of every day, whether we realize it consciously or not, whether we are writing criticism or, as Vanderbilt reminds us, driving a car. Perhaps even *because* we do not realize it. Every moment we are shutting out sensory, intellectual, emotional, as well as other inputs a lot more than we are taking them in. But we also engage in this conscious and unconscious perceptual triage because one fears that to try to take in and to remember consciously everything, to react to everything, to engage with everything is the way toward madness. We triage inputs in order to preserve ourselves.

Instead of merely drawing our attention to the ways in which we succumb to the temptation to talk like everybody else, though, Everett's work often appears to fight against the reading process itself. In another conventional gesture of criticism, it's worth classifying much of Everett's fiction among the works of writers whose work is difficult to read, and indeed may even appear to frustrate reading deliberately. Russell Hoban is quite explicit in this intention, as he describes some of the mechanics of Riddleyspeak, the worn-down version of English that his characters use to communicate with one another in *Riddley Walker.* Hoban says in an afterword to the novel: "Technically it works well with the story because it slows the reader down to Riddley's rate of comprehension" (225). Flann O'Brien's *At Swim-Two-Birds* speculates on the value of the convention of one beginning and one ending to a novel, proposing instead three beginnings and three levels of narrative, each of which threatens to interfere with another level over the course of what might be called the principal narrative. Texts like Hoban's and O'Brien's invite associations with the bildungsroman, on the one hand, while on the other hand, frustrating familiar associations with this recognizable mode and making the frustration all the more frustrating by having invited the association in the first place. This relationship between invitation and frustration is also characteristic of Everett's work.

So if conventions serve their functions and are all the more tempting to succumb to because of their familiarity and service, it is difficult to convince readers to participate voluntarily in the act of denying the conventional. Everett's work requires, however, that we confront this difficulty. The novels examined in this chapter demonstrate in ways that are different from those of the first chapter what is at stake in resisting the temptations of reading convention. Of course, where I am headed is toward an eventual discussion of why this resistance is especially germane to the body of work of an African American writer and to the work of African American writers more generally, with the implication that judging African Americans and other groups to whom one does not oneself belong might be nuanced or improved by adopting a similar practice of resistance to habit.

The conventions of aesthetic judgment are on full display and under the most explicit attack in all of Everett's work in *Erasure,* which brings with it the additional irony of being Everett's best-known novel to date. Published in 2001, *Erasure* tells the story of Thelonious "Monk" Ellison, the Everett-like main character (Southern California college English professor who writes novels that some criticize as not black enough) who writes a ghetto novel in furious response to and parodic resistance against the fame of what appears to be an unintentional parody of black life, *We's Lives in Da Ghetto.*[2]

Erasure thematizes associations related to convention in any number of ways and episodes. In fact, it must be said that there are moments in *Erasure* when it appears that the overstatement of a given character is intended to draw attention to itself as overstatement. These instances can, I am arguing, initiate the asking of better questions, a surefire encouragement to rethink our relationship to the conventions we already know. A couple of characteristic episodes in *Erasure* illuminate other moments in Everett's fiction and show what these episodes have to say about what we might learn from the encouragements repeated in Everett's work to look beyond the usual, beyond the conventional.

In one of the many interludes in *Erasure* that test Ralph's declaration in *Glyph* about digressions, Monk Ellison describes driving along Highway 395, on his way to fishing the South Fork of the Kern River. He notes that dusk is coming on "and so it was late enough and still eerie enough for the weirdos to be out" (45). This observation matters because of what happens in the diner where he stops to eat, providing along the way the useful bit of travel advice regarding eating, "When traveling, it is best to eat without regard to health or one might not eat at all" (45). Into this scene walk "a couple of stringy, gimme-capped, in-bred bohunks" (45), who pick up the sound of people speaking French, a "fern" language, as Monk describes it, in his second dismissive characterization of these two men. The two bohunks then ask the two French-speaking men if they are "funny," following this question up with the clarification "You know, queers" (46). The two Frenchmen turn out to be gay, at which point the two bohunks extend the following invitation: "Come on outside so we can kick your ass" (46). In many ways, this scene so far is as familiar as it is asinine, as anyone who has ever found themselves singled out for similar hate-based hostility can attest.

The first actual surprise in the scene occurs after the two bohunks invite the two Frenchmen outside for the aforementioned ass kicking. Monk speaks up, including himself in the defense of the Frenchmen. Monk's intervention is met with another stereotypical reply from one of the bohunks: "I think we got the nigger riled" (46). Monk also suggests that he "might be" when asked by one of the "provincial slugs" (47), as they are also called in the narrative, if he's "a faggot, too" (46). Monk even indulges himself in a threat, as he delivers the sort of line that seems ready-made for an occasion such as this one: "Okay, if we're going to do this, let's do it. Just remember that this is one of the more important decisions you will ever make" (46). This is the kind of overwrought line one associates with a western or a television crime drama.

The scene's payoff occurs when the two Frenchmen stand up to engage the two "rubes" in their challenge. Monk says: "I wished I'd had a camera to capture the expressions of those two provincial slugs. The Frenchmen were huge, six-eight and better, and healthy looking. The rubes stumbled over themselves backing away, then scrambled out of the diner" (46–47). The size of the Frenchmen says something to us about ourselves. Irrespective of how progressively minded we like to think ourselves to be, it is easy to imagine two gay men being accosted by two hostile bigots as potentially smaller and more vulnerable than these two Frenchmen turn out to be. The two bohunks share this expectation, as evidenced by their hasty retreat once they take in the Frenchmen's height and physical condition. Depending on how else we think of the French, their national identity may add to potential negative expectations. In addition, as we know from *Glyph,* how other people are spoken about provides some indication of who if anyone in a given scene is not white. Because Monk is called "the nigger," as opposed to "another nigger" or "this nigger, too" when he makes his intervention into the episode, we know not only that the two aggressors are white (we were probably assuming that in any case) but that the two Frenchmen are white, too, since they have only been singled out for their sexual orientation and for sounding "fern."[3]

Monk's observation about himself in the scene is notable, since he reiterates something that he already knows about himself, even if here he has to rethink what he knows. As the two Frenchmen invite him to join them after the abortive altercation, he thinks to himself: "I was laughing when the men asked me to join them, not at the spectacle of the rednecks running out, but at my own nerve and audacity, to presume that they needed my help" (47). On the one hand, Monk gives voice to what we may have been thinking as well—that these two gay Frenchmen needed the help of someone else in order to defend themselves. On the other hand, as he has already noted in thinking about his brother, Bill, who has recently come out as gay: "Effeminate behavior, I learned when young, served as no measure of sexual orientation" (45). Old habits, like new ones, die hard.

Monk draws attention to his presumptions on at least one additional occasion early in *Erasure*, when he visits his sister's abortion clinic. He sits down in the waiting room next to a "young woman with curling, blue fingernails" (20). He engages the woman, who remains unnamed (we can easily imagine that Monk never learns her name or has forgotten it) in the sort of waiting-room small talk at which academics seem particularly bad. As their conversation turns to books—including *Their Eyes Were Watching God* and *Cane*—and the woman makes several reasonable observations about them, Monk asks, "Have you gone to college?" (21). She laughs, and Monk tells her not to laugh, that she's really smart, and that she should at least try to go to college. She replies, finally, "I didn't even finish high school" (21)

Monk's self-reflection is characteristic of himself and of many of Everett's protagonists: "I didn't know what to say to that. I scratched my head and looked at the other faces in the room. I felt an inch tall because I had expected this young woman with the blue fingernails to be a certain way, to be slow and stupid, but she was neither. I was the stupid one" (21). As in the episode with the Frenchmen and the hostile bigots, Monk is not really guilty of very much in the way of transgression, as social transgressions go. He does in these two episodes what probably all of us have done at some point. He has judged books by their covers—something he resents, especially when it's literally the covers of his books being judged. But as he does this, he then draws attention to the important commitment to learn something from his erroneous judgments, something that might interfere with the reflex of judging next time. That's worth something. The issue is not to pretend that we do not make these judgments. We do, and we will. The hope is that we might get better about how we react when we make these judgments. Maybe we'll ask better questions of ourselves next time.

An additional instance from Everett's fiction makes a similar point about what is available to our perception at the point when we reexamine how a convention affects our judgment. It comes from one of his short stories. "The Appropriation of Cultures," from the same 2004 collection, *Damned If I Do*, that features "The Fix." "The Appropriation of Cultures" presents Daniel Barkley, who is, in many ways, a characteristic Everett protagonist and another who in some ways, resembles Everett.[4]

Everything we will have read or been trained to read and think suggests that a character with Daniel Barkley's background will probably be white. He has "money left to him by his mother" and a "house that had been left to him by his mother" (91). His mother's sister has also left him money "because she had no children of her own" (91). In addition, he has a "degree in American Studies from Brown University that he had in some way earned, but that had not yet earned anything for him" (91). He "didn't work and didn't pretend to need to, spending most of his time reading" (91). In all of these ways, what is most important about Daniel is less that he is an unusual black character in literature than the very fact that he is an unusual black character in literature because of these characteristics. His financial status—resulting from the passive receipt of inherited money from several family sources—and his Ivy League education (not to mention his dismissive attitude toward it) conspire to focus our attention on what that usual assumption (that Barkley is probably white) might mean to how we move around and take in the world. Daniel occasionally plays in a jazz band "with some old guys who all worked very hard during the day, but didn't hold Daniel's condition against him" (91). Based on the descriptions so far, Daniel's "condition" appears to be his financial independence, a state of affairs rarely if ever characterized as a condition—something to be endured, overcome, or cured—when it happens to white literary characters.

The notion of Daniel's "condition" becomes all the more significant and double-voiced, though, because of what happens in the next paragraph, during the scene on which the entire story turns: "One night, some white boys from a fraternity yelled forward to the stage at the black man holding the acoustic guitar and began to shout, 'Play "Dixie" for us! Play "Dixie" for us'" (91). Daniel's *condition* now looks like it might equally be his wealth and his color, as he is *the* black man on the stage playing the acoustic guitar. The frat boys, after all, can't just look at him and tell that he's wealthy. They probably see him and make the same kinds of assumptions that we make when we encounter a black character in our reading. Of course, syntax makes it possible that he is the only black guitar player; hence *the* black man playing the acoustic guitar, but the way he is singled out in what follows at least suggests that he's the only black musician in the band. Otherwise, they would demand of the whole group that they play the song. Black characters are often identified in this by-the-way fashion in Everett's work, as made clear by Ralph's observations and self-description in *Glyph*, that white characters do not need to be legitimized to exist on the page. We continue to assume characters are white, in other words, until we are told otherwise.

We are told that the frat boys are white, which punctuates the hostile intent of their song request. The frat boys in "The Appropriation of Cultures" are easy stand-ins for the "couple of guys" (45) who challenge the French strangers to a fight in *Erasure,* and like them, the frat boys are eventually the butt of the joke and the occasion for a lesson. As in *Erasure,* the expected confrontation takes an unexpected turn when Daniel plays "Dixie" as requested but plays this song "he had grown up hating, the song the whites had always pulled out to remind themselves and those other people just where they were. Daniel sang the song. He sang it slowly. He sang it, feeling the lyrics, deciding that the lyrics were his, deciding that the song was his. *Old times there are not forgotten.* . . . He sang the song and listened to the silence around him. He resisted the urge to let satire ring through his voice. He meant what he sang. *Look away, look away, look away, Dixieland*" (92). Just as when the two men in the diner skulk out after the event turns on them in *Erasure,* so here: "One person clapped. Then another. And soon the tavern was filled with applause and hoots. He found the frat boys in the back and watched as they stormed out, a couple of people near the door chuckling at them as they passed" (92).

Daniel does not yet know what he has learned at the end of his heartfelt rendition of "Dixie." Like Monk, though, he does reflect upon what the incident means to him. In the diner scene, Monk laughs at himself for intervening in a way that he sees as unwise, ill-advised, and, as it turns out, completely un-necessary. But he nevertheless feels good about himself for having done so and having learned something important about his judgments of others. Daniel's reflections are more complicated because of his difficult relationship to this heavily freighted song:

> Daniel didn't much care for the slaps on the back, but he didn't focus too much energy on that. He was busy trying to sort out his feelings about what he had just played. The irony of his playing the song straight and from the heart was made more ironic by the fact that as he played it, it came straight from his heart, as he was claiming Southern soil, or at least recognizing his blood in it. His was

the land of cotton and hell no, it was not forgotten. At twenty-three, his anger was fresh and typical, and so was his ease with it, the way it could be forgotten for chunks of time, until something like that night with the white frat boys or simply a flashing blue light in the rearview mirror brought it all back. He liked the song, wanted to play it again, knew that he would. (93)

Daniel's anger is "fresh and typical." He, too, is a convention, in other words, a stereotype of young, black male righteous anger. In any number of ways, most of us are enacting typical, conventional responses much of the time, whether we know it or not. But this does not mean that we cannot grow, change, get better at whatever it is we are doing. As Daniel's relationship to this once-hated song is changed as a result of an unbidden intended insult, he learns something very important about himself, something unavailable if he persists with his fresh and typical anger.

The story ends in an expression of Daniel's discovery: "I've decided that the rebel flag is my flag. My blood is Southern blood, right? Well, it's my flag" (98). He begins to drive a pickup truck with a large Confederate flag displayed across the back window of the cab. Eventually, other black Columbians start joining in, and "Soon, there were several, then many cars and trucks in Columbia, South Carolina, sporting Confederate flags and being driven by black people" (102). The more black people embrace the flag, the more the "symbol began to disappear from the fronts of big rigs and the back windows of jacked-up four-wheelers" (103). Finally, "the piece of cloth was quietly dismissed from its station with the U.S. and State flags atop the State Capitol. There was no ceremony, no notice. One day, it was not there" (103). Once he is inspired to think about "Dixie" in a different way, he is able to realize the possibility that he might be able to *take* an artifact of a cultural expression initially intended to dehumanize him. He puts it very plainly: "You should have seen those redneck boys when I took 'Dixie' from them. They didn't know what to do. So, the goddamn flag is flying over the State Capitol. Don't take it down, just take it. That's what I say" (99).

Of course, it's not as simple as that, and his large-Afroed friend, Sarah, chimes in as the voice of reason: "That's all you have to do? That's all there is to it?" (99). Daniel replies, with an inadequacy that is palpable, "Yep." But what Daniel now sees in the song and the flag is not even ponderable if he is still mired in his fresh and typical anger over emblems like the Confederate flag and "Dixie."

It's difficult not to think of Bud Powell's advice to a young Craig Suder, after Powell decides to release a neighbor's dog that has been barking, even after another neighbor threatens to shoot the dog. When Craig reminds Powell of this threat, Powell says, simply, "That's called a chance. . . . If Mr. Simpson shoots him, then he shoots him. At least the dog is free to get shot" (161). The dog is in fact subsequently shot, and a frantic Craig yells at Powell, "It's your fault" (161). Powell "stared at me without expression. Then he stepped into the house" (161). He is gone from the Suders' house the next morning, but seems to know something important that Craig eventually learns. Freedom is not about guarantees and sometimes comes at a high cost, like the risk you won't be able to land safely after jumping off of a high rock and flying over a pond with wings made out of garbage bags.

So the gesture of *taking* is not as simple as "The Appropriation of Cultures" might first appear to imply. *Taking* is complicated and unpredictable. Daniel's independent wealth means he doesn't have to work, for instance, and so all of his acts in the story express his individual will. He doesn't, for instance, have to worry about getting fired for stirring up trouble in his South Carolina hometown. But the same thing could be said about pretty much all of the main characters in *The Great Gatsby* (excluding the Wilsons) or *Mrs. Dalloway* (excluding Miss Kilman). Everett's story draws our attention, finally, to the sorts of questions that we don't tend to ask of those canonical (read: white) novels, but perhaps we should.

The conventional vignette that finds an anticonventional expression takes on another form familiar to readers of Everett's work. This is the case where a character finds profound meaning in what is not there. It's worth returning to *Erasure* first. These moments of interstitial meaning serve as effective arguments against the force of convention, stereotype, or more mundanely, the usual. The questioning of what is and is not art that pervades *Erasure* appears in places other than Monk's writing of *Fuck* to protest the predictable and essentializing reception of *We's Lives in Da Ghetto*. He reflects on the status of art as he thinks: "Even as it's thrown out of the museum, what has been called art, it is still art, discarded art, shunned art, bad art, misunderstood art, oppressed art, shock art, lost art, dead art, art before its time, artless art, but art nonetheless" (227). While this example might initially appear to be the coup de grâce, it is not. That is applied next, taken from, if we might use the term, real life.

This is the episode in which Robert Rauschenberg asks Willem de Kooning to draw him a picture of whatever de Kooning chooses. The picture's content is irrelevant because it is Rauschenberg's intention to erase it. After four weeks, we're told in the novel, Rauschenberg tells de Kooning that it took him forty erasers to complete his work, but he has completely erased de Kooning's picture. "Your drawing is gone," Rauschenberg says. "What remains is my erasing and the paper which was mine to begin with" (228). What happens next illustrates why this movement into the interstices is significant, and what it enables within the world that Everett creates, and that his characters inhabit:

De Kooning: You put your name on it.

Rauschenberg: Why not? It's my work.

De Kooning: Your work? Look at what you've done to my picture.

Rauschenberg: Nice job, eh?? It was a lot of work erasing it. My wrist is still sore. I call it "Erased Drawing."

De Kooning: That's very clever.

Rauschenberg: I've already sold it for ten grand.

De Kooning: You sold my picture?

Rauschenberg: No, I erased your picture. I sold my erasing. (228)

De Kooning's observation, "That's very clever," is persuasive in itself, since Rauschenberg literally sees value (in at least two senses of that word) in what is not there and makes meaning out of this absence, an absence that he has created through much physical exertion. In a manner of speaking, he has made what is not there.[5]

The experience of actually seeing the "Erased de Kooning Drawing," as it is actually titled, illuminates (to put this one way) what Rauschenberg has seen and created. What is disarming is how alive the erased drawing is, even in its state of not representing something. As you stand in front of the picture, you become aware of the erasing marks almost etched into the paper. It becomes possible to imagine—even picture—a man exerting the physical effort necessary to erase a picture large enough to fill a frame approximately fourteen inches square. Of course, within all of this imagining is the very present experience of seeing your own reflection as you look at the picture behind its glass covering. As is usually the case in a gallery, you can become aware of the movement of other patrons around you as you observe the work in the frame. The difference with the "Erased de Kooning Drawing" is that it almost encourages this awareness of others because of the reflection in the glass. The "Erased de Kooning Drawing" conveys the sense of observing the mirror, in all of its complications, that Ishmael Kidder reflects upon in *The Water Cure*. Rauschenberg's work requires us to observe the mirror, which Kidder says we never actually look at. At this point, you become aware of the prospect that some of the other patrons may be wondering why you are standing in front of what appears to be an empty frame. You can become aware of simultaneously looking like you are the butt of a joke and like you are also very much in the know. You might even be guilty of a sense of superiority as you think about what *other* patrons of the gallery might be looking at, not having the same tutored eye that you have, the tutored eye necessary to appreciate an erased picture. I get it, you might think. They don't. As you observe "Erased de Kooning Drawing," you cannot help but think about other things. Perhaps we always do this when we look at art, but it is difficult to not be aware of it when you are looking at what appears to be—at first glance, at least—an empty frame. That moment of being aware that you are thinking about other things is made manifest by the nature of the picture's erasure. And yet, for all of its power in its absent presence, Rauschenberg's work can leave one with a mixed sensation. There is great anticipation leading up to seeing it, but this anticipation can be followed by equal anticlimax, perhaps because of the work that this work of art leaves for us to do.[6]

Jacques Derrida might have been writing about Rauschenberg's erasure of de Kooning's drawing in "Différance," when he describes the trace:

Since the trace is not a presence but the simulacrum of a presence that dislocates itself, displaces itself, refers itself, *it properly has no site—erasure belongs to its structure*. And not only the erasure which must always be able to overtake it (without which it would not be a trace but an indestructible and monumental substance), but also the erasure which constitutes it from the outset as a trace, which situates it as the change of site, and makes it disappear in its appearance, makes it emerge from itself in its production. The erasure of the early trace . . . of difference is therefore the "same" as its tracing in the text of metaphysics. This latter must have maintained the mark of what it has lost, reserved, put aside. The *paradox* of such a structure, in the language of metaphysics, is an inversion of metaphysical concepts, which produces the following effect: the present becomes the sign of the sign, the trace of the trace. It is no longer what every reference refers to in the last analysis. It becomes a function in a structure of generalized reference. It is a trace, and a trace of the erasure of the trace. (134; emphases added)

At the risk of sounding like I'm literalizing Derrida, what he says here says much about how the erased picture works as the simulacrum of a presence. It is this simulacrum that Rauschenberg and de Kooning argue over when they appear briefly in Everett's novel. The work of art that we expect to see is stood in for by this simulacrum. Instead of *art*, we get erased art, which we can add to the list provided by Monk Ellison as he thinks about the different statuses art may take while still remaining art. Because the sign *art* carries such weight, such signifying power, its simulacrum also carries power, part of which is to draw to our attention how art itself might work in ways that we had not expected. Art is still present, in other words. But in this form, it is less important as art and more important in what it makes us think about when we conventionally think about art. The trace gives another form to the potential of the anticonventional.

A less elaborate cognate example of this kind of trace occurs in *The Water Cure,* less elaborate because it does not carry the signifying weight of the work of art as its referent. It is nominally just about eating dinner. Ishmael goes to dinner with his agent, Sally. When the waiter arrives at their table, Ishmael says, "I need a big plate and a bowl" (152). The waiter replies, understandably, "We serve food here, not dinnerware" (152). Ishmael, sounding sham-compliant, looks at the menu and seizes upon the most expensive item: "I'll have the Kobe steak and the blanket-wrapped asparagus, but hold the bacon. In fact, hold the steak and asparagus, and bring me the plate. Now, for the soup. Sally, what soup shouldn't I have?" (152). Like Daniel Barkley, Ishmael Kidder can get his way, as he says at the end of this scene, in part because this possibility occurs to him— also like Rauschenberg—but also because, as he describes himself, "Luckily, I am wealthy" (25), and has "more money than I need" (153). Like Daniel, then, Ishmael is an unusual black character in part because of his financial circumstances and in part because of his occupation. But he is also unusual because of what he sees that others do not. This ability includes seeing traces of objects,

objects that others would not even be able to say are not there because they would not have noticed them in the first place.

Ishmael registers that he is unusual in his explanation for the pseudonym under which he writes the romance novels that enable him to indulge in his peculiar restaurant etiquette, which I cited in chapter 1. His status, as both Estelle Gilliam and Ishmael Kidder, suggests that he is always trace, too, as is his dinner order. But he is not willing to leave his relationship to the rules of convention without comment, and he does so bluntly: "You're just like everybody else in this country, hung up on silly rules" (153). It matters that he, again, like Daniel, and also like Monk, reflects upon what it is that he is doing that other people—not just other black people—are not doing.

By the time the elk stew that Ishmael cooked himself and brought to the restaurant has attracted enough attention that another patron in the restaurant attempts to order it, Ishmael sums up his behavior as follows: "Well, I know what I like. I'm paying thirty American dollars to rent a plate. I don't think they really mind. Besides, I'm what you call local color" (171). Immediately following this statement, that single line of text stands alone: "roloc lacol llac uoy tahw m'I" (171).[7]

As he transposes his description of himself as local color, then, he also alters the conventional relationship we have with restaurants. This time it's fair to say that nothing revolutionary comes of this alteration, but then again, sometimes that's the way life is. Sometimes the reversal or alteration of convention can be revolutionary or politically progressive, like Daniel's taking of "Dixie" and the Confederate flag. But sometimes the mere act opens possibilities of one kind or another. The premise of simple negation opens up such possibilities in *I Am Not Sidney Poitier*. Rare is the person who would have seen this title for the first time and thought that "Not Sidney" was in fact the given name of the main character. Even the seasoned Everett reader would most likely have assumed that the title was some kind of frustrated negative declaration, probably made by a black man with some other name altogether who has spent too much of his life disabusing strangers who mistake his superficial resemblance to the famous actor for his being the actor himself—an elaborate counter to the thoughtless suggestion that "they all look alike to me." The title perhaps answers any question before it is raised, making it in some sense an antititle, but a title nonetheless, thus offering a further and different suggestion of negation. Of course, the same might be said of the title of *Erasure* and, in still another way, *Assumption*.

One important characteristic that Not Sidney shares with Daniel Barkley and Ishmael Kidder is that he is wealthy. In fact, he may be the wealthiest of the group. In 1970, his mother invests "every dime she had in a little-known company called the Turner Broadcasting System," when Not Sidney is two years of age. "Every dime" was about $30,000: "It turned out to be enough to make her filthy, obscenely, uncomfortably rich. Not as *filthy* rich as she would have been had she lived a little longer" (6; emphasis in original). Because Not Sidney's mother dies when he's seven years old, "Instead, I became *filthy* and insanely rich" (6; emphasis in original). In fact, Ted Turner's entrance into the story is based on the premise that Not Sidney's mother has such a large share in TBS that Turner visits her shortly before she dies. Upon Turner's arrival, Not Sidney thinks of him as "a pale, mustachioed, talking tornado" (6).

From the beginning of the novel, it is established that *Not* is an integral part of the character's name, and so not a negation at all, as evidenced in this early conversation between Not Sidney's mother, Portia, and Ted Turner:

> "Tell me, Portia, just what kind of name is Not?" he asked.
> "It's Not Sidney," my mother corrected him. (7)

Not Sidney goes on to reflect further on what he doesn't know about his name: "One might have thought that my mother imagined that our last name, rare as it was, was enough to cause confusion with Sidney Poitier, the actor, and so I was to be *Not* Sidney Poitier. But her puzzled expression led me to believe that my name had nothing to do with the actor at all, that *Not Sidney* was simply a name she had created, with no consideration of the outside world. She liked it, and that was enough" (7). His name is an example of the difference between anticonventional and unconventional. It is unconventional since his mother appears completely unaware of the antecedent name at all when she bestows her chosen name on her son. It would be anticonventional if she had been so aware and given it to him in order to make some sort of point. But his name is also a trace, carrying with it a presence and an absence simultaneously. Even though Portia Poitier had no intention of naming (or not naming) her son after the well-known (to everyone else) actor, the actor's name nevertheless exists in the world. As Derrida says of the trace, "Erasure belongs to its structure." So the trace of *Sidney Poitier* cannot help but exist within the structure that is the name *Not Sidney Poitier*. The confusion occasioned by the name throughout the novel, in fact, is caused by the trace, not by the name as such.

Like the Confederate flag or the song "Dixie," or how one is expected to order dinner in a restaurant or draw and sell a picture, how we name our children carries with it a great deal of symbolic but also conventional freight that we think about when naming our own children but maybe don't think about when encountering others' names, unless a name is really unusual, according to our own evaluations of what an unusual name might look or sound like. Not Sidney's mother behaves toward her son's name in the same way that Ogden Walker does when he is told Detective Hailey Barry's name in *Assumption*.

> "I'm Detective Hailey Barry," the woman said. She reached up and shook Ogden's hand. "Don't even mention my name."
> "What about your name?"
> The woman cocked her head and looked at Ogden. "Halle Berry, the actress?"
> "Listen, Detective. I find pot growers and throw sticks for my dog. I don't know much about movies. I just found out about Craigslist this morning." (137)

These jokes about names reveal something else about how convention works. The jokes only exist as jokes if the hearer shares a key bit of information. Without that information—in these cases, actors' names—these are just names without jokes, nothing more, nothing less.

Ogden is not wealthy, like these other men, but he is unusual in his environment because of where he is. There is a lot more to say about Ogden, but for now it is worth noting how Hailey Barry's name resonates with Ogden no more than another actor's name seems not to resonate with Not Sidney's mother, except in what are, to her, the most important terms. This is her son's name, not a reference to someone she's never met, and his name is not to be shortened to "Not," although Turner's accent has him consistently truncating Not Sidney's name and pronouncing it "Nu'ott" throughout the novel. But by then, Not Sidney's mother has died and is not in a position to correct Turner, as she did when she was alive.

While the convention of the strength of a mother's love is to be found all over Everett's work—from Craig's mother (in her way) in *Suder* to Ralph's mother in *Glyph* to Monk's mother in *Erasure* to Medea in *For Her Dark Skin* to Ogden's mother, Rita, in *Assumption*—the importance of a child's name to its mother carries particular resonance in such literary work as Everett's. After all, names, like all words, are just metaphors and only derive any resonance from how they are used. It's difficult not to think back to how Deleuze and Guattari frame this question: "Why have we kept our own names? Out of habit, purely out of habit. To make ourselves unrecognizable in turn. To render imperceptible, not ourselves, but what makes us act, feel, and think. Also because it's nice to talk like everybody else, to say the sun rises, when everybody knows it's only a manner of speaking." They keep their names, even though the names, according to this formulation, mean nothing. Except, as they make clear, names mean a great deal. Not only is it nice to talk like everybody else; it is a necessary evil if we are to be understood at all. The jokes about names stand right on the brink of not being understood because of the difference between the associations some people have with these names as opposed to the associations others have.

How jokes rely on convention is another subtext to *I Am Not Sidney Poitier*, since the text is littered with references to the actor Poitier's films. When Not Sidney is asked by a character named Percival Everett to deliver the line "They call me Mr. Tibbs," for instance, it is safe to assume that a given reader has probably heard of that quite famous Poitier line, even if they do not know that it comes from *In the Heat of the Night*. The same may be said about the elaborate allusions to *Lilies of the Field*. But a reference to Roscoe Lee Browne will take a minute for some and send other readers scurrying to IMDb.com or Google before recognizing a photo of Browne. By then, the joke has run its course, or at least lost its steam.

The way convention expresses itself and makes itself available for critique and rethinking in *I Am Not Sidney Poitier* is, as with most of Everett's fiction, almost without limit. Not Sidney's trip to Washington, DC, to visit the family of his girlfriend, Maggie, for instance, blends a convention that Everett highlights with another more explicitly political one. The one highlighted is the appearance of upwardly mobile or simply wealthy African Americans. Whereas Not Sidney's wealth, like Daniel's and Ishmael's, contributes to his mobility of body and of mind, the wealth of Maggie's family creates something approaching a prison for them. Their house is a large "midsixties split-level with a three-car garage" (126). The attention to detail, in the house and in the description of the house, both convey something uncomfortable and slightly unsettled, if not unsettling: "We stepped into an anteroom, what might have been called a mudroom in a farmhouse. It was a room that might have been bright and cheery if not for the heavy red drapes covering the windows on either side of the door. From that room I could see into the kitchen and beyond that into what I would learn later was the breakfast room. The walls were painted red, the tiled floor of the kitchen was red and white, the refrigerator and stove were red" (126). The wealth on display in Maggie's family home—not to mention the existence of the family's housekeeper—about whom Not Sidney thinks, "The word servant seemed more correct but less appropriate" (127)—might put one in mind of the Daltons' house in *Fuck,* the novel within the novel in *Erasure.* But that similarity seems less important than the explicit fashioning of the family home in a way that would put most visitors—not to mention most readers—in some dis-ease. Maggie's drawing attention to the room's decor—"My mother loves red" (126)—has the kind of inadequate, drawing-our-attention-to-something-significant quality that encourages some reflection on what else might be going on in a given situation. Red also carries the association of political color with the Republican Party and American conservatism, which only seems right considering who we discover Maggie's family to be.[8]

Maggie's father refers to Not Sidney's name as "some kind of ghetto nonsense, no doubt" (131) in an attempt to make sense of—and demean as a bonus—Not Sidney's name in a way that allows the name to fit a category that the father thinks is familiar to him. In addition, the name's "Who's on first?" potential is played out (as it almost necessarily is several times in the novel) when Not Sidney is introduced to Robert, one of Maggie's friends.

> "Then what is your name?" he asked.
>
> "My name is Not Sidney," I said.
>
> "Not is a part of Not Sidney's name," Maggie said.
>
> "Knot, with a k?" he asked.
>
> "Not with a k," I said.
>
> "That's what I said," he said.
>
> "N-O-T," Maggie said.

"Sidney?"

"Not my name is not Sidney. My name is Not Sidney. Call me Not Sidney."
(139–40)

The whimsy of this scene is tempered in a couple of ways. "Call me Not Sidney" should put us in mind of *Call me Ishmael*, as deployed by both Everett and by Melville. As both *Moby-Dick* and *The Water Cure* represent quests that cannot be fully satisfied, perhaps *I Am Not Sidney Poitier* does so as well, if in a minor key. Also, the space in between categories can cause genuine hostility for those who find themselves floundering within it. They don't like it. As a result of this exchange, Not Sidney finds himself thinking, "Though he was the one being dense, I was the one in the middle, feeling stupid, trying to explain the unexplainable. And for no good reason" (140). Not Sidney recognizes himself as in the middle, if not the infinite middle so central to Everett's fiction. His name is unusual, to be sure. But it is not unexplainable. The unexplainability of his name to Robert registers nothing more than Robert's having failed a simple test of his imagination.

Not Sidney articulates his role in this joke in a way that helps identify what is actually going on here. In effect, it's a joke that is being played on Not Sidney in one sense and on the members of this exclusive and excluding club of young people in another. As Maggie's friends continue interacting among themselves as if Not Sidney is no longer in the room, he has a clear thought about what is going on: "Instead, I was kindly excluded and I felt somewhat happy about that. I had a sneaking realization, however incapable I was at articulating it, that my presence was essential to them, not in some singular, specific way, but in a broad and pervasive and insidious way that none of them would or could understand or acknowledge" (141). He articulates this observation just fine, because he's not doing it for the other people in the room. He's making sense of the situation entirely for his own comprehension. In another of these self-reflective moments, Not Sidney articulates his point of view for us to hear or see. There are possibilities available here to see things in at least slightly new ways. But these possibilities are lost on the people in this room.

When Not Sidney seizes upon the idea that Maggie's family exhibit a "classic case of self-loathing" (133), he is noticing something important, not about the essentials of being black but about how this group of black people are trying to be black not only in a less recognizable way (which is not necessarily a bad thing) but, because they are so conventional and stereotypical of another ethnocultural and class-identifiable group (i.e., rich white people) in how they go about expressing whatever sense of identity they have arrived at. They have merely reproduced many of the strictures, categories, and limitations that, under other circumstances, would have oppressed them, and have then used these familiar criteria to oppress others when they can. They have missed too many points for Not Sidney to try to convey any of this to them now, even if he were inclined to try.

Consider where the prospects of the character who situates himself (in almost all of Everett's novels, anyway) in between established or familiar categories might lead us. Many of Everett's characters may be called schizophrenic, not in the familiar but inadequate sense of the "split personality" way that is still occasionally encouraged in television programs and movies, nor, for that matter, in the properly clinical sense that is diagnosed by medical professionals, but in the version offered by Deleuze and Guattari.[9] According to Eugene Holland, Deleuze and Guattari's schizophrenic is "a spontaneous or unpredictable form of desire freed from social coding" (66). The notion of the spontaneous and the unpredictable both signal someone not just unusual but also an unusual nature that is potentially constructive, perhaps even revolutionary. This idea of freedom from social coding implies a freedom *to* in addition to whatever freedom *from* might be at stake. Sometimes the latter potential can facilitate the former.

While the schizophrenic—for Deleuze and Guattari—embodies a desire freed from social coding, that in and of itself is not an adequate positioning if the objective is some sort of social and/or political progress. The social coding—the Oedipus in whatever form it might take—is much too powerful to be counteracted via mere embodiment. There must be something much more thoroughgoing in play to confront the Oedipus on anything approaching its own terms. The Oedipus is not just the complex, but anything dominating and, as a result, disfiguring of our abilities to desire, to resist, to imagine. As they write, "Oedipus is one of those things that becomes all the more dangerous the less people believe in it; then the cops are there to replace the high priests. The first profound example of an analysis of double bind, in this sense, can be found in Marx's *On the Jewish Question:* between the family and the State—the Oedipus of family authority and the Oedipus of State authority" (*Anti-Oedipus* 81). The image of coercion inherent in the structure most dangerous when people be-lieve in it less is a haunting one, as it points to those moments when interests are imposed on the population. Such prospects only add to how complex the task of the schizoid is. So for Deleuze and Guattari the monumental task at hand is to do justice to the notion of the schizorevolutionary, who, as discussed in chapter 1, enacts the freedom from social coding and releases revolutionary potential, since social coding can be enforced by the police as well as the clergy, if necessary. The theorists also bring home the problem of the double bind in their characterization of American literature, a description that cannot help but put one in mind of American culture more broadly: "Isn't the destiny of American literature that of crossing limits and frontiers, causing deterritorial-ized flows of desire to circulate, but also always making these flows transport fascisizing, moralizing, Puritan, and familialist territorialities?" (*Anti-Oedipus* 277–78). The setting of these contradictory flows, both obviously at work in American culture as apparently equal and opposite investments, declares the folly of taking inflexible, certain, absolute positions within such a fluid, com-plex, and eminently changeable social and political framework. That Deleuze and Guattari focus on these flows within American literature highlights the po-tential for literature as this schizophrenizing force, if we receive some training in thinking along these lines.[10]

But the formulation of the schizorevolutionary is not a simple opposition of the paranoiac-bad/schizorevolutionary-good variety. While Deleuze and Guat-tari certainly explicate the paranoiac as imprisoned and therefore hegemonic, they do not guarantee, by any means, that the schizorevolutionary positioning is unproblematically beneficial or liberatory, which is why it is crucial here to talk in terms of potential. In fact, in *Difference and Repetition,* Deleuze later, writing on his own, usefully articulates the imbrications implied within the schizo-revolutionary: "A problem does not exist, apart from its solutions. Far from disappearing in this overlay, however, it insists and persists in these solutions. A problem is determined at the same time as it is solved, but its determination is not the same as its solution: the two elements differ in kind, the determination amounting to the genesis of the concomitant solution" (163). This imbrication of solution within problem that Deleuze highlights is probably more visible to the schizorevolutionary if for no other reason than the schizorevolutionary, as opposed to the paranoiac, is freed from social coding in a way that enables the perception of possibilities that entrapment within or by the Oedipus forecloses upon or proscribes.

Many of Everett's protagonists are schizorevolutionary in the ways that Deleuze and Guattari theorize. After all, the many gestures of self-description, self-awareness, and self-critique found among these characters demonstrate their attempts to free themselves from the various investments of the more segregative (as opposed to nomadic)[11] motivations and desires these characters encounter in the world of others' making. Not only do they carve out and live in the infinite spaces in between conventional categories; they also oppose these categories in ways that reveal previously unforeseen revolutionary prospects. It is possible to see this kind of potential in many of the protagonists I have discussed up until now, but perhaps no protagonist in Everett's body of fiction exemplifies this figure of the schizorevolutionary as profoundly, or as chillingly, as does Ogden Walker, the small-town sheriff's deputy at the middle of *Assumption*.

Obviously, a title like *Assumption* from a writer like Everett (to the extent that there are a lot of writers like Everett) is one of those moments when even casual readers cannot help but wonder if they are in on the joke or being set up to be the butt of one. The title appears at first too suggestive, too on the nose, but this is especially the case if one is familiar with the body of this writer's work. And, of course, when we come to realize that Ogden Walker, almost cliché in his mild-mannered demeanor, has actually been doing at least some of the killing that has engulfed small-town New Mexico, the sense of having been the butt of the joke is overwhelming. But Ogden's presence in *Assumption* and the concluding revelation about him make a significant point about the schizorevolutionary about which it is crucial not to lose sight. In encountering Ogden Walker, it's worth retrieving once again the statement made by Bud Powell to a young Craig Suder toward the end of that novel. Powell says, simply, "That's called a chance," after the dog is shot by the neighbor who had earlier threatened to shoot it. And so it is. A chance to be freed of the social coding that determines so much of our lives cannot help but bring with it a chance of an outcome that we might find undesirable. This is why I assert that Deleuze and Guattari do not pose the schizorevolutionary as a simple good in opposition to the simple evil of the paranoiac. Hoping for some sort of guarantee is conventional and understandable, within conventional boundaries. But as

Gulliver learns when told about the Struldbruggs in book 3 of *Gulliver's Travels*,[12] it is the height of arrogance and folly to assume that being able to live forever presupposes eternal youth. Likewise, it is also the height of arrogance and folly to assume that the potential of the schizorevolutionary will only express itself in ways that we would wish, like, or prefer.

In stark contrast to, say, *The Water Cure* or *Glyph*, *Assumption* looks quite conventional in its narrative presentation. *Wounded* comes to mind as another conventional-looking Everett novel that culminates in a way that is, at the very least, morally unsettling. The same may be said of *Cutting Lisa*, obviously. *Assumption* even relies upon a third-person narrator, thus keeping at bay the hard-wired associations of tendentiousness with which it is easy to associate first-person narration.[13] Ogden Walker moves through the narrative investigating crimes, interacting with secondary characters like his mother and a woman in whom he has a burgeoning romantic interest until she conspires to try to kill him, and expressing his own misgivings about what might be called his subjectivity. He is described by the narrator, for instance, as he confronts an old woman, Mrs. Bickers, who has fired two shots from her "long-barrel .22 target pistol" (7) through the same hole in her front door, after having been startled by a noise. As Ogden attempts to defuse the tension between himself and the aptly named Mrs. Bickers, he is described this way: "He always sensed that the old woman didn't like him because he was black, but that was probably true for half of the white residents of the county" (6). Ogden's fish-out-of-water self-consciousness and his self-awareness of the vulnerability that accompanies it invite anyone reading *Assumption* to trust him somewhat reflexively, without really thinking about this effect or how it might encourage a reader to let down whatever guard that reader might otherwise have in place when confronting a new narrator for the first time. This letting down of a guard enables *Assumption* to perform a feat that resembles something close to a magic trick by its end.

The truly anticonventional nature of *Assumption* only draws attention to itself when it is read a second time, at which point we realize that it has been signaling its true nature at every turn. The number of people we see Ogden alone with and who then turn up dead really begins to pile up. We don't necessarily notice this coincidence as anything other than coincidence because of our conventional associations with police officers, sworn as they are to protect and serve. Even in a time when the commitment of some police officers appears conditionally applied depending on the citizen in question (To protect what? To serve whom?), it is difficult to completely divest oneself of that association enough to suspect Ogden early on in a first reading of the novel. But as Deleuze and Guattari point out in their acknowledgment of continuing to use their own names, we do any number of things out of habit. Believing that a police officer must be trustworthy appears to be one of those habits. Our inclination to give the benefit of the doubt to a third-person narrator appears possibly to be another.

So once Warren Fragua, Ogden's police partner and occasional fishing buddy, finally puts all the pieces together for us, it is difficult not to feel yet again that we have fallen into a trap we really should have seen there under that thin covering of leaves and brush, of police uniform and narrative point of view. Warren says: "I think you killed this man right here. Somehow Terry Lowell found you with the body and you shot him, too." Ogden replies, "That's pretty much it" (224). Warren's revelation makes it difficult not to think back to Mrs. Bickers, to whose house we are told by the narrator Ogden is called at the beginning of *Assumption,* and whom, as we are told subsequently, Ogden is the last person to see alive. About now we have to consider that not only has Ogden fooled us but that the third-person narrator has been his accomplice all along, dispensing information that furthers Ogden's dissimulation and not our accumulation of evidence, as we have come to expect the narrator to do for us. After this exchange between Warren and Ogden, the urge is inescapable to cast one's mind back to the various drug dealers and prostitutes whom Ogden was arresting and protecting, respectively, several of whom also turn up dead. On a first reading, it's easy to ascribe the unfortunate ends of these many characters to the risky lives they lead and not to their bad luck of having come into contact with the wrong sheriff's deputy. We also cannot help but think back to what at the time sounded like a joke, as Ogden, the ostensible and conventional good guy, is explaining to a member of the underworld of the novel the string of deaths he is nominally investigating. An unnamed bartender, noticing how many of these dead people have crossed Ogden's path says, in passing, "It don't pay to know you, does it?" (149). And later, but before Warren's discovery about his friend, when Ogden provides another update to someone, it is Ogden who says, "I'm trying to find Carla Reynolds before Hicks does. Maybe not everybody has to die" (161). We finally realize that he has been making on his own at least some of the decisions about who has to die all along and that we are drawing exactly the opposite conclusions about whom Carla Reynolds's safety actually depends upon.

Perhaps most of all, we might cast our minds all the way back to what at first seemed like one of the few interior monologues that *Assumption* allows itself. The narrator tells us, as Ogden thinks to himself while alone, as he pursues yet another lead in this unusual string of murders in and around Plata, New Mexico: "Ogden could feel his heart racing and he wondered why and realized the answer to that was obvious. Nothing makes people more interesting than their being dead. Sad, but true. He really didn't want to see dead people. It made him feel queasy to see dead people, but damn if it wasn't interesting. The sky was so blue that it was almost ironic" (43). On first reading, this observation about how interesting people are when they're dead sounds like just an observation made by a cop in over his head and unused to dealing with so many murders. On subsequent reading, though, it sounds like the partial confession of a conflicted but compulsive psychopath who "didn't want to see dead people" but seems not to be able to control himself. Same words. Same character. Completely different reading. But a trace of the initial reading persists, and it is the challenge of reconciling the opposing readings that makes the ending of *Assumption* so unsettling, and weirdly invigorating. The trace of the virtuous cop doing his job does not recede into our memories any easier than does the name of a famous actor even as someone else's name negates it. We still see a trace of the Ogden we first met in the version who confesses to the murders. Our well-trained reading habits and familiarity with certain types of story (here, the crime drama) have a lot to do with our *not* having heard this unnerving resonance the first time. But why would we? After all, Ogden is one of the good guys.

During the novel's finale, to which I'll return in chapter 4, in response to Warren's complaint that Ogden's actions don't make any sense to him, Ogden concurs: "I wanted some drug money. I'm hooked on meth. Do any of those reasons help this make sense? I was tired of being a good guy. Was I ever a good guy? How about that? Does that have it make sense for you? How about that? Does that have it make sense for you?" (225). Ogden seizes upon Warren's need for an explanation, for the certainties of causality, and for the synchrony of convention and explanation. He does all of this while his own story stands in direct contravention to any of it. Ogden is a homicidal Bartleby, whose meaning is left for others to judge, and is all the more unsettling for it. But more than Bartleby, because of the murders, there is an additional urgency to make some meaning of Ogden's actions. Of course, what matters most to Ogden is to draw attention to his refusal to provide the answers and to the convention that is the desire for them. Instead of providing answers, he toys with Warren's (and our) desire for them, piling question upon question, casually dismissing each as he goes along.

Ogden wonders about his own sanity, as Ishmael does about his. These considerations appear to bother Ishmael more than they bother Ogden—perhaps a function of the different narrative points of view in the two texts—but both commit acts that conventionally good people try to avoid. As Mark Seem writes in his introduction to *Anti-Oedipus*, "A schizoanalysis schizophrenizes in order to break the holds of power and institute research into a new collective subjectivity and a revolutionary healing of mankind. For we are sick, so sick, of our *selves!*" (xxi; emphasis in original). Both characters are haunted by their attempts to break the holds of power, the conventions that have run their lives, which are not unlike the conventions that run all of our lives, to a greater or lesser extent. An escape from the holds of power of which we are all sick, to return to Seem, can appear frightening at the point when what looks most conventional—belief in good and evil—begins to look like nothing more than an opening bid or a closing argument. But in order to draw our attention to the tyranny of everyday convention, Everett's characters traverse a path far away from where most of us stand at any moment. Convention need not be everything, just as it cannot be nothing. Perhaps this proffered resolution explains the recurrence of Zeno's paradoxes in Everett's work—the "ubiquitous musings" that Ishmael characterizes as "dismissible yet true, superficially simple but persistently gnawing and troubling, a thorn in the side of any traveler" (25). The way in which Zeno is both right and wrong enlivens a movement through the world that requires our constant and conscious attention to sometimes the smallest details.

Habits will always persist, after all. We need them. The challenge laid down by Everett's work is discerning which habits continue to do us any good and which do not. This is a perpetual discernment that is the constant responsibility of citizenship as well as critical reading practices. Otherwise, before we know it, we will find ourselves caught in some trap that we probably should have seen, if only we'd been paying attention.

II

RELIGION, ART, AND RACE IN EVERETT

3

PLATEAUS OF INTENSITY IN A WORLD BETWEEN CATEGORIES

Democracy is such a sightless word, a condition rather than a practice, easily spoken of by its participants and drooled over by its estranged.

—*Frenzy*

The final irony is, beautifully, that they think they perceive the irony.

—*Percival Everett by Virgil Russell*

So far my argument has been that Everett's fiction carves out an infinite space in between categories and then shows what appears to be the potentially revolutionary nature of that infinite space. Of course, as *Assumption* makes clear, that potential revolution—like all revolutions—can be one that we are inclined to approve of in theory, or just as likely, one of which we might be expected to disapprove in practice. The infinity of revolutionary space necessitates an infinity of potential outcomes, a prospect it is sometimes preferable to overlook but toward which Everett's fiction invariably draws our attention. Now that we've examined more and less explicit areas of this argument as they help illuminate Everett's work, this chapter and the next will take a more thematic approach by concentrating on a couple of recurring subjects in Everett's fiction, in the hope of demonstrating how these subjects further nuance and complicate the notion of the infinite space between categories. This chapter will examine the treatment of one subject that is relentlessly mocked in Everett's fiction and one that is just as relentlessly defended—the former being religion, the latter art. Chapter 4 will explore how race is and is not approached in Everett's work and—considering his work's instruction on how to see the world in between conventional categories—whether or not, and why, we should even discuss race in Everett's work at all.

Religion and art are two sites for the sorts of disinvestments, counterinvestments, and overinvestments that Deleuze and Guattari identify as fascisizing in their tendencies, and both are particularly illuminating to examine in the context of Everett's fiction. What Deleuze and Guattari have to say about religion in *Anti-Oedipus* helps focus the discussion on art as well and enables a further kaleidoscopic effect as the two interweave toward the end of this chapter:

> And if one were to ask when it all started to go bad, how far back must we go for an answer, back to Lenin, back to Marx? So true is it that the various investments, even when opposed, can coexist with one another in complexes that are not the province of Oedipus, but that do concern the sociohistorical field, its preconscious and unconscious conflicts and contradictions, about which it can only be said that they fall back on Oedipus, Marx the father, Lenin the father, Brezhnev the father. Fewer and fewer people believe in all this, but it makes no difference, since capitalism is like the Christian religion, it lives precisely from a lack of belief, it does not need it—a motley painting of all that has been believed. (375)

This observation about how the belief of fewer and fewer people makes no difference to the power of capitalism or religion is reminiscent of what the two theorists say earlier in *Anti-Oedipus* about Oedipus being one of those things that becomes all the more dangerous the less people believe in it, because this diminished belief serves as the entry point for the police or some other form of explicit repression. So religion, like capitalism, does not rely upon belief as such but upon habitual investments that stand in for belief, thriving under a lack of belief, in fact, as the theorists say. Actual belief might not be as problematic, is the suggestion here, because perhaps at least actual belief would presuppose some sort of conscious engagement. (That said, it is difficult to imagine Deleuze and Guattari making an argument in favor of "actual belief," whatever we might imagine that to be.) The "motley painting of all that has been believed" is a particularly fraught and apt way of expressing the distinction to be drawn here between actual belief (in the provisional way I have already qualified this term) and what can often pass for belief.

Of course, *Anti-Oedipus* provides a necessarily provisional engagement with the motley painting of belief in the form of the schizo, here sometimes schizophrenic and sometimes schizorevolutionary:

> For what is the schizo, if not first of all the one who can no longer bear "all that": money, the stock market, the death forces, Nijinsky said—values, morals, homelands, religions, and private certitudes? There is a whole world of difference between the schizo and the revolutionary: the difference between the one who escapes, and the one who knows how to make what he is escaping escape, collapsing a filthy drainage pipe, causing a deluge to break loose, liberating a flow, resecting a schiz. The schizo is not revolutionary, but the schizophrenic process—in terms of which the schizo is merely the interruption, or the continuation in the void—is the potential for revolution. To those who say that escaping is not courageous, we answer: what is not escape and social investment at the same time? The choice is between one of two poles, the paranoiac counterescape that motivates all the conformist, reactionary, and fascisizing investments, and the schizophrenic escape convertible into a revolutionary investment. (341)

The clarification here is worth dwelling on for a moment. The schizophrenic process, as defined in *Anti-Oedipus,* is not necessarily revolutionary in and of itself. To suggest such a thing would be to accede to the kind of habitual association that is under such relentless attack in a Deleuze and Guattari critique. Such an association is never an option. But they make clear that while the schizophrenic escape may be convertible into revolutionary investment, this revolutionary investment cannot arise from within the paranoiac (the schizophrenic's opposite), because the structures that the paranoiac inhabits and by which the paranoiac is imprisoned are intended in their inception to short-circuit any revolutionary potential. With all of this said, it is no small wonder that the schizorevolutionaries who so often reside within Everett's fictional landscape do not find any comfort in the world of religion. From there, it is not surprising that the world created by an author so preoccupied by the spaces in between categories holds up to frequent ridicule the world of religion.

A relatively benign characterization of how religion often appears in Everett's work arises, not surprisingly, from within Everett's work. Monk, as he narrates

Erasure, makes this observation about himself, pertaining to religion: "When younger, I despised religion. Later, I didn't care, viewing the trappings with vague amusement and almost always finding the practitioners somewhat dull of spirit and thought" (50). Primarily, religion appears in two expressions in Everett's work. It's either an outrageous prayer of some sort or a specific verse from scripture. The juxtaposition of these two kinds of text aids in making sense of how religion's depiction in this fictional world may be reconciled with the rest of the provisionality that is otherwise so critical to what transpires in so much of Everett's fiction.

The prayers are the kinds of irreverent expression that one gets accustomed to when moving around within the fictional world Everett creates, especially when religion is involved.[1] In *Suder,* Dr. McCoy, the dentist and spiritual guru whom Kathy Suder embraces for a short period of time, comes to the Suder house for dinner and says grace before the meal. Disdain for the man and his religious exploitation of Kathy is expressed by the continuation of an ongoing conversation between Bud Powell and Craig's father as the dentist says grace:

> We sat at the table and McCoy closed his eyes and put his hands together.
> "Heavenly Father, we thank you for this mea . . ."
> "Just fine," said Mr. Powell, glancing at McCoy. "It was real hot there. People don't come out when it's hot."
> "And bless these peas and sweet potatoes . . ."
> "Atlanta's going to be even hotter," Daddy said.
> "Lord, help us through these trying . . ."
> "Yeah, well, at least people down this way are used to the heat."
> "And Lord God, bless these good colored folks who I'm eating with."
> Daddy shook his head and smiled and Mr. Powell laughed out loud.
> "Amen." McCoy opened his eyes and looked sternly at Daddy and Mr. Powell.
> "If you folks believed more strongly in God, maybe you wouldn't be colored."
> (53–54)

McCoy's exposure of his extreme racial feelings is striking in its juxtaposition to his ostensible devoutness, and yet it is not actually surprising in the least. He is, in fact, another type of category, the cliché sophist of the "hate the sinner, but not the sin" variety. When Craig's father asks him "why a peckerwood like you comes to a Negro house for dinner" (54), he registers not shock or even surprise but just the sort of annoyance borne of familiarity with and recognition of a type. McCoy's response is no less surprising, except for the spectacle of his having actually said it out loud: "Well, Dr. Suder, I just wanted to see what colored folks was like. So, I could pray for you, like real people" (54). To this, Craig's father replies, again, understandably, "McCoy, you half-baked, Bible-headed redneck, just get out of my house" (54). The scene's effect relies, of course, on its religious overlay and the ways in which Dr. McCoy's investments in his faith and his equivalent investment in his racism coexist unproblematically for him, perhaps because he has spent so little time consciously considering either. Leaving aside how many horrors have been underwritten in human history by religious belief, this juxtaposition of faith and racism here is not, in and of itself, even remarkable. The prayer and the stated purpose of the prayer are what matter. Were McCoy just Kathy Suder's dentist, without any declared religious faith, his performance in this scene would carry a completely different, and it's fair to say lessened, significance.

Watershed presents another grace to similar religion-satirizing effect, although without the racist undertone. Here the somewhat pedestrian concern is household propriety, especially when visiting one's parental home. Whereas Dr. McCoy is eventually revealed to be hateful, James Reskin, the author of this grace in *Watershed,* is more embarrassing in a recognizably familial way, even if with the kind of edge that Everett's fiction often displays. Reskin, the father of the house, has shot a turkey and now says grace before the family eats it. But having shot the bird is not his only trauma, as his grace also reveals some unresolved feelings about the decision of his daughter, Karen, to have sex with Robert Hawks, the novel's main protagonist and her boyfriend for a time, in her parents' home. Reskin works out both anxieties as he says grace:

"Dear Lord," he said, his voice a bit deeper. "First of all, let me ask you a question: Why such a big bird? This is a large tom and I'm not sure I'm worthy of him. But I thank you. We thank you. And thank you for allowing us once again to sit at this table as a family. Please watch over us, protect us, though we may screw our brains out in the room next to our parents." Karen sighed loudly, but Reskin didn't miss a beat. "And watch over our guest. He is a good man. One might hope better for him than my daughter, but you do work in mysterious ways."

"James," Edith complained.

"So, Lord, let us finally say thank you for the lovely meal before us and our health and this fine home, the walls of which continue to reverberate with moans and gasps."

"James!"

"In Jesus' name, amen." (114)

In addition to the role of religion as both source of humor and the butt of the joke, Reskin's grace also lifts the covers of the potential Electra component of the Oedipus that Deleuze and Guattari anatomize. One wonders if Reskin's grace might have sounded the same if it had been his son with a woman in the next room the evening before, not to mention how Edith, Reskin's wife, might have reacted under those circumstances. In either case, the attitude conveyed toward religion in *Suder* and *Watershed* is derisive, or at least dismissive, as evidenced by the amount of interruption to which each grace is subjected. The novels' attitudes do not venture into much that might resemble sympathy to believers, for instance, but relentlessly mock the notion of belief, whether expressed with benevolent or ill intention. As Dionysos says to Vlepo, his sprite, in *Frenzy*, "'This sadness that you see,' he said, 'is for no one but me. Creatures of such power can have no concern but for the self. Godding is tough work, my Vlepo'" (19). And, no doubt, it is. And the godding that the gods do does not translate into the worshipping done by mere mortals. Perhaps mere mortals are not up to the challenge of worship in all of its complexities. Perhaps the act of worship is so constrained by its investments that it cannot be anything but tendentious and, as a result, fraudulent and laughable. It is, however, suspect when shown in the form of prayer. And yet, even though there is a pretty consistent tone toward religion in much of the kaleidoscope that is Everett's fictional world, there is nevertheless sometimes a level of seriousness accorded to religion as well. At the very least, there are times when religion is nevertheless represented in ways that suggest gravity and value, even if practitioners are not necessarily up to the challenge.

One consistent expression of this latent seriousness about religion in Everett's work is the recurrence of one verse of scripture in several of his novels. What can be made of this verse and its appearances in his fiction is quite generative in terms of where the notion of religion in particular, and structures into which we are tempted to invest thoughtlessly in general might take a reading of Everett's work, and where that reading might take us in broader terms. References to Isaiah 38:1 appear at least three times in Everett's novels—"Set thine house in order: for thou shalt die, and not live." It stands as one of the epigraphs to *Cutting Lisa* and is referred to in *Watershed* and in *American Desert*. Each of these allusions holds the sort of multilayered and in-between resonances characteristic of Everett's work, even in relation to a subject usually held up to ridicule.

The recurrence of this verse in these three novels is useful in illuminating a point about how the same attitude toward religion is expressed differently in Everett's work. The overlap of both parts of this discussion involving *Watershed* only adds to the complexity of the stance relating to religion apparent in the novels overall. *Cutting Lisa* presents a very serious position on questions of family, fidelity, truth, and patriarchy. It might even be said that John Livesey's *final vocabulary*—to use another formulation from Richard Rorty[2]—is largely made up of these four fraught words. But in setting his house in order, Livesey tramples on the rights of everyone else in his family. This trampling is facilitated by his certainty, his investments in his beliefs, rather than any sense of a continuum on which they might be located, a continuum that might accommodate the beliefs of others. It is easy to imagine that he destroys his family in order to preserve some abstract notion of *Family*, whose existence supersedes the personal interests of anyone else to whom he might be biologically related. This kind of fidelity to an abstract convention—especially one as pervasive as family—can look extremist under the wrong (or right) light.

I will concede the point that perhaps epigraphs are only read by critics who study a given text. With that concession, it is reasonable to argue that this reading may overstate the importance of this verse's appearance at the beginning of a novel that begins with a man with no medical training delivering his wife's baby by caesarean section and ends with the suggestion that a retired obstetrician is about to abort the fetus of his grandchild on his daughter-in-law and son's kitchen table. But at the same time that I make this concession, the novel does force upon us the challenge of making sense of these two men's decisions, both expressions of a man setting—as he sees it—his house in order. After all, the scripture is there to be interpreted, as is the novel. This opening up of prospects and the requirement that the reader contend with the implications of competing readings makes the instance of the biblical verse here very serious, as a provocation for thought—which may be the highest calling of scripture, instead of the more secular purposes to which it can sometimes be put. All this from an epigraph.

A return to *Watershed* brings with it a more extended and fraught application of this verse. Sometime after Robert Hawks has broken up with Karen Reskin (the other half of the couple who *screw their brains out* in the bedroom next to her parents' room, the subject of much of her father's grace), her father shows up unannounced at Robert Hawks's apartment in Denver, having somehow made his way there from Santa Fe. There is understandable tension between the two men, since Robert has only recently ended his relationship with the other man's daughter, but as Reskin reiterates his low opinion of his daughter, initially expressed as part of the grace, the nature of the tension changes from Robert's uncertainty about why the man is in his home to the inappropriate feelings expressed by the man about his daughter. While it is true that our expectation that Reskin would love his daughter is itself an expectation steeped in the conventions governing how we think of family relationships, it's fair to recognize that we all (whether wittingly or not) draw our lines somewhere regarding which conventions we accept.

The tension of Reskin's arrival is punctuated by his resorting to the verse:

> "You know that I am an unhappy man." There was no need for his waiting for a signal of agreement from me. "Isaiah 38:1 says, 'Set thine house in order: for thou shalt die, and not live.' Well, Robert, you've seen my house."
>
> I nodded.
>
> "'Thou shalt die and not live.' How about that? What do you think?" He leaned forward and started to push around the photographs on the coffee table. (141)

One could not be blamed for imagining another tableau not unlike that between Ishmael Kidder and the unnamed man he tortures in his basement. The kaleidoscopic interrelations between Everett's novels encourage at least some reflection on the theme of water central to both novels, a theme that recurs in his 2015 collection of short fiction, *Half an Inch of Water.* Depending on how much tolerance we have for this free-associative moment, we might also include

Swimming Swimmers Swimming (2011) and perhaps even *Grand Canyon, Inc.* (2001) and *Trout's Lie* (2015). Again, there is no such thing as digression.

Reskin's ruminations on death in the biblical verse, and the tension in the scene, both begin to make sense when Hawks notices that "Reskin was holding a pistol. He held it in his lap, rubbing his hands over it as if it were a smooth ball" (142). As their conversation continues, Reskin comments that the .32-caliber pistol he is holding is "not a big gun," and when he asks Hawks if he thinks it will nevertheless "do the job," Hawks cannot help but answer, "What job would that be?" (142). Reskin answers with another question: "If I put the barrel in my mouth and pull the trigger, will this pistol kill me for sure?" (142). Hawks squeezes off a good line here: "You're the doctor" (142).

Reskin is a physician, and he takes up Hawks's remark with another reference to scripture: "Yeah, I'm the doctor. 'Physician, heal thyself.' Is that how the saying goes?" (142). Reskin is nominally a religious man, but here doesn't appear to recognize Luke 4:23 as anything other than a cliché, which it also is. As their conversation continues, Reskin registers that he is deriving no solace from his faith, such as it is: "Yea, though I walk through the valley of death, I shall fear no evil. His staff, blah, blah, blah" (143). Reskin appeals here to Psalms 23:4, another ecclesiastical cliché that is, nevertheless, a Christian staple in times of crisis and/or death. And yet he truncates it—it's "though I walk through the valley *of the shadow* of death"—and then loses interest in the verse altogether. As he eventually allows Hawks to take the gun from him and unload it, it becomes clear that Reskin doesn't really care about shooting himself, but this moment of relief is short lived, once Hawks realizes that Reskin has already taken an overdose of pills as well. That Reskin is gotten to the hospital, has his stomach pumped, and survives is all entirely beside the point of the sequence. Reskin's religious faith is powerless in the face of his earnest desperation, but the demonstration of this religious powerlessness is itself moving as an example of something human that takes place between two men who do not know each other very well at all. The religious accompaniment expresses itself more as a futility beside the beauty of the actual (secular more than holy) communion between the two men, even as each refuses the communion in his own way. The religious scriptures are integral to the scene in order to display how unnecessary they are to the most important aspect of the exchange between the two men.

The significance of Isaiah 38:1 here is obvious enough, I would think, as

RELIGION, ART, AND RACE IN EVERETT

to need little additional comment as such. The combining of the notions of answering for one's own choices, actions, preferences, priorities, beliefs, in the face of the relentless pressure of our mortality and the judgment of God requires a humility that rarely appears to accompany religious faith among the believers in Everett's work. There is an irony in the coincidence of such sage counsel emerging from a text whose lessons appear so frequently to be applied tendentiously instead of with generosity. The verse's wisdom could undermine the kind of certainty that can—in its worst expressions—masquerade as faith. After all, the suggestion is, I must be right (and others must be wrong) if I'm following God's word, because God is right. The willingness to look into the possibilities of one's own uncertainty is obviated by religious faith in this application. It needn't be, of course, but it can be. The results of refusing the constructive, perhaps even revolutionary, potentialities of facing up to one's uncertainties open up possibilities for genuine horror.

The scriptural and the irreverent come together in the eulogy delivered by the Reverend Larville Staige at Theodore Street's funeral in *American Desert*. Perhaps the early stage of the clergyman's development has something to do with the nature of his eulogy, tempting one to wonder what the pupal (pupil?) stage of his eulogy might have sounded like. As he attempts to cool himself with "a fan bearing the image of Martin Luther King, Jr. on one side and advertising a funeral home on the other" (8–9), Rev. Staige says the following:

"But we must send our brother off to his final resting place with the proper blessing and the love of Christ, our Lord. Poor, poor Theodore Street met a violent and senseless death on the streets of our sin-ridden city. His blood spilled into the same gutters that carry away our daily filth and urine. Yes! Brothers and Sisters, Theodore Street is nothing less than a neon marker in the road of life, having looked both ways before crossing perhaps, but like so many of us, having failed to look up. He is a marker telling us that at any second—any second!—everything earthly can end. One minute, you're driving along and the next, your head is over there and your body is over there!" A yelp escaped one of Ted's children and then both buried their faces in their mother's sides. Staige spread his sausage fingers wide and wrapped them over the edge of the lectern in front of him. "Theodore Street was a teacher and he is teaching us even now. He is teaching us that life is temporary and that we had better have

136

our affairs straight. The Book of Isaiah, chapter thirty-eight, verse one, says, 'Set thine house in order: for thou shalt die and not live.' Never were truer words spoke. Just ask Theodore Street. But finally, I must admit that I did not know Mr. Street. But Jesus knew him!" (9)

Here the reverend fixes not on setting one's house in order but on the imminence of death and the judgment of God that necessitates this setting in order. This emphasis suggests a completely different reading of the passage from that which focuses on the setting of one's house in order. While we needn't choose which part to emphasize, the setting of one's house in order is the more readily available encouragement from the passage. It is easy to skim over the second part altogether. But it is the caution about imminent death and facing God's judgment that provides the passage with its urgency. Rev. Larville Staige's acknowledgment at the end of not even having known Ted is the icing on the cake, as yet another believer is exposed as lacking the true faith, whatever that might entail.[3]

An expression of the religious that takes a somewhat different and perhaps slightly more respectful (or at least less irreverent) tone is the appearance of the Penitentes, who are in the background of "Warm and Nicely Buried," another short story from *Damned If I Do,* and who take center stage in Everett's 1997 novel, *The Body of Martin Aguilera.* The Penitentes are described in "Warm and Nicely Buried" as "a secret order of Catholics who practiced rather severe bodily penance and recondite burials of their dead" (118). This definition matters because the story revolves around the body of José Marotta going missing from a funeral home after he suffocates to death with three other men in a mistake involving the fumes from a stove the men had been using to keep warm. The mystery is resolved, although not solved, in the realization by the police officers investigating the disappearance, Lem Becker and Warren Fragua,[4] that the Penitentes have taken Marotta's body because of their faith. Fragua describes the nature of his realization in terms somewhat typical of an Everett character: "Hell, I don't know, but I knew they had him" (127). Becker follows up this remark with an equally characteristic, "Enough said on the matter" (127).

Both characters do the kind of work many of Everett's central characters do. They are self-questioning schizoid types, whose in-between natures are invariably highlighted in the narrative. Becker is especially significant in this regard, as—like Ogden Walker in *Assumption*—he spends a fair bit of time reflecting upon his status as a police officer in comparison to the other police officers he encounters. His situation is different from Walker's, though, in that his cohort seems a lot like him. He is not only between categories but between generations, as he sees himself: "He wanted to be a part of another generation" (110). As he continues to think about how he is situated, this occurs to him: "He wasn't like a lot of people who became policemen, didn't want to be like them, but then most of the lawmen in those parts weren't like that, not *tough,* not *hard,* but doing a job that made them feel pretty good. He worked the grizzly hackle around the body and turned his mind again to trout" (110; emphasis in original). He is a very interior man who typically is unlike many who do what he does for a living but very much like the other men who do what he does for a living *where he happens to do it.* Fragua is another such man, which might help explain why he doesn't press for an arrest or something as predictable as that when he also figures out what happened to Marotta's body. They are not committed to the expected motivations that we are encouraged—at least by representations of the police in popular culture—to associate with the police.

The narrative goes a step further in singling out Becker from conventional associations with the police when he is investigating the death at the heart of the story: "A mouse or a small rat bolted from the garbage and across Lem's feet and he let loose with a short scream. So much for the macho front" (123). It's less important that Becker reacts this way than it is that the narrator—presumably through Becker's consciousness—comments on the un-macho nature of the "short scream" that Becker lets out. As with so many of Everett's central characters, it is in these moments of self-reflection, when they appear to separate themselves from others but also in a way from themselves, that these characters enable something that is not conventionally legible to the reader. His unsettling relationship with the Penitentes and their practices leaves Becker on edge, but he is already predisposed to see things—including the religious practices of this sect—differently enough that he is willing to respect their wishes as the story concludes.

In *The Body of Martin Aguilera,* a version of what happens to José Marotta takes place. A man named Martin Aguilera dies in his home, where his body is found by Lewis Mason and Mason's granddaughter, Laura. Aguilera's body is lying face down with blood pooling around his head. When the police arrive, having been called by Lewis, they find "no body, no blood, but there was a stain on the floor" (8). And so the mystery begins. The main police officer in the novel, Manny Mondragon, agrees with Lewis that perhaps a police report might not be the advised course of action, because the people in the town "are superstitious" (9), and "A dead man is one thing. A dead man without a body is something else" (9).

When Aguilera's body turns up again, it now appears that he drowned in a fishing accident, giving the (now second) impression that there is nothing unusual about his death. This is certainly the effect all of this has on those who did not originally see him dead in his home, but not for Lewis. At first we could not be blamed for thinking of *American Desert*, where a dead man revives at his own funeral and proceeds to narrate the tale. Even death is not a conventional line in Everett's fiction. And the deceased Martin Aguilera is a significant character in the text, making several appearances after each of his deaths. But Martin Aguilera's death is not the most important thing about him. That would be his role in illuminating the in-between nature of Lewis Mason, who emerges as the kind of central character we have come to anticipate in an Everett novel.

Most remarkable about how *The Body of Martin Aguilera* treats religion, then, is how comparatively respectful it is about the particular subdenomination at the center of the mystery. Perhaps because the Penitentes have a private belief system and do not express a religion that is doctrinaire, proselytizing, or expansionist, they enable a lens through which to see the characters in the novel, revealing them as free from the paranoiac investments of convention, able to engage with the world on more schizoid terms, the terms on which Everett's main characters tend to interact with the world. To put this another way, there is a consistency between this unusual religious sect and the unusual characters Everett prefers. Instead of the kind of religious zealotry found and mocked in secondary characters in *Suder* or *Watershed* or *American Desert*, and at least implied in John Livesey's actions at the end of *Cutting Lisa*, the Penitentes appear to exist in between the traditions of organized religion instead of insisting upon them. This in-between status will inevitably make such a group vulnerable to those who are unable to allow them to exist without external, and conventional, interference. In this way, they are similar to Lewis Mason himself.

Lewis is not terribly interested in the Penitentes at all until their world overlaps with his. The overlap is not Martin's death, as significant as that event is for Lewis, but it is the duplicity, violence, and finally the tragedy (marked by the murder of his friend Maggie Okada) that accompanies the intrusion of those who cannot leave this group or this slightly unusual man to themselves. His reassurance to one of the adherents, "You have my word, Salvador. I have no wish to compromise you or your beliefs" (82), is characteristic of his attitude toward those whose beliefs are different from his own. As in "Warm and Nicely Buried," the group is described, briefly, as "a Catholic sect that practiced self-punishment," who "buried their dead in secret graves" (58). While Lewis acknowledges to himself that it all "seemed a little far-fetched" (58), he nevertheless respects their unusual belief system.

The novel presents a clear opposition of the paranoiac to the schizoid, with both terms signifying in their more familiar, if inaccurate, ways as well as in the applications derived from *Anti-Oedipus* and *A Thousand Plateaus*. It must also be added that there is nothing so absolute about the distinction, even though Deleuze and Guattari imply such a distinction at times. Both Cyril Peabody and Manny Mondragon, for instance, suggest in themselves elements of both the paranoiac and the schizoid, and these suggestions contribute to the tensions in the novel, in which Lewis cannot be certain at different points which of the two men he can trust. The paranoiac/schizoid orientation, then, does not supply us with simple Bond-villain-type characters. Cyril might remind us of John Livesey from *Cutting Lisa,* for instance, since, like Livesey, he exploits the sorts of habitual associations that are easy to develop about physicians, or, in Cyril's case, veterinarians.

Cyril initially comes across as open to the world around him, without the impression that he is protecting some predetermined position or belief system. He puts Lewis at his ease, implying at least a similarity of spirit between them. When Lewis drives to meet Martin's grandson, who has mysteriously appeared on the scene shortly after his grandfather's death, Cyril tags along. Lewis tells Cyril much of what has been happening, although not everything: "He did not repeat his observation that there were no animals in the canyon [where Martin is found dead the second time]. That sounded too strange and it scared him too much" (27). Lewis's thoughts also go to the following place: "Lewis wondered why the man was taking such an interest and coming with him, but he was glad to have the company. He felt a little less scared. Strength in numbers and all that, he thought" (27). Cyril is a calming presence for Lewis, whose daughter has just started at Bennington College, where Lewis used to teach. The two have much in common, which encourages a sense of trust of Cyril on Lewis's part (and perhaps ours).

It is finally after Cyril gets the name of the college wrong—he says "Brown" instead of "Bennington" (104)—that Lewis believes that Cyril is not all that he has led Lewis to believe that he is. Lewis discovers that Cyril's daughter does not attend Bennington, realizes that Cyril (a veterinarian, remember) may have deliberately injured a horse that Cyril had been riding on, and wonders, "Who was Peabody? What did he want?" (105). But the kind of trust that Lewis had built up in Cyril does not go away easily: "Maybe he was just lying about his kid because she was a junkie or something and was ashamed of her. Maybe the mare really did pick up a stone. And then again, maybe Peabody didn't want them going farther down into the canyon" (105). Lewis's back-and-forth rationalization of Cyril's behavior also suggests a vulnerability in the schizoid position. A determination to resist convention may also leave one open to second-guessing one's own better judgement, for instance, and as a result, to possibly being manipulated by the paranoiac, who, by definition, might be able to justify such subterfuge to protect his or her own interests, as Cyril ultimately does.

Whereas Cyril Peabody creates an initial impression of trustworthiness and sympathy, Manny Mondragon can appear at first to be the stereotype of the crooked cop. If the veterinarian inspires confidence, maybe this police officer (maybe police officers more generally) invites a bit more suspicion, at least at first. Cyril appears sympathetic to Lewis's problems from the beginning, while Manny actively doubts Lewis's early conclusions. After all, he is the officer that Lewis calls after he finds Martin's body, and then when Manny arrives, Martin's body is gone. This would lead any normal person to have some doubts.

After Lewis is directed to where he can find Martin's body, in order to turn it over to Cyril in exchange for the safe return of Maggie (in another of the intricate plots that Everett characteristically creates), it is Manny's blue lights that Lewis sees flashing in his rearview mirror as he drives away with Martin's maggot-riddled body in the back of his pickup truck (145). Manny's opening conversational salvo, "Early for you to be out" (145), sounds like the sort of thing a suspicious cop might say to a black man on an isolated dark road. Here, although not always in *The Body of Martin Aguilera*, Lewis's being black should be at the forefront of the reader's imagination. But at least Manny acknowledges his suspicions of Lewis, in the kind of gesture that implies his own schizoid tendencies: "I'm sorry, Lewis. I thought when you called you were just overreacting. She still hasn't shown up?" (145). But now it's Lewis's turn to express suspicion, since he doesn't trust the cop now. Lewis thinks: "If Manny knew he had the body, he might take it, might have to take it" (146). For the rest of this exchange, each speaks past the other, intensifying the impression that Manny is not to be trusted and that Lewis is correct in withholding the truth about Maggie from him. When Manny asks Lewis about the smell coming off of him and the mud on his boots, Lewis tells him that he's been to the dump because he found a dead coyote in his pasture and is disposing of it. The scene concludes with Manny looking at Lewis "like he wanted to say something" (147). This lack of resolution only adds to the sense of suspicion that Lewis conveys about and toward Manny.[5]

But in the end, it is Manny Mondragon who saves Lewis's life, shooting Cyril Peabody before Cyril can murder Lewis. While Manny performs one of those definitive cop-at-the-end-of-the-movie gestures, as he kicks "the gun away from the fallen man's hand" (163), he has left behind whatever beliefs he had held earlier. He does, however, acknowledge this change in beliefs: "I just nodded and turned away. I should have seen what was happening. I'm sorry" (163). Lewis presses him on this change, though: "'Were you scared?' Lewis asked" (163). And again, Manny demonstrates his constructively schizoid investment: "Yeah, I suppose that was it" (163). This behavior is as un-cop-like as we can expect to find, as Lewis also implies that perhaps Maggie would not have had to die if he had abandoned his own paranoiac investment earlier in the proceedings.

Lewis's schizoid investment is clear throughout *The Body of Martin Aguilera*. In fact, he is able to describe his in-between status in the self-reflective way most reminiscent of Monk Ellison. In Lewis's case, he thinks about his relationship to the blood ritual of hunting, an annual rite in which he participated with his father as a child. He remembers his wife asking why he continued to go on these trips, since it was obvious that he did not enjoy them: "He didn't have an answer for her. It was the killing, though. It was the killing that kept him going back out there. He couldn't do it, but he wanted to see it" (106). Lewis's separation from the act itself, and his concomitant desire to witness the act of killing, is suggestive of a character with a deep commitment to understanding something important about himself rather than a commitment to some ritual of masculinity, for instance, another of those limiting conventions. Lewis sounds a bit like Ogden, when Ogden thinks about how interesting people are when they're dead. But Lewis's reflections are not the prelude to our discovering something abhorrent in him, as is the case with Ogden, even if the schizoid investment contains the potential for such a discovery.

Toward the end of *The Body of Martin Aguilera* is an instance of the quint-essential Percival Everett sentence: "He wondered if they were on the lookout for an elderly couple, a black man and a Japanese woman, driving a Ford F250 pickup with a dead Mexican in the back" (157). *Suder* provides another such sentence: "So, I'm in this truck and I've got an elephant in the back and I'm driving into the Cascade mountain range of Oregon" (133). And *Glyph* provides still another: "It is not important unless you want it to be and I will not say more about it, but a physical description of one kidnapped baby would have to be released to the police and that description, being delivered by my parents, would be more or less precise and therefore, two, rather pale, white people trav-eling up the California coast with a baby possessing at least one of the attributes of the rendered portrait might have a problem" (54). In each case, the narrator reflects upon an absurdity that is nevertheless necessary to the plot, and upon which it is critical that the reader pause for a moment or two. These gestures of slowing the reader down or redirecting readerly focus to the absurdity itself suggest a meaning in the absurdity that is different from the meaning we con-ventionally educe from arriving at a more recognizable place of meaning, like the resolution of a mystery. While that kind of resolution is satisfying, it can cloud over our ability to find meaning in those moments that do not provide resolution. It is at these moments of nonresolution that Everett's novels often encourage us to look and spend some time.

In *The Body of Martin Aguilera* a man's belief in what is right and his desire to save his friend are aided by the obscure religious sect whose burial practices proscribe embalming or cremation. The burns on Martin Aguilera's body are significant in resolving the novel's mystery, although that resolution, in and of itself, hardly matters by the end of the novel. The evidence of some form of official wrongdoing is preserved by the Penitentes' practices, enabling Lewis to find out and attempt to expose and enabling the wrongdoers to attempt to conceal. Their unconventional beliefs and practices are helpful to the schizoid in this case, an unusual role for religious practices to play in the world that Everett creates. And perhaps it is because of the unconventional nature of this expression of religious belief that they come in for considerably more sympathetic, or at least benign, treatment than is usually the case when religion appears in an Everett novel.

♦ ♦ ♦

If religion is usually represented in Everett's work as the butt of a joke that makes very clear who is in and who out, then a subject that stands out for rarely if ever providing the kind of in-between, distanced, provisional, contingent source of meaning that appears constitutive to this fictional world is the subject of art. In other—more accurate—words: in the same way that if there is a subject that will almost certainly be treated with humor if not disdain, it will be religion; if there is a subject in Everett's work that is most likely to be treated somewhat earnestly, it is the subject of art. Whether it be art being desecrated, art being struggled over, art being argued about, art being misunderstood, or just art being loved, the subject itself is usually encountered as a very serious subject for consideration indeed. This is not to say that the subject of art does not occasion jokes, riddles, puns, and the modes of expression that make up much of the work to be found within this fictional world. It is, however, to say that even these jokes belie a sense of and a demand for respect for the subject. That's the difference between how art is treated and how religion is treated here.[6]

Art is one of the many names that Ishmael Kidder inflicts upon his torture victim in *The Water Cure*, and this is a compelling naming decision on Ishmael's part. He is, after all, bringing the man into being in a new way. If that isn't a definition of art, what is? But like the potential in the schizorevolutionary, the potential in art is unpredictable, too. The subject of art in its innumerable expressions is meditated upon in Everett's work in ways that some might find a flaw, if taken without the context I am proposing here. It is less that art is an absolute value than that its importance lies, in part at least, in its existence within a world with so few, if any, absolutes. The juxtaposition of how religion is treated here and how art is treated further suggests the potential dimensions of the infinite, since both subjects bring with them prospects for ridicule as well as for respect. On balance, religion is ridiculed, but not in the case of *The Body of Martin Aguilera.* Art comes in for almost reverential treatment, but there is still the treatment in *Erasure* of the erased de Kooning drawing.

In addition to Monk's rumination in *Erasure* that "it's incredible that a sentence is ever understood" (44), he recounts an exchange between himself and his father when Monk was in the middle of his freshman year in college. Monk, with the certainty characteristic of many a college freshman, remembers saying this to his father, Ben, at the dinner table, about *Finnegans Wake*, no less:

> In spite of the obvious exploitation of alphabetic and lexical space in the *Wake* and in spite of whatever typographical or structural gestures one might focus on, the most important feature of the book is the way it actually conforms to conventional narrative. The way it layers, using such devices as metaphor and symbol. What's different is that each sentence, each word calls attention to the devices. So, the work really reaffirms what it seems to expose. It is the thing it isn't perhaps twice, and depends on the currency of conventional narrative for its experimental validity. (185)

To pipe the whole thing down a bit, to start, the narrative renders the title of Joyce's novel as *Finnegan's Wake*, in another instance of the linguistic syncope that Sylvie Bauer has identified, and which I discussed in chapter 1. The title is deliberately wrong in Ben Ellison's rendering of it aloud to his son. But more than this, Monk's freshman dissertation, is—like Zeno again—both right and wrong. Its earnestness, like his evaluation of Joyce's text, undoes itself, depending on the currency of critical discourse for its exegetical validity. The deconstructive move of exposing how the text is undone by itself is the sort of aporetical parlor trick that certainly impressed me when I was an undergraduate, being introduced to Derrida for the first time, for instance.[7] But its earnestness also, or rather, nevertheless, suggests a possible critique not only of Monk's exegesis, but of Everett's novel. *Fuck*, the novel within the novel that wins the book award at the end of *Erasure*, is also "the thing it is" and depends on a similar currency of authentic representation of ghetto life—in its case—for its gritty, realist credibility. One might do this continually, although this reading of *Fuck* suggests further that the adult Monk who authors *Fuck* seems to have forgotten about literature what his younger alter ego already knew. Had the older Monk remembered this obvious fact, he might not have found himself so overmatched by the momentum that gathers around the parodic novel that he writes in a fury, to which he cannot sign his own name, but for which he accepts large sums of money. The fact that the novel ultimately hits the publishing home run of being both commercially lucrative and critically acclaimed enables the parody of Ellison's position quite efficiently to do its work twice over.

And then there is the matter of how the *Finnegans Wake* passage finishes, with Monk's father looking at his son "for a long time. He then looked at his other two children and put his fork down. 'I hope before you go to bed this evening, you kiss your brother.' Then he stood and left the table" (185). One of the many instances that signal to Lisa and Bill (Monk's sister and brother) that Monk is special, this moment lends the considerable symbolic weight of their father's authority to Monk's words. Ben Ellison, the patriarch, no longer dismisses these as the words of youth but anoints them with his familial stamp of approval for all three of his children to see.

And it's worth remembering what inspires Monk to write his parody of a ghetto novel in the first place. We get our first glimpse of his motivations when he is told that Juanita Mae Jenkins's *We's Lives in Da Ghetto* has been optioned as a movie, for the price of $3 million. He thinks to himself: "The reality of popular culture was nothing new. The truth of the world landing on me daily, or hourly, was nothing I did not expect. But this book was a real slap in the face. It was like strolling through an antique mall, feeling good, liking the sunny day and then turning the corner to find a display of watermelon-eating, banjo-playing darkie carvings and a pyramid of Mammy cookie jars. 3 million dollars" (29). Monk's comparison of Jenkins's novel to artifacts that are only called art under very specific circumstances (themselves difficult to imagine) suggests (as does my preceding parenthetical) that for him the definition of art is finite. While this is not to attribute to this character named Ellison any sort of *I don't know much about art, but I know it when I see it* incapacity, the comparison is significant in its implication. The invocation of *popular culture* in the passage does similar work, drawing a bright line between this form of expression and the *serious literature* Monk remembers beginning to read as an undergraduate, the kind of reading that leads to his dinner-table appraisal of *Wake*—which is always art— and to his father's expression of approval, perhaps even more importantly, also probably contributes to his viewing Jenkins's novel as he does. These aesthetic judgments, which leave very little room for the kind of in-betweenness that characterizes so much of Everett's fictional world, certainly help explain why when he is finished writing *Fuck,* he sees it as a novel "on which I knew I could never put my name" (62).

Everett's 2017 novel, *So Much Blue,* balances the demands of the *real world* with the demands of Kevin Pace's painting, which he conducts in closely guarded privacy in "this structure that looks like a foaling barn; I suppose that it is. No one enters but me. Not my wife. Not my children. Not my best friend Richard" (4). The real world includes a remembered trip to El Salvador with Richard in order to rescue Richard's brother and a present-day trip to Paris for an opening of an art show featuring Pace's work, which results in an affair with a much younger woman. Pace introduces the idea of the painting that he is working on in secret by describing its dimensions, "As one should" (3). But then he moves to what appear to be the more important points about the painting, which have to do with the privacy and mystery that surround it. In addition to no one seeing it, no one even speaks of it:

> My canvas, my private painting, has a title, a name. It has never been spoken aloud to anyone. I have said it only once, under my breath while I was alone in my studio. It is a bit like my email password except that it cannot be retrieved if I forget it. I have not written it down. One reason I will never let my children see the painting is that they might try to name it and so ruin it and everything. I will not let my wife see it because she will become jealous and that will ruin it and everything. I know that my family and friends, though they love me, I imagine, whatever that means, are somewhat eagerly anticipating my death or, just because I love the word, quietus. They all want to see the canvas. (5)

He considers whether or not this private painting is his masterpiece and equiv-ocates, "Perhaps. Probably not. I don't know what that word means. This notion of a masterpiece has something to do with eternity, forever, I am told. I will have no truck with such concepts, not out of philosophical principle, but as a matter of taste" (6). He continues to equivocate, even on the concept of a masterpiece—even on the concept of his masterpiece—and concludes: "My *masterpiece* is apparently of great concern to so many. It is not a good feeling to know that one is more interesting dead than alive, but neither is it a terri-bly bad feeling" (6; emphasis in original).[8] This final statement about how his interest to others will increase upon his death, and how this does not create a good feeling, nor a terribly bad one either, suggests something important about how Pace views his world, his place in it, and the place of art and his art in it as well. His ability to make relative a concept as ostensibly absolute as the "masterpiece" draws attention to just how tendentious such a judgment actually is. By reminding us that the notion of the masterpiece is a matter of taste, he destabilizes the putatively absolute term with one as transient as one can find. After all, what is more fickle than taste?

His resolution to the ideas governing why no one can see his painting, and why no one can name it, opens up some possibilities previously hinted at in *Erasure*. Monk remembers being in a museum with his father: "He once said to me in a museum, when I complained about an illegible signature on a painting, 'You don't sign it because you want people to know you painted it, but because you love it'" (32–33). While this may be true—and there's no saying that it is or isn't—its opposite is just as plausible, maybe more so. That is, an artist does *not* sign a painting because of an intense love for it. In some sense, this might be more plausible because the privacy of love would appear to have been betrayed at the moment of its public declaration, as with signing. Perhaps this is why large weddings always seem just the slightest bit strange, in their capacity as elaborate and approximate public declarations of intimacy.

Victoire, the very young woman with whom Kevin has his affair in Paris, paints watercolors, which do not impress him, but then shows one to Kevin after they've made love: "The paper was about twenty by thirty inches. The work was green, green leaning into blue in places, edged with blood in the southeast corner. It was abstract, stunning. It was so unlike the country scenes and city-scapes of hers that I had seen before. The painting was rich, dense, and deep. Too deep, I thought, for a work on paper, no matter how heavy the stock, too rich to be anything but oil colors, but it was surely watercolors. I was surprised by it, confused by it. I began to cry" (115). The intensity of Kevin's reaction may be associated in part with postcoital bliss. But his close analysis of the painting—its dimensions, the medium in which it is produced, the material onto which it's been painted—situates him very much in the moment with the painting. He also reevaluates his earlier judgments, since he has seen others of her paintings by which he's been disappointed. She catches him in at least one of his possible prejudgings: "You think a young, pretty French girl cannot paint this picture?" (115). He defends himself by saying: "I don't believe anyone could make this picture" (115). It's fascinating that he says he doesn't believe anyone could make it, not he *didn't* believe it, since now he knows it is possible, since he is sitting in front of it. He continues not to believe that anyone could make this painting. All he can do, finally, is immerse himself in the painting itself: "I wanted to get up and walk over to it, to get right up on it, but I also did not want to end the experience I was having with it" (115). Eventually, all he can say is "I love it" (115). He declares of the painting what she might hope he would declare about his feelings for her.

Kevin rarely matches the emotional intensity he expresses for Victoire's painting anywhere else in *So Much Blue*, whether in his feelings for his wife or either of his two children. Even his feelings for Victoire are attenuated for the most part. But once he is able to release himself from his presuppositions about watercolors, he is able to experience and express a level of emotional profundity that is uncharacteristic of him most of the rest of the time. Art, perhaps like nothing else in his life, or in the novel, means that much to him. Only art brings him to this place of emotional self-expression and self-awareness. The painting is called *Verdant*, and its greenness carries with it a further dimension for Kevin, since its "green leaning into blue in places" harkens back to his admission to Richard about how he likes the color green, but he doesn't use it much because he can't "control it" (50). *Verdant* appears to be Victoire's masterpiece. She can control the color and at least this composition, and her mastery adds a further resonance to her exhibiting it for Kevin, and perhaps his reaction to it.

The importance of art illuminates where we end up at the novel's conclusion. Even when Kevin is able to return to the scene of one of the most traumatizing moments of his life—where he saw the body of a little girl who had been murdered in a Salvadoran village—he cathects the memory through an association with art. This is another moment in the text when Kevin cries, this time with the father of the murdered girl: "A light rain began to fall, but I remained outside the house, in the middle of the road. I blurred my vision and stared at the rocks on the road and found it looked like a Pollock" (233). His most intense emotional register expresses itself through associations with art, whether Victoire's, Pollock's, or his own, as is the case as the novel ends.

Throughout *So Much Blue,* Kevin's relationship with his wife, Linda, is fraught, difficult, and largely silent. As they come to a new understanding of what has been a thirty-year relationship at the novel's end, he reflects on the changes in her, and does so through the eyes of a visual artist: "She was thirty years older than she was when we first met. She was slightly heavier. Her face was interestingly lined. Her hair was mostly gray. She had never been more beautiful than she was as she poured that tea" (233). He sketches her in his mind as if doing a preliminary study before embarking upon another painting; maybe this one is his masterpiece. But again, this artistic sensibility lends itself to emotional expression: "And I loved her. I understood that I had always loved her and I was so sad that I had never allowed her to feel that love" (233). This intense moment of love mixed with sadness is characteristic of how Kevin Pace enables his emotions, not as themselves but as mediated through art. It makes sense, then, that he ultimately expresses his love for his wife through his decision to show her the painting he has been obsessively hiding: "I was about to say I was sorry, but I was done with apologies, pointless apologies, empty words. Instead I said, 'I want you to see something'" (233). The artist's attention to detail is everywhere in the scene's description: "I took Linda's hand and walked her out the back door toward the shed. I could feel the muscles in her hand tense. I said nothing. I unlocked the door. 'I should have let you in here a long time ago.' I opened the studio. I let her walk in in front of me and I switched on the lights. It was another world, the lights flooding everything inside, the covered windows keeping out everything else. Linda stood in front of the painting, moved slowly to the middle of it. I stood behind her" (233). When he says that he should have let her in *here* a long time ago, *here* could just as easily be himself as the foaling barn where the mystical painting has been secreted away. What he has to give her of himself, he can express most completely through his art. In between her repetitions of "So much blue," he tells her, "Now you know everything" (233).[9] It's both significant and insignificant that the contents of the painting are only revealed to Linda and not to the reader. This is the way privacy works. He shares the painting as an expression of his love for *her.* He signs the painting by showing it only to *her.* The exchanges that take place with the painting as a conduit are all the more emotional because of how they are beholden to Kevin Pace's relationship to the mode of expression that means the most to him, so much so that he can use it as a medium of translation to explain himself to his wife, if only to the extent that he can explain himself to her.

The emotional investment that art represents in Everett's fiction is perhaps most compelling in another of his more recent novels, *Percival Everett by Virgil Russell*. *Percival Everett by Virgil Russell* is all art. It's about storytelling, at the expense of what we might conventionally call *plot*, and at times keeps characters alive entirely through storytelling, through art. The notion of plot being almost beside the point is not to be dismissed out of hand. The main premise of the novel is an elderly and hospitalized father and his middle-aged son exchanging and sometimes trading stories. By *trading* I mean to refer to how sometimes a story that one starts is given off to the other, as opposed to the more conventionally I-tell-one-you-tell-one arrangement of an exchange of stories, the narrative equivalent of trading fours between musicians. The narrative itself draws attention to this arrangement of and relationship between storytellers and stories on at least two occasions relatively early in the novel. First: "I could begin my story here or your story there or you could begin my story, from the beginning or middle or end, depending on how you want it or I need it" (45). The notion of trading stories also reinforces an impression that no one really *owns* a story. Once other storytellers emerge, sometimes from within a story already being told, the kaleidoscope of stories begins to appear reminiscent of O'Brien's *At Swim-Two-Birds*, which also features characters within so-called *primary* stories who are then brought to life and empowered in some way to tell their own story. Again, no one owns a story in the mundane sense that this expression might be employed. The kaleidoscopic sensation of *Percival Everett by Virgil Russell* is again expressed in the observation, "I'm an old man or his son writing an old man writing his son writing an old man. But none of this matters and it wouldn't matter if it did matter" (63). The arrangement is reminiscent of the title of Everett's 2011 collection of poems, *Swimming Swimmers Swimming*. The joy in the artful arrangement of words is expressed in all of the poems in the volume, perhaps nowhere more aptly than in a poem entitled "A Novel":

We had no ordinary meeting,
We were no less than two strangers.
And no fewer. (46)

This poem might have served as a fitting epigraph for *Percival Everett by Virgil Russell,* with the "no fewer" correction of and addition to "no less" playing the part of the father (or the son) correcting but also adding to the words of the son (or the father).

This novel lends itself aptly to a Deleuze/Guattari reading. Like most elements to be examined in an Everett novel, the subject is addressed in the novel itself: "In a dream, in the repetition of the dream, the riddle is solved. I kill myself as my father in order to commit incest with myself as my mother, but as my father I prevent my own conception" (147). This expression of the Oedipus, here in its most Sophoclean/Freudian form, creates what is at times an uncomfortable and disorienting interchangeability of father and son, which serves as part of the tension in the novel, not to mention the taboo in the Oedipal drama.

The relative importance or unimportance of the actual plot again presents itself in a repeated formulation that appears near the beginning of the novel and concludes it. After a characteristic exchange, in which father and son argue over the purpose of the stories they write, trade, and discuss, this happens:

> Dad, you realize that I'm dead.
> Yes, son, I do. But I wasn't aware that you knew it. (14)

A moment like this cannot help but remind us of Ishmael's anguish at the loss of Lane in *The Water Cure.* The exchange creates uncertainty and bewilderment but also a sadness that suffuses the rest of the discussion about their stories. And the sequence repeats, in reverse, in a way reminiscent of Vladimir and Estragon in *Waiting for Godot:*

> You hold my hand.
> I hold your hand.
> I write this for you.
> If I wrote, this would be it.
> If you wrote.
> Yes.
> I will always be here.
> And I.

I'm dead, son.

I know that, Dad. But I didn't know that you knew it. (226–27)

Like the first exchange, this one carries a sweetness and tenderness to it in its mutuality, accompanied by the interchangeability that threatens to undercut the tenderness, to make it look more like yet another art game. Religion is never treated like this. But the final moment leaves us not even sure where we stand and—again—saddened by the poignancy of the scene's resolution. Art, as in *So Much Blue,* enables profound emotion in two characters who may not be willing or able to express themselves on such a deep emotional register otherwise.

While the interchangeability of the father and son carries with it the Oedipal confusion that the complex mandates—although in the absence of the mother figure—the narrative presents at least one moment in which who is who is most significant. As with Kevin Pace, whose ability to express his emotions is mediated through art, so here with the father and son. In one of the most emotionally arresting moments in the novel, as, again, father and son meditate over the form, function, meaning, provenance, structure, and progress of their stories, they consider in about the middle of the novel a *preface,* which is not out of place (how could it be?) so much as drawing attention to itself because of its location. One speaker says, "How bizarre a reader you construct, because you do construct her, him, it, don't you? How bizarre that reader must be to ingest your preface and believe it or at least not abandon your projected desires concerning your so-called novel" (151). From there, the larger point is "However, in fact, your book might seem to begin in the manner of a definition dialogue, setting out to identify rhetorical stratagems, but concludes, as perhaps all things conclude, appearing as little more than an attempt to discern how one can best find some happiness in this life" (151). Here, the introduction of the subject of happiness (not to mention subjective happiness) shifts the discussion to an emotional register approaching desperation. But this connection of aesthetics and emotion draws the meditation to what has to be its logical conclusion, considering who the two speakers are: "Whereas we might be moved to plausibly regard the novel as just this, we would still be wrong, wouldn't we? Because all it is, all it ever will be, all it ever can be, is an effort at saying how much you love your old man. And a day late at that" (151). This concussive conclusion is shocking in its unadorned emotional resonance and makes the connection between art and life itself visible for all to see, even among everything else happening within the novel's style.

Art, then, serves a mediating role even in its almost absolute value in Everett's work. That it enables the vital communication that appears otherwise impossible for Kevin Pace or the father and son in *Percival Everett by Virgil Russell* discloses another importance that the space in between categories reveals of itself. Art's recurrence in Everett's work, like that of religion, demonstrates the recurring, revivifying, and destabilizing potential that Deleuze and Guattari identify in the rhizome, a natural metaphor that is useful to discuss as a way of concluding this chapter.

◆ ◆ ◆

Brian Massumi's translator's foreword to *A Thousand Plateaus* concludes with an injunction that I cannot help but read as instructive in my thinking about Everett and the kaleidoscopic approach I am taking to his work here, and that I try to put into play in whatever I read more and more. This injunction might serve as a critical template more generally for others as well. At the heart of Massumi's observation is how he uses the word *challenge*, which is how I've been thinking about it throughout this book: "The best way of all to approach the book is to read it as a challenge: to pry open the vacant spaces that would enable you to build your life and those of the people around you into a plateau of intensity that would leave afterimages of its dynamism that could be reinjected into still other lives, creating a fabric of heightened states between which any number, the greatest number, of connecting routes would exist. Some might call that promiscuous. Deleuze and Guattari call it a revolution" (xv). It's impossible not to ruminate on Massumi's mischievous suggestion of a "greatest number" in his invocation of thought in describing Deleuze and Guattari's work. Granted, some texts pose more challenges than others. And while Massumi's task is different from mine, in that he is responsible for approximating the mind and intentions of his subject, I have no such responsibility here. That said—and if I might put things this way, just for a moment—to characterize Everett's fiction as a challenge would probably not come as a foreign or unwelcome concept to him, especially when using the word as Massumi does. And as is always the case with intentionalism, it doesn't matter. What does matter is that Everett's texts do issue challenges collectively and individually. And these interrelated challenges reemerge at intervals, not unlike the rhizomes that Deleuze and Guattari theorize as hermeneutic symbols in *A Thousand Plateaus*.

When Deleuze and Guattari speak of rhizomes, they have in mind characteristics that, as with schizoanalysis, free up potentialities that do not exist under hierarchical structures, whether Oedipal or arborescent (their word for the vertical, hierarchal structure, whether of thought, nature, capital, or power):

> Subtract the unique from the multiplicity to be constituted; write at $n-1$ dimensions. A system of this kind could be called a rhizome. *A rhizome as subterranean stem is absolutely different from roots and radicles.* Bulbs and tubers are rhizomes. Plants with roots or radicles may be rhizomorphic in other respects altogether: the question is whether plant life in its specificity is not entirely rhizomatic. Even some animals are, in their pack form. Rats are rhizomes. Burrows are too, in all of their functions of shelter, supply, movement, evasion and breakout. The rhizome itself assumes very diverse forms, from ramified surface extension in all directions to concretion into bulbs and tubers. When rats swarm over each other. The rhizome includes the best and the worst: potato and couchgrass, or the weed. Animal and plant, couch grass is crabgrass. (*Thousand Plateaus* 6–7; emphasis in original)

The relentlessly vertical (read: hierarchical) nature of the root and radicle system closes off the kinds of associative structures made possible by the horizontally oriented rhizome, and these associations are as structural, natural, and earthly as they are metaphorical, theoretical, and hermeneutic: "A rhizome ceaselessly establishes connections between semiotic chains, organizations of power, and circumstances relative to the arts, sciences, and social struggles. A semiotic chain is like a tuber agglomerating very diverse acts, not only linguistic, but also perceptive, mimetic, gestural, and cognitive: there is no language in itself, nor are there any linguistic universals, only a throng of dialects, patois, slangs, and specialized languages" (7). The patois grow uncontrollably out of and away from the standard language, then. Deleuze and Guattari prefer the nonstandard languages in their many forms over the standard languages of hierarchy and power and standardization. The nonstandard languages only ever gesture toward an opening up of possibilities and speak in order to draw our attention to multiplicities: "Multiplicities are rhizomatic, and expose arborescent pseudomultiplicities for what they are" (8). Put still another way, "A rhizome has no beginning or end: it is always in the middle, between things, interbeing, *intermezzo*" (25).

The commitment of these theorists to the significance and potential of the middle, contingent, provisional is complete (to the extent that within this theoretical framework such completeness would be possible). The authors' note that precedes *A Thousand Plateaus* provides instructions that themselves reside somewhere on the continuum between mandate and option. They characterize the second volume of *Capitalism and Schizophrenia* as "composed not of chapters but of 'plateaus.' We will try to explain why later on (and also why the texts are dated). To a certain extent, these plateaus may be read independently of one another, except the conclusion, which should be read at the end" (xx). The questions that immediately arise from these instructions are: How can we know when is the end? Are they supposing that we will only read *A Thousand Plateaus* once? Maybe most obviously, when is the end? Of each reading of the whole? How are we to know when we are at the end of any individual reading? These instructions are obviously provided without the slightest intention of their being followed, or even of their being followed being possible at all, strictly speaking. They do, however, ask questions about the status of authors' notes. More than most suppositions available, this note undercuts the notion that *A Thousand Plateaus* (or, for that matter, *Anti-Oedipus*, and, at least potentially, any book) is, in any way, complete or definitive. And, of course, they aren't because of the infinity of potential readings, although we may convince ourselves that they are complete at any one time, because of the finite number of actual readings. Again, Zeno is both right and wrong. This intermezzo state of the instructions themselves suggests meaning on its own, but not a meaning of a kind to which we have become accustomed or that is based upon criteria we are in any way used to trying to follow.

When the rhizome makes a couple of appearances in *Percival Everett by Virgil Russell*, these appearances are suggestive as multiplicities in ways resonant of *A Thousand Plateaus*. In fact, they serve as additional instances in which Everett passages read like they come almost straight from Deleuze and Guattari: "The dark-purple irises that you were sorry you planted, though you loved to look at them, always needing to be divided, always being given away as gifts in paper bags saved from the market, the rhizomes lying there like bodies in a mass grave" (41). The uncontrollability of the rhizome frustrates arborescent certainty, especially in the conventional gardener. And then: "The role of all this last act, as it were, is to provide a context for the impossible, a home for the contradictory, a bed for the irreconcilable. What I have planted, am planting, are like rhizomes, easy to put in, *but you have to divide them before you know it. So much work*" (166; emphasis added). Again, the frustration of having to divide them because of their resistance to the conventional treatment of planting and uprooting, their potential for invasion, but also here there is the further, and more explicit, notion of how much work the rhizome becomes. This work would gesture toward why we tend toward the arborescent and have to be instructed in, encouraged toward, nudged in the direction of the rhizomatic. It does not come naturally to us.

Even when the phenomenon we attempt to understand is purely rhizomatic in nature, we are still inclined to impose an arborescent, hierarchical, and limited structure upon it. There are few such rhizomatic structures—whether of thought, belief, emotion, interpretation, or judgment—in American life as persistent as questions of race. As I turn next to how race is and is not represented in Everett's fiction, it is worth keeping Deleuze and Guattari's thoughts about the rhizome close to hand.

4

THE TRACE OF RACE AND DIFFICULT LIKENESSES

I really liked the part about little white boys holding hands with the little black girls.
Double fives.
Lucky bastard.
Lucky, my ass. I cheat. I always cheat. I cheat whenever I can. I have to cheat. Slaves have no luck.
Of course they do, Heston says. It's just all bad.
—Charlton Heston and Nat Turner in conversation while playing backgammon on the top step of the Lincoln Memorial in *Percival Everett by Virgil Russell*

D. W. Griffith: I like your book very much.
Richard Wright: Thank you.
—*Erasure*

It should be obvious by now how a discussion of the anticonventional potential of looking at the infinite space in between established categories might appositely apply to a discussion of race as it is lived, perceived, and experienced in the United States. At the same time, perhaps the subject that most makes a critic discussing the work of Percival Everett feel like the butt of the joke rather than being in on it is the subject of race and, more importantly, how the subject of race is addressed in Everett's work. But as it turns out, the prospect of being the butt of the joke when talking about race is always in play for the American; it's just that with Everett's work it is less easy to pretend that this prospect does not always already exist. Race is the great Oedipus of American life with no parallel, and like any Oedipus, it encourages the kind of paranoiac, arborescent, hierarchical, conventional thinking that inevitably issues in bigotry, fixity, stagnation, and all of the other enemies of thought that Deleuze and Guattari theorize about in order to suggest an opening up of our thinking that might move us away from these fixities. Bigotry relies on certainty, inflexibility, fixity. The schizoid investment offers at least some way to think beyond these restrictions. Deleuze and Guattari describe the notion of the Oedipus in psychoanalytic terms, in familial terms, in political terms. But they also describe it in metaphorical terms, which lends their version of it the kind of application to which I am putting it here. Race is a matrix of traps in American life. To redeploy the governing metaphor of my discussion here, it has kaleidoscopic possibilities that dazzle, bewilder, confuse, and disguise the world as we attempt to perceive it, no matter our best intentions. As Deleuze and Guattari write about the Oedipus, we might think of how they may be read as writing about how race imprisons so much of American life and thought:

Oedipus is like the labyrinth, you only get out by re-entering it—or by making someone else enter it. Oedipus as either problem or solution is the two ends of a ligature that cuts off all desiring-production. The screws are tightened, nothing relating to production can make its way through any longer, except for a far-distant murmur. The unconscious has been crushed, triangulated, and confronted with a choice that is not its own. With all of the exits now blocked, there is no longer any possible use for the inclusive, nonrestrictive disjunctions. Parents have been found for the (orphan) unconscious! (*Anti-Oedipus* 79)

Deleuze and Guattari describe the Oedipus as all-encompassing, inescapable, while at the same time largely incomprehensible, a labyrinth that draws us into itself and encourages us to draw others in. You would be hard pressed to arrive at a more effective metaphor for race in America.

In the case of Percival Everett's work, in fact, the argument might even be made that the extremity of the circumstances in which many of his characters find themselves demonstrates how far an African American writer must go in order to distract a readership acculturated to fixate on a subject it has also been acculturated not to understand. Whether a flying baseball player, a three-hundred-pound fertile woman in a world where fertility is illegal, a possibly murderous Greek demigoddess, an actually murderous small-town sheriff's deputy, a torturing and murderous romance novelist, a hyper-genius toddler, an alive-dead-undead-dead college professor, a hydrologist in the wrong place at the wrong time, and so on. And since I have been arguing for the ways that Everett's work carves out an infinite space in between categories and then creates a large, complex world within that infinite space, the reasonable question to ask of me is whether or not it is necessary, or even advisable, to include a discussion of race in this study at all. What could be more conventional when examining the work of an African American writer than to discuss how this writer engages with questions of race? If I'm unsuccessful in this section of my discussion, in a way that does not obtain in any other section, I run the risk of looking like an unwitting character in *Erasure*. More than this, I would look like I was unnecessarily capitulating to a temptation (perhaps a desire) to discuss race when, in fact, such a discussion is ill-advised and adds little or nothing to my overall considerations here.

While such queries would be entirely valid, I would argue that to avoid questions of race would be even more ill-advised than addressing them is. When something looks difficult or perilous, it is understandable that we attempt to avoid it, if we can. At least we can hope that is always one of our available alternatives. But more than this, to do so here would do a great disservice to Everett's work, since how it deals with questions of race is, in fact, central to the question of the infinite space in between categories. Put another way, instead of speaking about race from the position of explicator to white America, as is so often the case with race in the mouths of nonwhite characters in much American art, Everett motivates many of his characters with the anti–double consciousness that I mentioned earlier. Instead of seeing themselves through the eyes of other people, as Du Bois so presciently put it all those years ago, many of Everett's black characters insist upon seeing themselves as the multiplicities that they know themselves to be. This self-perspective is not resolution, of course, but a recognition of the inner complexities that so many white characters—not to mention white American citizens—are able to take for granted. This anti–double conscious posture might be described as claiming the privilege of seeing oneself as being as complex as any white person, without trying to *be* a white person. If many of Everett's characters are guilty of anything, it is the temerity to see the experience of being black as a complex, unresolved subjectivity and not as a problem to be solved, a condition to be endured, an oddity to be explained. This important challenge has its own value, irrespective of whether or not others are up to it. This perspective on race is worthy of critical attention. So I am not ignoring race, nor am I suggesting that race doesn't matter in Everett's work.[1] I see race operating in his work as issuing another anticonventional challenge to the reader. The challenge here is to imagine how race operates in America and what it might look like if it operated—and were approached—differently.

In order to discuss what we might learn from Everett's representations of race, we could do worse than examining his epistolary novel that features Strom Thurmond as both subject and object, talking and talked about. But before turning to *A History of the African-American People [Proposed] by Strom Thurmond as Told to Percival Everett & James Kincaid,* it is worth noting a minor point about how this novel illuminates the argument about the importance of art in Everett's work that I was making in the preceding chapter. It is significant that the book named in the title of the novel is never itself produced. Such a work would surely stretch the definition of "art" farther than perhaps even Everett might dare, especially when we remember the elevated status the notion of art tends to occupy in his work. Also on the status of art, Ben Ellison chastises his precocious undergraduate son in *Erasure* for not using the entirety of book titles: "I see they've refrained from using complete titles in university these days" (184). Nevertheless, I will refer to the novel as *A History of the African-American People,* in the interest of manageability if not brevity.

The authors' note to *A History of the African-American People* sets a tone similar to that established by the authors' note to *A Thousand Plateaus,* complete with a similar escape clause built in:

> *The authors wish to make clear to the reader that this is a work of fiction (i.e. none of it is true). Though there are many references to actual people, all of our interactions with those people (and the fictitious ones as well) are, in fact, fictitious. This includes all of the characters and events in the novel involving the Simon & Schuster publishing company. If any of the matter of this novel should be found offensive by anyone, we understand (if not completely) and suggest you find another book to read. We wish we could say that we mean no disrespect.* (4; emphasis in original)

The authors' note establishes a mischievous tone appropriate to satire but also identifies where the reader should be looking, as much of the novel takes place in an imaginative space in between the real characters and companies named in the novel and the fictional world created by the authors. And is this not where all fiction takes place, in one way or another? Of course, this declaration is relegated to a note that, I will admit, many would not even notice, let alone read, let alone think seriously about, because of the nature of authors' notes. The note does not even carry the title "Authors' Note," leaving it all the more both anonymous- and innocuous-looking—simply some additional front matter to be ignored by all except critics working on the novel, along with information like the mailing address of Akashic Books. This novel is a selection of the Akashic Urban Surreal series, which seems about right; although we encounter here again the designation *urban* and cannot help but wonder if it is code for *African American,* as it so often is.[2] But the note is worth noting for its relationship to what follows, a satirical account of the difficulties obtaining to the inevitable nonpublication of a most improbable work of history.

The Percival Everett character in the novel refers to Thurmond as "the Reddest Neck" (151), in a use of the superlative that appears here at least defensible, considering the long record of the former very senior senator from the state of South Carolina. Thurmond comments quite tellingly on this record:

> Well, for one thing, I may have already said this, I repeat myself a lot these days. I didn't used to do that, not so much anyway. About the colored people, I reckon that more than any other living political figure I have affected the lives of these people. I honestly believe that any progress that the Negro race has experienced is not due to the efforts of emancipators, but to the kind of decent and honest white Southerners. It doesn't bother me that coloreds can stay at white hotels and go to white theaters and eat at white restaurants. Not now. Now white people are accustomed to their presence, but back in 1950, we weren't. I have to tell you that I was against the North forcing the South to desegregate. Especially when the North was more segregated than the South. You have to admit that the South has been the national whippin' boy. I have never in my life used the word "nigger." (164)

Where to begin? Thurmond's reconstruction of his past views still consists of a world in which hotels, theaters, and restaurants are still *white,* and black people are allowed to patronize them. His sine qua non about his avoidance of the word *nigger* as proof of his racial enlightenment is the kind of declaration one still occasionally hears from white people who consider themselves progressive on racial issues. And yet, if I can put it this way, some of Thurmond's words here ring true. He is not so much a caricature as a believable portrayal of the man as we might easily imagine him to have been, if we are inclined to turn our minds in his direction. As he resorts to the conventional defense that the North was more segregated than the South, he nudges up against Martin Luther King's famous indictment of "the white moderate" as the primary impediment to black progress and not the members of the Ku Klux Klan or the white citizens' councils, as he famously writes in his "Letter from Birmingham Jail."[3] All of this, however, is modulated by Thurmond's easily missed concession, "Not now," when talking about objecting to blacks eating in *white* restaurants, etc.

But first, there is much waiting to be done before Thurmond appears in the novel. He is almost a white whale figure, to put this one way. In fact, Thurmond does not appear until nearly halfway through *A History of the African-American People*. By this point, he has been spoken of, speculated about, referred to, and ventriloquized by others. A couple of his presumably handwritten—and largely incoherent—notes appear in the early going, but he does not surface finally until Kincaid and Everett are invited for lunch at the senator's home in Edgefield, South Carolina. When he finally makes his entrance, as evidenced by the lengthy self-rationalization quoted above, he is very much worth the wait. Thurmond's two appearances are presented as transcripts of the conversations that take place at two meals that Everett and Kincaid have with him, one a lunch at Thurmond's home in Edgefield, the other, dinner at a tony restaurant in Washington, DC. At this second meal, Thurmond dies while standing on his head against a wall in the restaurant, bringing to an end the prospect of the *History of the African-American People* being completed at all. So Thurmond is not always just lampooned—although he is sometimes—in keeping with the provisional nature of Everett's work. Or, rather, Thurmond, by being represented in a way that we can imagine to be fair and accurate—for better *and* for worse—lampoons himself in *A History of the African-American People*.[4]

The Edgefield lunch is a complicated affair. There is, understandably, tension when the men introduce themselves to one another and sit down. The preliminaries out of the way, the drinks ordered from Thurmond's black servant (*Old times there are not forgotten*), the principal conversation is initiated by Jim

Kincaid: "Senator, that's why we wanted to actually meet with you. We'd like to understand what you mean by history vis-à-vis our current project" (153). Thurmond approves of Kincaid's directness, surmising correctly that he's from the Midwest. Turning to Everett, Thurmond confirms that he's a "fellow South Carolinian," with which Everett will not agree: "I was born in Georgia" (153).[5] Thurmond then moves on to a point of contention between the two men: "You're the one who gave that speech at the State House" (153). Thurmond's reference to the speech about the importance of the arts that Everett began at a session of the South Carolina state legislature in 1989 is significant for a couple of reasons. First, it inserts into this conversation the kind of real-life event (to put this one way) referred to in the authors' note at the beginning of the book. Second, it highlights the way that Thurmond does remember some things quite clearly while forgetting others, drawing our attention to which might be which and what his motivations might be for conveniently forgetting certain details from his long personal history. Third, and perhaps most importantly, Thurmond's remembering and forgetting emphasizes a distinction that he draws between thought and belief. When he states, "You gentlemen forget that I did vote for the Civil Rights Act of 1964" (160), Everett and Kincaid cite chapter and verse refuting this assertion, prompting them—during one of the senator's frequent restroom breaks—to wonder if they "went at it too much like an interrogation" (160). But even in the face of this interrogation, Thurmond's response is simply "Well, I remember supporting it" (160). There is no disputing what someone chooses to remember or how they choose to remember it.

It's easy to see the Thurmond we encounter in the novel as being a lot more fascinating than might have been the experience of meeting the real Thurmond in the flesh. The novel's Thurmond *is* a fascinating character. His memory comes and goes, which is to be expected of a man of his advanced years. But the manner in which it departs and returns depends a lot on the topic under discussion. He remembers, for instance, details of the infamous 1999 New York Police Department shooting of Amadou Diallo, in order to make a point about the difference between how that story was covered and how the 1998 murder of James Byrd in Jasper, Texas, was covered. In the New York case, the police officers were called "racists and pigs and such, but no one suggested anything about the character of the city of New York" (156), while in the Texas case,

"When those rednecks, those dumbass peckerwoods down in Texas dragged that poor boy to death behind that pickup, all you heard was how awful Texas and the South remain" (156). His intermittent memory is a convenient device, though, for incorporating a pretty nuanced discussion of race, memory, and—most importantly—the relationship between thought and belief into the conversation. It is Thurmond who discusses the relationship between thought and belief, unwittingly revealing his own prejudices but also illuminating how prejudice can work more generally.

Thurmond actually lectures Kincaid and Everett in the difference between thoughts and beliefs, as a way of explaining his success as a politician: "Let me tell you what the secret to politics is. It's got nothing to do with issues or even rights. It's got to do with people and what they believe. Not even what they think. Hell, they don't know what they think. But they know what they believe. The great thing about beliefs is that you can convince people they have them" (161).[6] Among other things, his account helps explain why his having voted in favor of the Civil Rights Act can exist in his mind as true—as a belief—in spite of the historical fact that he voted against every iteration of it that made its way to the US Senate. Thoughts are cultivated through study, reflection, consideration, and time. They may even be said to be somewhat dispassionate. Beliefs can remain deep, pure, rigid, and unexamined without losing any authenticity as belief. This distinction helps explain his assertion that people know what they believe but not necessarily what they think. Beliefs can be manipulated by a skilled observer, while thoughts make their appeals to some sense of authority, expertise, growth, flexibility. Belief, when manipulated skillfully, can lead to ghastly consequences, as Thurmond makes clear in an anecdote about a lynching he witnessed as a young boy:

I saw that man hanging there and that was gruesome enough, but to this day the ugliest thing I remember seeing was the smiling faces on my own people. Fact was, I learned later, that Negro man hadn't done anything but frighten a white woman, probably by coming around a corner or something. But all my life I heard of raping and lynching all tied together and it was hard to separate the two. I know that the poor crackers around here used it as an excuse, but they really believed it too. How'd I get on that? I guess it's the belief stuff. (162)

"The belief stuff" tends toward the inflexible, too, and starts to resemble as a trace the status religious faith occupies in Everett's work. As difficult as it is to rethink something, as I've acknowledged any number of times over the course of trying to make an argument in favor of rethinking, it is easy to imagine that it is probably impossible to rebelieve something. The fact that the English language does not even have a word that accommodates this act is telling. Thurmond is presented as complex and horrible, amusing and repellant, but more importantly, he's many of these things to varying degrees at the same time. Cognitively, he poses a similar challenge to that posed by Ralph or Ishmael or Craig or Ogden or John. It is easy to imagine the actual Thurmond this way. It would be easy to present him as an unrelenting caricature of bigotry, but what is disarming about the portrayal of this character is how human he is. His portrayal, again, issues a difficult challenge to the reader. And now we really should reflect back to how Brian Massumi uses the word *challenge*.[7] There are, after all, racists in the most conventional sense of that word in *Erasure* and *Wounded*, not to mention Rhino Tanner in *Grand Canyon, Inc.* But Thurmond is not like these other characters.

But as we know already, if only from our reflections on Zeno's paradoxes, something (or in Thurmond's case, someone) can be both compelling and all but completely wrong at exactly the same moment. We know, for instance, that our beliefs can be theorized into thought without ever traversing the barrier into correctness, based on some evaluation of what *correct* might consist of. As Jonathan Lear has noted, in a discussion of Zeno's paradoxes,

> The skeptical puzzle is not refused, in the sense of being dismissed on the basis of absolutely incontrovertible assumptions; it goes away. However, sincere beliefs, no matter how sincerely believed, are not guaranteed to be stable over time for an individual or a community. Should the assumptions of a theory used to answer a skeptical paradox come in question, the puzzle which one may have thought buried forever will be resurrected. One may be able to construct another theory which will answer the paradox, but there is no theory which can guarantee that one will forever be able to keep a good puzzle down. (101)

Lear could be talking about race in America, a puzzle whose very nature, as it expresses itself in oppression, must be enforced, theorized, dismissed, re-enforced, retheorized, and redismissed ad infinitum by those holding power. This enforcement, theorization, etc. is, paradoxically, often presented as an expression of the natural order of things, even as it is being enforced, theorized, etc. Not only is it the labyrinth that Deleuze and Guattari describe in the Oedipus, it is also the belief that the skilled politician (Thurmond) can manipulate to his ends, be they the gathering of votes or the continuation of Jim Crow. But this self-fulfilling mechanism has the ability always to imbricate into its narrative even those who resist it. The imbrication is part of how convention works, not unlike how *Finnegans Wake* relies on conventions of the novel to enact its potentially unconventional nature, as a young Monk Ellison notes. The enforcement part of this set of investments, as Deleuze and Guattari would class them, explains why the choice of Strom Thurmond, a legislator, as the titular mover of this history of the African American people, is so compelling. Who else but a legislator is in a position to continue this cycle of puzzles and solutions, as Thurmond himself did in his run for the American presidency in 1948 as a segregationist, during his infamous filibuster against the Civil Rights Act of 1957 and in his opposition to the Civil Rights Act of 1964? As Lear continues his point about puzzles and solutions: "We know that there is a temporal dimension to our experience, but the attempt to explain our *experience* of the present, the period of time in which we are self-consciously existing, tends to induce vertigo. Such vertigo motivates the desires for a theory which will explain our experience to us. We do not have clear intuitions which dictate the shape of an adequate theory; rather we seek a theory that will help us conceptualize our intuitions" (101; emphasis in original). Lear's point about vertigo characterizes well the experience of attempting to match some theory with our intuitions—our thoughts with our beliefs. Again, a skilled politician is well placed to provide such a theory for a potential supporter to justify their already-held beliefs. While Thurmond insists that he is not trying to clean up his image, he does selectively work to explain his experience to himself as well as to Everett and Kincaid. His beliefs do not appear to have changed, but his thoughts may have. It is his thoughts that he tries to convey to his two visitors, because they are easier for him to articulate to them. Perhaps what is compelling in this portrayal of thoughts and beliefs, or intuitions and theories, is that we all stand in this vertiginous relationship to something. The schizorevolutionary at least might develop a vocabulary for understanding this vertiginous relationship in a productive, or at least less duplicitous, way. Thurmond's point is not exactly undermined by Lear's points, but it is complicated by them, as Lear's argument makes much more fluid than Thurmond's does the relationship between thoughts and beliefs. This fluidity is of little consequence to Thurmond, except in how he—as a politician—might capitalize upon and manipulate that vertiginous relationship as it occurs in others. Part of his problem with Everett and Kincaid is that he cannot do the same with them. What Lear points to is a much more dynamic relationship in which thoughts and beliefs exist on a continuum, and the really interesting stuff, as almost always, exists in the space between the poles. But it is this space between the poles that we are acculturated to overlook as fluid and infinite, focusing instead on the categories, on whom we will and will not vote for, rather than on these potentially infinite spaces. Even with a figure like Thurmond, the infinity of this space still emerges.

The second appearance that Thurmond makes in *A History of the African-American People* takes place in Washington, DC, at Estelle's Southern Cuisine, an upscale restaurant in Georgetown. This episode is considerably more chaotic than the first, if for no other reason than Thurmond dies at the end of it, standing on his head in the restaurant in an attempt to get the attention of Kincaid and Everett as they rise to leave. Clarence Thomas also makes an appearance. (At least a character whose name is Clarence Thomas, who is an associate justice of the Supreme Court of the United States and appears to know a woman named Anita Hill, makes an appearance.) Thurmond cannot remember the justice's name, calling him by turns "Judge Tom," "Charles," and "Clevon." He also refers to Thomas as "a good boy, that Clevon. Dumb as a plucked chicken in a truck, but a good boy" (308). Calling a sitting Supreme Court Justice "boy" seems the least of Thurmond's transgressions. But they add up over the course of his representation in the novel.

The sequence with Clarence Thomas points to another aspect of the Thurmond character that situates him along some sort of continuum of humanity instead of as a purely malevolent caricature. He is mischievous in a way that is part (maybe mostly) dirty old man and part prankster schoolboy. The juxtaposition of his willingness to talk about the murders of Amadou Diallo and James Byrd, on the one hand, and then to imply that he slept with at least one of his maids (hardly a stretch to imagine, considering the revelation after the actual Thurmond's death of his having fathered a black daughter), on the other, leaves Thurmond somewhere along a continuum that makes him very difficult to pin down definitively. It would be completely understandable to expect a representation of Thurmond that fulfills our very worst expectations of him. But where is the art in that?

Very few moments with Thurmond in the novel demonstrate these points about the character's mischievousness, as well as his situation on a continuum, quite as vividly as his reflection on the Battle of the Bulge, and where that reflection leads him. As Kincaid and Everett continue to press Thurmond over dinner regarding his attitudes toward race and his role in a history of which many would not necessarily be proud (not to mention a *History* that eventually does not get written), Thurmond uses a recollection from his time as a tank commander at the Battle of the Bulge to make a point about his belief in racial equality, "however separate" (309), as he makes clear. To this qualification he adds, "But that's all changed now. Heck, mercy, man, you teach with Kincaid here at that College of South California?" (309). But his central point has to do with the crucial role a group of "diggers" played during a particularly unpleasant scene for the (white) soldiers during the battle: "Where it wasn't muddy, the ground was frozen hard," he says. Or, at least, this is how he remembers it as he tells the story now: "So when those Negro soldiers showed up, we put them right to work digging us some latrines. Boy, they really saved the day for us. As I remember, they dug real nice latrines. They tickled me too, the way they wanted to go fight some Germans. Those diggers were a godsend" (309). The humor that Thurmond finds in the desire of the African Americans soldiers to fight the perpetrators of what for him appears to be the only racism in the Second World War that matters again suggests this peculiar nature to his character. At first, this rhyming slang of "digger" appears to be just an easy racist caricature. But as he goes on to *compliment* the soldiers—as he sees it—his usage becomes more pointed and contemporary in its resonance: "You see, that's partly why I want to write this book. I want the diggers of the world to know that I appreciate them. I want them to know that we white people don't think of them simply as dirty diggers or lazy diggers or even agitating diggers" (309). The story that Thurmond tells is remarkable because it is, at the same time, brazen and cowardly, as perhaps all racist acts must be. He can do pretty much all the work that he wants his story to do by resorting to and relying upon a rhyme that is actually a trace, since it carries all of the resonance of the actual word (especially when accompanied by adjectives like *dirty, lazy,* and *agitating*) without having to sully his account of this event with the actual word itself. But *we* know what he means. This is how the dog whistle sounds, at a frequency (clearly, here, the lower ones) that separate groups of hearers from nonhearers, as well as supporters from opponents to his version of history. After all, he's just telling a story about men digging latrines. Right? Thurmond finally exposes himself as the apologist we could not help but expect him to be. But it has taken some time to get here, and we are not afforded the luxury of forgetting where else we've been with him along the way to getting here.

At this point, Thurmond becomes, finally, the Thurmond that it would have been easy to be expecting from the beginning of the novel. He seems to turn a corner into an unrelenting apologist for himself, his region, and his history, but mostly himself. He admits, "I'm getting old. I don't know if you noticed. I know I'm not going to live forever. And when I die I'd like to have a seat at the big party, if you know what I mean. You probably don't. I'm talking about heaven, boys. I'm cramming for finals, trying to make amends, trying to have my parking ticket validated" (309). Thurmond is voicing the ghostly echo of Isaiah 38:1, without saying so. As he attempts to get his house in order, since he shall eventually die and not live, he acknowledges at least the possibility that he's been wrong in his thoughts, if not in his beliefs.

From here, things spiral out of control, culminating in Thurmond dying in the restaurant while performing a headstand, actually his second headstand in the novel. In the same way that the resolution afforded by the conclusions of many of Everett's novels are beside the point, Thurmond's death is, too. The more interesting aspect of Thurmond's character in *A History of the African-American People* is that he appears, and that he is not a simple caricature to be sacrificed to make some relatively obvious point about the nature of Thurmond's soul, or the nature of the bigot, for instance. Instead, he moves around within the dizzying possibilities that might actually be in play if two people like Everett and Kincaid were ever to meet someone like Thurmond. That imaginative space, into which we are invited, is infinite and all the more remarkable for it. As I mentioned earlier, the *History of the African-American People* itself does not ever get written (Thurmond's death militating directly against the book's completion), but in the end, that is beside the point, too.

In chapter 3, I signaled a specific moment in *The Body of Martin Aguilera* in which Lewis Mason's blackness was crucial to reading a scene, specifically because the scene involved his interaction with a police officer. At that time, I said that we don't always think consciously about Lewis's race, but in that moment we had better. In that chapter I also said that one of the challenges that Everett's work poses is to create a balance in how we interact with questions of race when we encounter them in his fiction. If his work is attempting something significant, after all, with respect to the status of the African American artist, then we should tread with great self-awareness when we succumb to what otherwise might appear to be a reversion to a default subject in his work. At the same time, one would be hard pressed to find a more pervasive expression of the Oedipus in American life than race. So it is worth coming to this question, now that we have interacted with questions of the Oedipus throughout this study, from a variety of perspectives. I have held off (and even that is a telling locution) discussing race until this chapter because it has seemed more significant to me to make the overarching point as clearly as possible first and then make a case for how race fits into this overarching structure, rather than beginning with race, at which point race risks becoming that overarching structure. As I've said, simply overlooking race as a subject of discussion in Everett's work would be to fail at least one of the numerous challenges that his work poses. It would be completely reasonable (or at least conventional) to expect that—if I were to talk about race in Everett's work at all—I would talk about race earlier in this discussion, quite probably first. An African American novelist—any African-descended artist working in English, really—will be expected to have much to say about race and to foreground race in his or her work. Even expressions of Afro-futurism, expressed in popular form recently in the film *Black Panther,* will be expected to have some sort of allegorical statement to make about race as it impinges upon, constructs, or constricts the realities of the central black characters or subjects in a work of art.

The ways that even someone as polarizing as Strom Thurmond might be read as an in-between figure when re-created by Everett (with James Kincaid) emphasizes the priority that may be discerned from his work more generally, perhaps like nothing else in his considerable body of work, especially where the subject of race is concerned. Like other members of his fictional cohort,

Thurmond draws attention to his own in-betweenness, a gesture that in turn draws attention to the more generally applicable and potentially revolutionary possibilities inherent when situating him with respect to the larger world. As with Ishmael Kidder, for instance, this schizorevolutionary potential may not be entirely to our liking, but the infinite nature of the space between categories cannot help but mean that negative potentialities must necessarily be part of the equation. These characters draw attention to how conventions limit our perceptions in ways that Deleuze and Guattari would characterize as schizoid. So the question may be asked now, with this said, whether or not race as a discursive field carries within it the same revolutionary potential that any other subject might. Clearly, I will suggest here that the answer is, at least, probably. But if Deleuze and Guattari are correct in identifying family, capitalism, and sex as limiting Oedipal forces that determine our lives and maintain the paranoiac status quo that they anatomize in their work, then surely, at least within the American context, race exerts the same force, at least to the extent of any of the others. In other words, in addition to race being America's original sin, as the cliché goes, it is also America's Oedipal complex. America's racial history finds its citizens believing they are living one life when at the same time they are sowing the seeds for their own destruction. Sometimes Everett's characters appear to emphasize their eccentricity as a way almost to distract the reader from the primacy of their being black. Eccentrics like Craig Suder, Ralph Townsend, Ishmael Kidder, Ogden Walker, and to lesser extents Not Sidney Poitier, Robert Hawks, John Hunt, Lewis Mason, and Kevin Pace may all be described this way. Additionally, the un-raced nature of the Livesey family in *Cutting Lisa* (as well as Ruth, Oliver, and Lorraine, whose race is also left unspecified), not to mention the lack of racial markers of the characters in *Walk Me to the Distance,* creates some level of discomfort in a reader acculturated to anticipate black characters—and preferably *representative* black characters—from a black novelist. But this discomfort, this expectation, is again a crucial component to the challenge posed by Everett's fiction.

The number of places where a black character is identified as black because of how other characters see *him* (usually) are almost too many to keep track of in the body of Everett's work. These moments reinforce Ralph's observation in *Glyph* about who requires legitimization to exist on the page and who does not. There is an art to introducing the obvious, and Everett's novels provide innumerable examples of this art, each time drawing attention to something that others are noticing, even if the character being noticed remains only slightly less than completely uninterested. In *Assumption,* to which I will return at the end of this chapter, Ogden is situated as one of these observed characters when he asks directions to the home of Lester Robbins, who is known to local residents for his antiblack bigotry. A fellow police officer from another force instructs Ogden as he heads off to meet with Robbins, "'You should be careful over in that part of town. It's kind of rough. Especially for someone like you. Being from out of town and,' he paused, 'black like that'" (86). Ogden replies, simply, "Got you" (86). There is both art and humor in the officer's "black like that" remark, as if, on the one hand, he is telling Ogden something about his appearance of which he is unaware, and yet, on the other hand, stating something wholly obvious and needing no actual mention, except as Ogden's being black activates any number of expectations and assumptions on the part of others. The caution about the neighborhood makes sense in the context, but the officer feels the need to say something, though he cannot say anything that is less than awkward and slightly ridiculous.[8]

Like any other expression of the Oedipus, race and racial difference are reinforced because on their own they cannot exert the kind of limitation and constraint they exert on a society. This is why the expression of the obviousness of race and racial difference stands out as art in Everett's work. So when the gay son of a friend of the narrator, John, arrives for an unscheduled visit, in *Wounded,* and he brings along his opinionated, and spoiling-for-a-fight boyfriend, Robert, the scene might be predictable, but for the way the question of race is addressed:

> "Ever have any problems?" Robert asked. "With race, I mean."
>
> "Of course I have, son. This is America. I've run into bigotry here. Of course, the only place anybody ever called me nigger to my face was in Cambridge, Mass." I let that sink in. "There are plenty of stupid, narrow-minded people around. They're not hard to find. There are a lot of ignorant people, a lot of good, smart people. Is it different where you come from?" (52)[9]

One would be hard pressed to find a black person living in the United States who hasn't wanted to say such a thing to a white fellow citizen who was working up the kind of momentum that will eventually issue in a lecture on race that Robert is here. John's *mot juste* moment here is reminiscent of another French expression, *l'esprit de l'escalier,* that expression describing the moment after the fact when we come up with the perfect riposte to a slight, but only after the moment has passed. John's awareness that this is exactly the right thing to say is registered in his decision to "let that sink in." The fact that such a moment seems only to happen in novels is mitigated by John's characteristic drawing attention to the incident itself and his role in it: "I felt a little like a bully and I didn't like it. I was a bit on the defensive and I liked that even less. I made myself relax, as when on a nervous horse. I viewed it as good practice" (52). As John studies and steadies himself, as he does this imagined horse, as well as the coltish young man, he manifests another of the advantages latent in the schizoid investment. Instead of laying into the unsuspecting young know-it-all, he waits and considers his actions. But most importantly, he makes sure to mention, for our benefit, his waiting and his consideration. The paranoiac binary is destabilized by this schizoid gesture. After all, he's right. But for the schizorevolutionary there is no comfort in just being right. There is invariably something else at stake.

Another encounter in *Wounded* that does a lot of the same kind of work in terms of redescribing how race looks and may be thought about also involves John and Robert:

> "Hey, I wanted to ask you about the painting on the wall," Robert said.
> "What about it?"
> "Is it a Klee?"
> "Yep. A real little Klee." I walked over to the small canvas. "And on that other wall is a Kandinsky watercolor. But that's the extent of my art collection."
> "How much is the Klee worth?" Robert asked.
> I bristled, but not noticeably. "I never think about it. I'm sure its value goes up and down. Why? You want to buy it?" (66)

Again, the character who reduces things to some prejudged value (in this case, exchange value) looks like he is missing some larger, more important point. (Think of Maggie's friends and their reaction to Not Sidney in *I Am Not Sidney Poitier.*) Or, put another way, Robert's insistent habit of mind, in which he keeps on translating whatever he encounters into a vocabulary that he already thinks he understands cannot help but ensure that he does not learn anything new. No matter what the schizorevolutionary does or says, the paranoiac continues to see in the same way, in a sort of conspiracy against the acquisition of additional understanding. It is not difficult to see the bigot's attitude toward race (or any bigot's attitude toward the object of their bigotry) working in this way. John side-steps the confrontation by attempting to reframe it somehow, but that approach can only go so far. Eventually, he will accept this impasse and find some value or utility in it. Perhaps after a point, we are all best advised to attempt such a reso-lution when faced with a position that is locked into its paranoiac investment.

In order to argue why a black writer need not always write about race, we need first to have as clear a sense as is possible what talking about race actually requires of us. This challenge, on several different registers, is the challenge is-sued by Everett's fiction. It should be clear by now that by *talking about race*, I do not mean in the common sense that this term usually invokes, which involves trying to resolve questions of race once and for all, in the dualistic, paranoiac way that is frustrated by the complexity of the problems under examination in the first place. If *race* were so easily solved, would it not have been so by now? I mean *talking about race* in the sense that recognizes the relatively obvious but difficult to drive home point that people who are actually racialized (everyone is potentially racialized, it just doesn't always seem that way) within and by the society in which they live are actually people and not Rubik's Cubes, that—once solved—may be put in a drawer and not thought about again, at least not until company comes over, at which point they are brought out so that someone can show off his or her mastery over what had appeared to be an insoluble problem. The anachronistic sound of the invocation of the Rubik's Cube is deliberate here, since this tendentious approach to talking about race should really have passed out of intellectual and social fashion by the end of the second decade of the twenty-first century.

Race as it expresses itself in Everett's work suggests its own insolubility and conveys this insolubility not as an end to be feared or frustrated by but as a be-ginning to countless considerations about how else we might mean conventions like *race*. Put another way, race changes over time, and so approaches to it must be similarly protean, malleable, schizoid. After all, just to limit ourselves to the American environment, race under slavery means differently than it does during Reconstruction, which in turns means differently than race under Jim Crow, or race during the Civil Rights and then Black Power eras, than again it means when we consider the "postracial" paradise (remember that?) immediately following the election of America's only ("first" suggests that I expect to see others) African American president. These iterations of race carry the consistent undercurrent of white supremacy, obviously, but they are perhaps more importantly distinguished by the countless differences of social, political, ethical, and legal policy and practice in place at any of these moments, not to mention the innumerable submoments they imply.[10]

By this stage of my argument, it couldn't come as a surprise that this challenging, schizoid way is how I argue Percival Everett's novels talk about race, when they talk about it at all. Putting this qualifier another way, Everett's novels are about race the way David Foster Wallace's novels, for instance, are about race. Since race is always a reality of American life, it is a reality in the stories Americans tell, even if they are not explicitly talking about it. *Infinite Jest* isn't *about* race except in the ways that it lends itself to a reading that is inflected by race because it is written by an American and situated in the United States. One of its settings, for instance—a junior tennis academy—resonates racially in ways that are completely different from what might be the case if those same sections of the novel had been set in, say, a high school basketball summer camp. Whether we like it or not, we imaginatively picture different kids when we say "junior tennis academy" and "high school basketball summer camp," and this visualizing is overwhelmingly influenced by what we know about race and wealth in the United States and about who tends to play which sports. Maybe at issue should be less how we discuss race in art produced by African American artists, and by members of other "racialized" groups, and instead more about how we do and do not discuss how questions of race resonate in the art produced by white artists. Of course, we are unaccustomed to doing our critical work in that way—with the occasional exception of criticizing white artists for the racism in their work or personal utterances. But such accusations of *racism* still do not discuss *race*, as such.

While not about race as such, then, *Infinite Jest* does provide a simple image of how our perceptual problems constrain us—as does the Oedipus—in terms of how we do and do not think about race. In one of the scenes set in a Boston Alcoholics Anonymous group, a member tells the following anecdote: "This wise old whiskery fish swims up to three young fish and goes, 'Morning, boys, how's the water?' and swims away; and the three young fish watch him swim away and look at each other and go, 'What the fuck is water?' and swim away" (445).[11] Well, race is water in America, irrespective of whether or not an individual citizen is aware of it. The anecdote that the AA member tells gets to the heart of this issue, just as Deleuze and Guattari's formulation of the labyrinthine nature of the Oedipus does. Race is everywhere, but it's difficult—sometimes maybe even impossible—to be able to gauge its presence, because of how profoundly we are immersed in it.

Every now and again, though, it expresses itself in a way that is particularly attention-getting, or attractive, or disturbing, and we end up paying to it the attention it always warrants, but like Wallace's account of the principle of induction, we cannot or do not always pay attention, because to do so all the time would threaten our very sanity. Nevertheless, to not pay this kind of attention holds a similar threat, and what Everett's work does is require us to pay this attention to race all the time, whether or not a given story is nominally *about* race. This is the nature of the challenge issued by his work generally. In the final analysis (if such a thing were to exist, of course), the basic question asked by many of Everett's protagonists is that question that white literary characters too many to name have always asked: Who am I? In fact, much of the lineage of philosophy, literature, and art in its various expressions through European history has held this question central, while at the same time suggesting that black people did not (perhaps even could not) think about such weighty matters or at least that it didn't matter if black people were asking such questions of themselves or not, since these questions were deemed only germane to the lives of the earth's white citizens. Black subjects (objects, really) have existed as significant only as reflections of white subjectivity, a sort of Conradian penumbra, always around the edges but rarely central in their own right.[12] I say all of this to emphasize the particular conventions against which Everett's fiction attempts to work whenever the subject comes up, as he brings it up in his work, or as it is brought up by critics or reviewers. Obviously, not all art by nonblack artists treats black characters this way, and other black artists problematize these conventions as well. But these individual examples cannot erase the history of such overwhelming convention. One of the more recent instances of a moment when race appeared to be rethought in America (but wasn't, actually) was the brief moment of the *postracial* in the days after Barack Obama's election. While the moment of the postracial should never have come into existence, and has now passed and been replaced by something at least as bewildering, with the election of November 8, 2016, the idea (or ideal) of the postracial serves as an instructive illustration of one of these moments when Americans have their attention focused anew on questions of race. The vertiginous transition from postracial to its backlash provides another example of the conflict between thoughts and beliefs. This moment can also teach us about how quickly convention can begin encouraging us to stop thinking critically, or perhaps at all. Everett's novel *Assumption,* in this context, helps us understand the lengths to which we may have to go sometimes to discipline ourselves to keep thinking— or start thinking—in productive and challenging ways.

◆ ◆ ◆

Imani Perry writes, in *More Beautiful and More Terrible* (2011), "Similar to the way Michel Foucault noted that Victorian mores about sexuality offered an opportunity to talk about sex, a lot; the 'postracial' discourse reflects both anxiety and confusion about what race means and doesn't mean now. In order to answer these questions, we must approach the enterprise with great rigor and sophistication" (2–3). Perry's discussion of these expressions of anxiety and confusion points up a peculiar difficulty when instances of what might otherwise be called *racism* (had America not reached its postracial moment, of course) are encountered. Quite helpfully, Perry notes that racism "is not deterministic these days, and it is frequently unintentional or unacknowledged on the part of the actor" (7). She goes on to say of racist impulses, whether acted upon by members of groups whose race is conventionally left undiscussed or by members of explicitly racialized groups, "that the practices of inequality are a matter of our collective culture" (7) and contends that attempts to mitigate racist attitudes through appeals to intent—since "no one wants to be called/ considered a racist" (16)—miss a central point. In order to think about race in the rigorous and sophisticated ways for which she argues, "We must look to how people make decisions to treat or respond to others, not just how they are situated" (19). Perry argues for a postintentionality where matters of race and inequality are concerned. This is a "post" that might actually prove useful. Her discussion of the postracial moment is helpful in emphasizing the difference between whenever racism was less intentional and when it was casually overt and explicit, in ways we had theoretically stopped encountering during America's putative moment of postracial bliss.[13]

This postintentionality regarding race cannot help but be determined, in part at least, by convention, by the constricting Oedipal frameworks that contain so much contemporary social and political thought and interaction. It is a completely logical and even predictable evolution of race and racism that did not require the election of an African American as president, although this unlikely event did help consolidate, for some, claims about the United States having slain its racial demons. And while the notion of the postracial has passed into history just as quickly as it had first emerged, it is worthwhile to ponder, by way of this discussion of race in Everett's work, what this resonant expression has to teach us about how we engage with the conventions to which our thinking and our beliefs so often conform, especially when questions of race arise.

A return to *Assumption* is especially illuminating now. What appears to be one of the many challenges issued by Everett's fiction, especially within the context of what is better described as the *desire for the postracial,* is the mundane—although apparently fine and difficult to strike—balance between being aware that a character is black, on the one hand, while simultaneously resisting the urge to become wholly preoccupied exclusively and reductively by this fact, on the other. We make a whole previously unseen world available to us at the point when we are able to hold at bay the impulse to make race a zero-sum game, an all-or-nothing proposition that depends on some other possible experience of the world necessarily being left unnoticed. The zero-sum game is animated in part by the desire for resolution of racial questions, a desire that is perpetually frustrated by its own paranoiac investments. Instead, *Assumption* leads down a completely unexpected road that makes clear that resolution cannot be the point of such questions. What, instead, can we learn from a lack of resolution? Ogden Walker's reflections toward the end of the novel draw our attention again to the meaning that derives from the lack of resolution, leaving the Oedipus of race looking different, perhaps all the more frightening, but also encouraging new, previously unasked questions.

One expression of the entrapping force exerted by the Oedipus of race and all of its limiting implications, as well as of the somewhat absurd consequences that follow from them, appears in a review of *Assumption* from the *Wall Street Journal*. First, the reviewer makes the following summary statement about the novel: "Mr. Everett's resistance to classification is most pronounced in his brilliant and often cathartically refreshing treatment of race and identity. He likes to introduce a character as black, tease out the reader's expectations of what that label means, and then either subvert such expectations or satirize them by way of startling exaggerations" (Sacks). Although reductive in the way that reviews sometimes must be, there is not too much to be bothered by here. It is later in the review where we run into problems, when the following statement is made, describing the organization of *Assumption,* and specifically how Ogden Walker appears in each section: "But in the second section—about a drug heist gone wrong that contains such mystery-novel archetypes as a one-armed villain and a daring escape from a moving van—Ogden's race is never mentioned as he investigates the crime; race is treated as irrelevant to his character." The assertion that "race is treated as irrelevant" to Ogden's character is the desire for the postracial on full display, trailing along with it the inevitably illogical implications of that desire. In similar ways that the desire for the postracial leads to counterfactual conclusions about the world in which we live, its history and its prospective future, this desire cannot help but result in insupportable readings, based solely in this irrational and tendentious desire. Again, race is like water. It doesn't just evaporate at the point when some readers happen not to have it drawn explicitly to their attention. It's still there. More to the point, we are all *always* swimming in it.

This kind of reading is probably best described by Judith Roof's exacting phrase "reverse reader response criticism" as she writes about how Everett's fiction manipulates readerly and writerly perspective: "And the ways that the narrator construction goes about simultaneously evading and reconstructing the performance of this *what* as a black, not-only-black, not-quite-black, so-what-if-black vibration that calls attention to the odd assumptions about race, genre, and style that wish always to cage the 'what,' in favor of the comforting 'we know who you are so tell us again' demand. This is a species of reverse reader response criticism, where the novel, having anticipated certain pleasures, refuses them" ("Mr. Everett," 42; emphasis in original). And while we have to concede that there is pleasure in having these assumptions satisfied, there is something at least as important, and perhaps more constructive, in having them artfully refused, if only so that we may review those assumptions through new lenses.

For its adherents, the age of the postracial was generally ushered in by the election of Barack Obama, although its specific genesis might be pinpointed to a particular moment. During his victory speech at Grant Park in Chicago on the night of November 4, 2008, Obama issues the following memorable proclamation: "It's been a long time coming, but tonight, because of what we did on this date in this election at this defining moment, change has come to America" (135). The declarative *that's that* tone of this statement encouraged for many the belief that with this one man's election, all was done. America's long racial nightmare was over. But, as with any *post*, there must be some antecedent, and for Eric Sundquist, that antecedent is the period following the 1954 *Brown v. Board of Education* decision. Sundquist, in discussing Obama's famous race speech of March 18, 2008, in Philadelphia, in the wake of a controversy over statements made by Obama's then pastor, Jeremiah Wright, points out: "Questions that have reached a stalemate, however, are questions that have yet to be answered. For all that Obama's diffusing the issue of race might seem to imply about an end to the post-*Brown* age, his choice to designate himself 'black'— and black alone—in the 2010 Census acknowledged that a national dilemma centuries in the making could not be resolved by one exceptional man's life story and aspirations, still less by one campaign-saving speech" (120). We might reasonably add that these stalemated questions have also not been resolved as a result of one exceptional man's election, even to the office of the president.[14] But it is from these stalemated questions, and that exceptional man's declaration and election, that the desire for the postracial gains momentum. Sundquist's use of the metaphor of the stalemate seems exactly right here, since the stalemate resolves nothing, but the two sides may play again.

Paul Gilroy speaks of "raciological thinking" in his book *After Empire,* and this idea carries significant weight in a consideration of how the desire for the postracial interferes with the ability of some to see and interpret the world, part of which is the ability to read. Gilroy writes:

> When the idea of "race" becomes a concept, it poses clear and incompatible alternatives. Once we comprehend racism's alchemical power, we do have to choose. We can opt to reproduce the obligations of racial observance, negoti-

ating them but basically accepting the idea of racial hierarchy and then, inescapably, reifying it. Or there is a second and far more difficult and rewarding alternative, in which for clearly defined moral and perhaps political reasons we try to break its spell and to detonate the historic lore that brings the virtual realities of "race" to such dismal and destructive life. (33–34)[15]

While Gilroy's formulation initially suggests a simple binary, it quickly becomes clear that he is describing the distinction between the paranoiac and the schizophrenic. The racial hierarchy and reification option is that of the paranoiac, arborescent, Oedipal thinker, while the one that attempts detonation and the breaking of spells is the schizorevolutionary. Detonation opens up the potentially infinite space. It is this latter position that Gilroy identifies as far more difficult, for what are, by now, obvious enough reasons. Call it the difference between thoughts and beliefs, call it desire, call it the quest for advantages in this stage of capitalism. Whatever it is, beliefs in racial superiority and a willingness to tolerate racial injustice through the moral exclusion of others inevitably comes with some sort of rationale, and some sort of payoff, which justifies the reproduction of the "obligations of racial observance," as Gilroy puts it. Gilroy's discussion of race as a concept points up the kind of tensions (he calls them "incompatible alternatives") that Adele Perry relates in her definition of race: "Race is a social construct that changes over time and across place. It has no physical or biological meaning, and its social meanings are always unstable and often subtle. But in the modern world carved out by capitalism, imperialism, and its attendant modes of thought, race has had palpable and enormously consequential meaning for individuals and the communities they reside and make meaning within. Race can include identities and experiences that we might otherwise register as the terrain of ethnicity, religion, or nation" (58). In theory, then, race means nothing; in practice, however, it "remains the self-evident force of nature in society," as Gilroy says, before continuing, "Our being resigned to it supports enabling analogies and provides legitimation in a host of historical situations where natural difference and social division are politically, economically, and militarily mediated" (*After Empire* 9). All of this discussion describes race as an ongoing trap or matrix of traps, culs-de-sac, nightmare boxes, and conundrums, which leave the subject seemingly without possible resolution. Race is both present and absent, another expression of Zeno's paradoxes, in which it is potentially infinite (a social construct) but actually very specific (palpable and enormously consequential). Monk Ellison characteristically suggests what might be called a conscious resignation in acknowledging the realities of race that give voice to the schizorevolutionary potential that I find central to Everett's work: "The hard, *gritty* truth of the matter is that I hardly ever think about race. Those times when I did think about it a lot I did so because of my guilt for not thinking about it. I don't believe in race. I believe there are people who will shoot me or hang me or cheat me and try to stop me because they do believe in race, because of my brown skin, curly hair, wide nose and slave ancestors. But that's just the way it is" (2). The "that's just the way it is" conclusion to this set of paradoxical observations may be as close as we honestly get when thinking about race, or whatever the subject is that stops us in our ethical tracks, that subject that does not allow us to be the conscious observers that Gilroy recommends that we be, and that Deleuze and Guattari insist is at the heart of the schizoid investment. Monk situates himself along that infinite continuum between the poles of the destructive racist he describes and some blithe ignorance in which someone, even for a moment, might forget the dire potential if he or she forgets that race is "the way it is." In the light of Monk's observation, the desire for the postracial emerges as not based on observation, historical happenstance, or, indeed, anything quantifiably material. The desire for the postracial is like any belief. It derives from the believer's need to believe, and belief as opposed to thought, as Thurmond (of all people) points out. The result itself is a belief that reinscribes the conditions that enable the believer to believe. This is pretty much exactly how Seth Morton describes the flaw in the ontological argument, a conundrum to which Everett's work return several times. The ontological argument "first defines god as 'that which none greater can be conceived' and then induces that because being is inherently greater than nonbeing, god, following the earlier definition, must exist. This smart piece of logic works perfectly when limited to its own linguistic frame— the proposed definition for god—but breaks down when one supposes any other frame" (198). Perhaps, like the schizoid in Deleuze and Guattari's sense, our responsibility is to spend our lives breaking down frames rather than investing in them.

This characterization of the desire for the postracial as a belief brings us back to the challenges to the "obligations of racial observance" that *Assumption* poses, and what might be read as instructions on how to meet the novel's challenges, as well as those it subtly poses to the society out of which it emerges. As I discussed in chapter 2, Ogden negotiates the tense scene with Mrs. Bickers—she is, remember, a good enough shot to have put two bullets through the same hole in her front door—quite skillfully, considering his sense of her prejudice toward him. His sense is just that, a sense, as we are later told: "Maybe she was acting strange simply because she was strange, because she had never liked Ogden's skin color, though she had never said as much" (9). His father's attitudes about race make the issue all the more complicated. Ogden remembers his father's attitudes "tinged with the language of race and social indignation" (13) and recalls that his father "moved to New Mexico from Maryland because there were fewer people and so, necessarily, fewer white people" (13). And finally, his father "hated white people, but not enough to refrain from marrying one" (13). Ogden finds it difficult "to think that his father hated half of him" (13). This possibly half-hateful relationship with his father situates Ogden where we find a lot of Everett's protagonists, unstably in between categories, even if that means occupying a space on the continuum between being loved and hated by one's own father.[16] All of this information is provided within the first few pages of the novel's first section, the (in retrospect) perfectly titled "A Difficult Likeness."

The second section of *Assumption,* titled "My American Cousin," is the section in which race is apparently irrelevant according to the review from the *Wall Street Journal* that I've already quoted. As the reviewer states, this irrelevancy results from Ogden's race not being "mentioned" in this section. But apart from the fact that the character has the same name, works at the same job in the same New Mexico town, we are also told he has the same mother—"Ogden Walker. Eva's son" (105)—as he confirms his identity for the police detective, Maggie Muddy, early on. In other words, we are not in the position of distinguishing the Percival Everett character in *A History of the African-American People* or in *I Am Not Sidney Poitier* from Percival Everett, the visual artist, fly-fisherman, dog and horse trainer, novelist, and university professor. Ogden Walker is not a ghostly echo, like Robert Hawks or Warren Fragua, and once we discover who he really is, his uniqueness may even register as a source of comfort. If it has been different black men all named Ogden Walker killing all these people, the novel is more about the weight of coincidence than it is about what is left unresolved at its end.[17]

In addition, while Ogden's race is not mentioned explicitly, it is mentioned obliquely by being gestured at in contradistinction to other characters. For instance, the following exchange he has with an unnamed motel clerk:

> "What does he look like?" Ogden asked.
> "Normal enough looking fellow. About your height. White guy. Light brown hair. Blue eyes." (123–24)

It's only after this description, and Ogden asks her if there is anything else that she remembers about him—to which she replies with the man's California license plate number, "5QTH769. I think it was a rental" (124)—that the clerk finally volunteers, "Did I mention he had only one hand?" (124). While it is true that black people can have light brown hair, and blue eyes, the description of the "normal enough looking fellow" makes clear that the addressee (Ogden) is, at the very least, not white; otherwise, convention would dictate that the whiteness of the one-handed man under discussion would not have warranted mentioning at all.

In another exchange, Ogden adopts the descriptive role, as he speaks to two unenthusiastic security guards in a casino: "Did a guy come through here with only one hand? White guy, brown hair, my size?" (129). Again, Ogden's nonwhiteness serves as a point of departure to describe the man he searches for. His race is instrumentally relevant to the scene, even as he searches for someone with a considerably more obvious and distinguishing physical characteristic than his race. The man only has one hand. The man's uncommon physical characteristic, however, does not tap into a centuries-old anxiety that might—with the election of November 4, 2008—finally have been put to rest for some of the members of the American populace.

All reviewers are not the same, of course. In fact, one particularly astute reviewer—Gregory Leon Miller—points up another of the ghostly echoes that recur in Everett's work: "Our assumptions are also upended by the novel's structure, whose three sections aren't connected in any conventionally satisfying sense. Some readers may see the book as a trio of related stories (in fact, Everett has embedded a revision of his nearly 20-year-old story, 'Warm and Nicely Buried,' into the first part)" (3). This identification of an earlier Everett text is very satisfying, even if the reviewer's desire for conventional narrative connections between the three parts of *Assumption* is not. But conventions soothe us in ways that resistance to convention does not. And even when convention makes an appearance during its own resistance, we may not recognize it because it doesn't appear in a conventional venue or form. After all, the arrangement of three related stories featuring the same central character is very familiar if we think in terms of police procedurals rather than what we expect from the novel form.

Ogden Walker is one of Everett's most fascinating creations, precisely in the ways that he enacts resistance to convention while introducing numerous aspects of the convention his character resists. He is not the sheriff, he's the deputy. He's the only black character in the novel, of any note, and he is actually biracial. As we're told, his mother is white. He mentions enough times that he's not necessarily very good at his job, although he appears committed enough to it, even driven by it. He doesn't fit in even with the unusual cops around him, in the manner of Lem Becker, the main police officer in *The Body of Martin Aguilera*. More than this, he appears motivated by an almost overdeveloped sense of right and wrong, which only complicates further the revelations about his crimes at the novel's end. This characteristic is commented upon by both Detective Hailey Barry and Warren Fragua, each of whom refers to him as having a messiah complex. Ogden puts one in mind of the version of Robert Hawks who appears in "Alluvial Deposits," in the collection *Damned If I Do* (the ghostly echo of the version who appears in *Watershed* [1996]), who also has bigger things on his mind than how other people see him, see race, or see race through him. Reflecting on his status as an oddity in Dotson, Utah, the town to where he has driven as part of some contract work for the Utah Department of Agriculture and the Fish and Game Commission, the Hawks of "Alluvial Deposits" thinks to himself: "For reasons too familiar and too tiresome to discuss, I was a great source of interest as I idled at the town's only traffic signal" (41–42). This statement enacts the kind of complex resistance to raciological thinking (Gilroy's expression) that confounds the need for resolution so paradoxically inherent in the desire for the postracial. Believers in the postracial think about race so that they will no longer have to think about race.[18]

For all of his ostensible detachment, though—from his sense of race, from his occupation, from his deceased father, from the region of the country in which he lives, from himself, finally—Ogden searches, looking for something, which turns out to be some version of himself, as the original Oedipus story has it, as it turns out that he is responsible for the murder of at least five people in the book, quite probably all of them, before Warren finally figures this out. Perhaps what is so terrifying about *Assumption* (not to mention our assumptions) is that where Ogden leads us by the end of the novel does not, in fact, resolve anything. This lack of resolution is completely, eerily, uncannily believable and makes complete sense with regard to the approach to race in Everett's fiction in particular and the overall approach to questions of category, convention, and the continuum between categories along which we live our lives. As Warren asks Ogden why he's killed all of these people, Ogden replies with a stream of his consciousness that is disjointed, harrowing, taunting, and refusing to provide resolution. I quoted a bit of this passage in chapter 2, but the paragraph warrants full inclusion here:

> Of course it doesn't make sense. What does make sense, Warren? Nothing in this damn world makes sense. Just look around. I'm out of my fucking mind. I must be. What do you think? Does that have it all make sense for you? I'm an evil man. *Live* is *evil* spelled backward or is it the other way around? I'm evil. I suppose that's what they'll say. I'm possessed by the devil, *lived* spelled backward. Does that have it make sense? I wanted some drug money. I'm hooked on meth. Do any of those reasons help this make sense? I was tired of being a good guy. Was I ever a good guy? How about that? Does that have it make sense for you? This is the way it is, Warren, simply the way it fucking is. Sad, sad, sad, sad, sad. Shitty, shitty, bang, bang. Nothing makes sense and that's the only way that any of it makes sense. Here I am, the way I am, not making any sense. Blood in the water. Blood on my shirt. (224–25)

The barrage of questions heightens the realization that there is no definitive answer. Life is like that. Race is like that. We do the best we can, and sometimes we don't. This is not nihilism. It is, however, also available from the notion of the schizoid. As we find in Ishmael Kidder, the schizorevolutionary potential may issue in ways that we do not like. But the negative potential must be part of the revolutionary potential. Ogden does some very good work in the novel, until, for his own reasons, he doesn't anymore. Warren's need to be given an answer, any answer, mimics the desire of "them" to ascribe Ogden's motivations and actions to insanity or addiction or metaphysics. This need to ascribe also mimics the desire for the postracial. It's not really about understanding at all. It's about some palliative belief, even if wholly inadequate, a gesture that can mask our lack of understanding and rescue us from having to face that lack of understanding, like the way we distract ourselves to preclude our reflecting on whether or not our bedroom floor will bear our weight this morning. It is not surprising that we distract ourselves from what Gilroy calls the "self-evident force of nature in society"—as he describes race—and what I'm identifying as the most American of Oedipal investments.

Perhaps the only salve that Everett leaves us by the end of *Assumption* is Ogden's death. At least he can't kill anyone else. Even though he is *only* a fictional character, this is still a relief because of how we turn fictional characters into people when we read. But Ogden's death ensures that we cannot find out why he did what he did. We will have to come up with some reason for it ourselves, and this deriving of our own answer may, if we're willing, take us through some of the uncomfortable terrain we usually try to avoid. But that, ultimately, is the point. Sometimes we cannot understand things. Ogden's final speech is a gesture of honesty that highlights the pointlessness of the desire for the postracial, a desire to resolve something we cannot definitively understand. But just because we cannot understand definitively does not mean we should give up in our continued quest for understanding, however provisional. Strangely, this is what Thurmond teaches us in his way, and Walker in his.

CONCLUSIONS
The Enduring Presence of Alternative Possibilities

Sometimes just making yourself at home is revolutionary.
   —Paul Beatty, *Slumberland*

But the irony was beautiful. I was a victim of racism by virtue of my failing to acknowledge racial difference and by failing to have my art be defined as an exercise in
racial self-expression. So, I would not be economically oppressed because of writing
a book that fell in line with the very books I deemed racist. And I would have to wear
the mask of the person I was expected to be. I had already talked on the phone with
my editor as the infamous Stagg Leigh and now I would meet with Wiley Morgen-
stern. I could do it. The game was becoming fun. And it was nice to get a check.
   —*Erasure*

As any work of criticism can only be partial and selective, so is any gesture at
conclusion. The only way to cover everything said and implied in a book-length
argument would be to repeat the entire text, word for word, running the risk of
turning the book itself into something approaching an Ionesco play. So, since
such a gesture is obviated by the prospect of revisiting parts of the book, I will
attempt here to draw out a few of the implications of what I've argued over
the course of these pages, in order to suggest something summative about my
argument as a whole.

   In a 2012 post titled "What Could a New Anthology of American Literature
Look Like?" in the *American Studies* blog, *Questions, Problems, Provocations*, Werner Sollors presented the following speculation:

In currently available anthologies of American literature there appears to be a general double standard at work, as "general American" texts by "mainstream authors" are selected primarily for their aesthetic accomplishment and historical-political significance as well as for the cultural fascination they hold, whereas African American, multiethnic, and many women's works are chosen primarily for their authenticity.

That means that a particular burden is placed upon authors included to represent racial, ethnic, or gender categories: their texts must not only be authored *by* members of these groupings (which is why it is so embarrassing when a false ethnic or gender ascription is discovered), but their works are also expected to be mostly *about* themes of race, ethnicity, and (perhaps to a slightly less intense degree) gender. (emphasis in original)

Sollors points up the double standard–cum-convention that it is difficult not to have gotten used to at some stage of one's development as a reader, critic, or artist who is a member of one of the groups he identifies as subject to the double standard. The work of straight white male artists is evaluated on its ability to produce something that we've never seen before, carrying the aesthetic, historical-political, and cultural fascination of which Sollors speaks in its unusualness, its novelty, all of which tends to be interpreted as *brilliance* or *genius.* By contrast, African American, multiethnic, and female artists, not to mention those artists who do not conform to conventional gender binaries, are responsible for creating the exact opposite effect. They are to produce work that we have seen before, work that purports to represent and reproduce the condition on which the conventions are established in the first place, what Sollors refers to as *authenticity.*[1] Within the world of establishing the canon of African American literature this dynamic appears to be at work and may even help explain why no text by Everett has ever appeared in the *Norton Anthology of African American Literature,* which is now in its third edition. We can all agree that Everett's work makes no claims to authenticity. An artist's willingness to shed a sometimes mocking light on the conventions and their adherents might contribute to such an omission. But more than this, the desire for such representativeness as a condition of acceptance for minoritized artists is another expression of what underlies the desire for the postracial, which is some resolution of the American problem of/with race. This Oedipal desire cannot help but carry substantial weight with it, and an artist whose project appears motivated primarily by a refusal to accede to this desire, and moreover, by drawing attention not only to this refusal but to the folly of those who persist in it, will continue to have a difficult time finding a place within that convention-bound space. But again, that refusal also conveys meaning.

Sollors draws attention to the Oedipal nature of the conventions that continue to dictate how literature anthologies look and make their selections. But the anticonventional implications of what he says imply at least the prospect of how else these anthologies might look and selections might be made. When we remember Daniel W. Smith's observations about the relationship between aesthetic judgments and moral judgments,[2] further implications of these double standards emerge as well. It's easy to be put in mind of the cogitations of Flann O'Brien's narrator at the beginning of *At Swim-Two-Birds:* "One beginning and one ending for a book is a thing I did not agree with. A good book may have three openings entirely dissimilar and inter-related only in the prescience of the author, or for that matter one hundred times as many endings" (9). Again, as Deleuze and Guattari have established, so much of what we do we do out of habit, purely out of habit. And if we're not careful, these habits will determine how we begin and end novels as well as how we select novels or any other literary texts for anthologies as they often do. No doubt, we can see resistance to these habits in many of Everett's characters. Ralph certainly might feel similarly to how O'Brien's narrator feels, as might Ishmael, Monk, and both the father and son in *Percival Everett by Virgil Russell.* It is equally imaginable that Deleuze and Guattari might have written O'Brien's words, expressing in yet another way how we are tormented by the Oedipus of our existence, irrespective of which specifically it might be. While writing a conclusion does accede to the sorts of conventions that the rest of this discussion has argued that Everett's work challenges, conventions that I am obviously arguing require such challenge, it is nevertheless worthwhile considering at this stage some of the implications of what has led up to this conclusion. O'Brien's narrator invites a further opening up of possibilities, a further imagining of challenges in terms of how we might picture and engage with some of the most oppressive of conventions and, as a result, perceive our world completely differently. Again, none of these possibilities come with any guarantees. Sometimes the freed dog gets shot by the neighbor, but at least the dog is free to be shot. Sometimes the sheriff's deputy is the murderer, but at least we are spared yet another crime drama, where the good guy prevails, leaving us further inured to how stories are told.

To consider some of these alternatives, I should stress here that Everett is hardly the only African American writer working in anticonventional ways. In fact, the second decade of the twenty-first century has witnessed something of a renaissance in the work of and recognition for specifically African American male writers, with Paul Beatty and Colson Whitehead winning major literary prizes for their fiction and Ta-Nehisi Coates garnering so much attention for his nonfiction that he spent some time as the target of negative attention from Cornel West, who in another moment occupied a position very similar to Coates's now. The fact that Everett continues to spurn the kind of attention that has become almost commonplace for some other male African American writers suggests something almost random about this attention, although the arc of his work may also suggest that as the mainstream acknowledges the margins, resistance dictates a further exploration of new margins. And so on.

◆ ◆ ◆

The differences between Paul Beatty's approach to fiction and Everett's illustrate what is available once the artist from the marginalized group determines to establish his or her own terms for his or her work's aesthetic value. To take one example: while numerous Everett characters comment lovingly upon the beauty of the American West (and except for the West, it is difficult to think of a lot of places that matter in Everett's fiction *as places*), Beatty's work explicitly calls up the meaning of or inherent in cities. Los Angeles plays a significant role in *The White Boy Shuffle, Tuff,* and *The Sellout,* for instance, as does Berlin in *Slumberland.* This latter novel is useful in demonstrating what makes Beatty's work distinctive, but also how understanding conventions' innumerable effects on us can engage us in necessary rethinking.

Beatty brings back to mind the notion of the anti–double consciousness that I argue is characteristic of Everett's work. While I have held off quoting Du Bois's paradigmatic coinage from *The Souls of Black Folk* until now, it does bear inclusion:

After the Egyptian and Indian, the Greek and Roman, the Teuton and Mongolian, the Negro is a sort of seventh son, born with a veil, and gifted with second-sight in this American world,—a world which yields him no true self-consciousness, but only lets him see himself through the revelation of the other world. It is a peculiar sensation, this double-consciousness, this sense of always looking at one's self through the eyes of others, of measuring one's soul by the tape of a world that looks on in amused contempt and pity. One ever feels his two-ness,—an American, a Negro; two souls, two thoughts, two unreconciled strivings; two warring ideals in one dark body, whose dogged strength alone keeps it from being torn asunder. (689)

Du Bois writes this familiar passage under a national, ontological imperative that says that white Americans (and African Americans) need to have it explained to them that African Americans are in fact human in the same ways that white Americans are human. This was an argument and an assertion that needed making at the time, not that it did a whole lot of good, but the circumstances dictated that it was better to be making the argument than not.

Beatty, in his way, is declaring in his fiction his outright rejection of the notion of double consciousness, specifically of its explanatory function. He is saying that the time has passed for such explanations and that one avenue through which to express this passage of time is art. He does not presume to speak as the *voice of African Americans,* since such a presumption would wholly undermine this rejection of Du Bois's explanatory formulation, at least tacitly lending credence to the impulse toward some totalizing explanation of African American life, experience, ontology, really. Instead his work suggests something more anarchic, more free, perhaps even more utopian.

What we get instead from Beatty is representations of what the African American self-consciousness that Du Bois posits as unattainable when he's writing might look like when rendered artistically in the twenty-first century. This is a self-consciousness that Beatty asserts forcibly and without concern for his work being measured by any tape other than that of his own choosing. Those who *get* Beatty's work get it not because of any explanatory concessions it makes, for it makes very few, if any. They get it because of their willingness to accept the challenge that his work lays down, on its own terms. In other words, the onus is on his reader at least as much as it is on him as artist.

And whereas the so-called voice of black America tends to sound from a quite limited, even prerevolutionary, place, and in quite narrowly circumscribed ways, the rejection of Du Bois's coinage is, by definition, infinite, and often unexpected. Ferguson Sowell, for instance, at the beginning of *Slumberland*, makes the following declaration: "You would think they'd be used to me by now. I mean, don't they know that after fourteen hundred years the charade of blackness is over? That we blacks, the once eternally hip, the people who were as right now as Greenwich Mean Time, are, as of today, as yesterday as stone tools, the velocipede, and the paper straw all rolled into one? The Negro is now officially human" (3). What Sowell states, at the same time matter-of-factly and portentously, is that black people are human, just like everyone else, that this news is no big deal, and that anyone who can't recognize this simple fact is dealing with their own impediments to the obvious reality. His use of "the Negro" as his nomenclature of choice resonates at least as far back as Du Bois and highlights the rejection of Du Bois's formulation, or at least the grounds upon which that formulation was based.

Beatty's invention of Sowell's auditory affliction, a phonographic memory, helps further articulate what is going on in *Slumberland*, since Sowell is, by definition, fixated with sounds, whether musical or lexical—the latter involving coming up with words for phenomena that exist but have yet to be named. In a way, he is appositely placed to try to name, and from there possibly resolve, the paradox of his own existence. Again, as Du Bois put it, "How does it feel to be a problem?" The problem, long-standing in America, is the humanity of the African American. But instead of resolving the problem on the terms dictated by others, Sowell seizes upon his own interests, some of which cannot help but run counter to the interests of those still mired in the terms established by Du Bois's turn-of-the-twentieth-century formulation.

Sowell's phonographic and lexical compulsions bring him into conflict with the senior editor of the *Kensington-Merriwether Dictionary of Standard American English*, Cutter Pinchbeck III, because, according to Pinchbeck, the neologisms Sowell tends to suggest to him do not possess the "straight, gully, niggerish perspicuity" of entries like "*badonkadonk, bling, bootylicious, dead presidents, hoodrat, peeps,* and *swol*" (14). The ways in which these words transit through popular culture, and specifically through the hip-hop most associated with African American artists, makes clear that Pinchbeck's animating philosophy concerning which neologisms to introduce into his dictionary continues to rely upon the versions of African American expression that are most reliably salable to white Americans, like Pinchbeck himself.

Sowell, by contrast, is more concerned with a "series of English words for 'the day before yesterday'" (15). He considers and rejects "*penultidiem . . . prepretoday . . . yonyesterday*" (15) before landing, with genuine excitement, upon "Retrothence!" (15). It is perhaps telling that Cutter Pinchbeck III (whose very name cannot help but conjure quite specific mental images of moneyed white America) is the editor of a dictionary, since he clearly still needs definitions like *double consciousness* and probably relies on others of similarly unexamined or anachronistic provenance in order to make sense of the world around him. Sowell does not need such definitions, or at least not in the ways Pinchbeck does, and can light out for new intellectual and artistic territories, irrespective of whether Pinchbeck and others of his ilk recognize his right to do so or not.

Whereas his lexical obsession centers primarily on Pinchbeck, Sowell's musical obsession is most clearly expressed in the character he travels to Berlin to find. Charles Stone has been nicknamed the Schwa by Sowell and his dj contemporaries because his sound "like the indeterminate vowel, is unstressed, upside-down, and backward. Indefinable, but you know it when you hear it" (36).[3] It is this last part—indefinable, but you know it when you hear it—that captures the sense of the infinite in Beatty's work. The challenge is not to make the one thing into the other, to translate one set of cultural associations so as to be legible to those arriving with a contemptuous and pitying set of associations (to return to Du Bois's formulation) but instead to recognize it when you see it, as laid out on its own terms.

Du Bois emerges with the notion of double consciousness at a time when a desire to explain black people to white people, and perhaps black people to themselves, is completely understandable. The prospect of someone in a position of some authority to be able to tell black people, *You're not crazy. This is actually happening to you,* was necessary at a time even before many southern blacks began what has come to be known as the Great Migration, the extended pilgrimage across time and space that articulated the desire of a large group of people to assert for themselves the kind of treatment, freedoms, and humanity they knew they deserved, and that their nation had putatively promised them.

Beatty's novel articulates the challenges that his work lays down for his reader in ways that highlight what is at stake when one must argue for one's humanity when immersed in a world established on premises that only undermine, diminish, and reject that humanity. Part of what happens is existential, part philosophical, part psychological. In *Slumberland*, once Sowell finds the Schwa, he makes the great man available to all who wish to pay homage. Charles Stone, the Schwa, is "a well-respected musician proficient in the improvisational techniques of the free-jazz movement of whom little is known" (37), as his "scant entry" (37) in *The Jazz Encyclopedia* describes him. Sowell acknowledges that he admires aesthetes like Stone "for withdrawing into themselves knowing they have nothing further to say, and even less desire to hear what anyone has to say to them" (39). This withdrawal starts to sound like a version of the self-possession Du Bois laments as lacking for African Americans. As others pay the Schwa the obeisance that Sowell and his small group of contemporaries feel is his due, Sowell also has a moment to reflect on where Stone has been and what the world requires of men like him:

> Those men of my father's generation, especially the black men, were a different breed. Fiercely independent, brilliant, and slightly touched, they were the type who'd represent themselves in court—and win. Children of the civil rights movement, they were the first generation of African-Americans with the freedom to fail without having to suffer serious consequences. They're the Negronauts the black race sent off into the unexplored vastness of manumission.
>
> Race, the final frontier. These are the voyages of the mother ship Free Enterprise. Its five-hundred-year mission: to explore strange, new, previously segregated worlds, to seek out new life and new civilizations, to boldly go where no niggers had gone before. (162)

The chronology from Du Bois through Stone to Ferguson Sowell (by way of a revision of the introduction to the *Star Trek* television series) is, here, acknowledged in terms of what the chronology itself has cost those who have embarked upon it over time.

But the question of chronology is, characteristically, not a simple one. The touchstone example, to which the narrative devotes a lengthy and eviscerating critique, of much that is wrong with how the story of African American culture has conventionally been told, is a musician born in 1961, making him almost thirty years younger than the Schwa: "I hate Wynton Marsalis in the same manner Rommel hated Hitler. Whenever I hear Marsalis's trumpet playing I feel like the Desert Fox forced to come to grips with the consequences of totalitarianism after the war has been all but lost. At least Rommel had Wagner. All I've got is Wynton. His musical Valkyries arrive not on winged steeds but astride caged birds" (96). Sowell describes listening to Marsalis's music as something approaching a tedious ordeal: "The song labored on, Wynton's band, like the critics, playing in the past tense" (97). Whereas Marsalis, "New Orleans born and New York praised, is jazz's most famous living musician" (95), Sowell cannot help but heap opprobrium upon Marsalis's music for what he sees as its pretension and presumption, primarily regarding an explanatory and representative posture that it conveys: "The tune, like most contrivances of the black telegentsia, seemed lost, a corny cacophonic search among the ruins of a romanticized African history for a self-affirming excuse to love being black" (95). Clearly, an excuse to love being black is not the same as loving being black. The juxtaposition of Marsalis and the Schwa about who tells the stories that matter about African Americans resolves itself when Sowell declares the terms on which he sees this musical debate being fought: "The existentialists say the flap of a butterfly's wings in the jungles of Mauritania can cause a hurricane in the plains of Kansas, but a high C from Wynton Marsalis's trumpet doesn't even change your mood, much less your mind. And I don't know whether or not Marsalis's music is an allegory for race, American democracy, or black fascism, but I do know the Schwa's music is anarchy. It's Somalia. It's the Department of Motor Vehicles. It's Albert Einstein's hair" (97). Marsalis's double consciousness–inflected musical orthodoxy stands in the sharpest possible contrast to the "Do your thing, motherfucker" (226) unpredictability of the Schwa. Doing *your* thing, as opposed to the thing that others dictate you do is, for Sowell, the test that he establishes, that the Schwa passes, and Marsalis abjectly fails.

That Sowell himself is not a musician in the traditional sense but a dj, who moves to Berlin to become a jukebox sommelier at the Slumberland bar, in the service of finding the Schwa, articulates another mode of musical expression, holding at bay the easy binary of the purism of Marsalis and the anarchy of Stone. The hybrid musical status of Sowell, whose stage name is DJ Darky,[4] invites us to consider the limitlessness of the possibilities between purist and anarchist, necessarily acknowledging the prospect of inventions not yet in existence, as rap was before the 1970s, or perhaps the 1940s, depending on how we feel about Louis Armstrong. How the stories get told literarily is also under pressure in *Slumberland,* as evidenced in part by Beatty's reliance upon his own auditory symbology, which necessitates the recognition of different allusions that members of different parts of his readership will not necessarily be able to identify: "For us the Schwa is the ultimate break beat. The boom bip. The *oo-ee oo ah ah ting tang walla walla bing bang.* The *om.* He's the part in Pagliacci where the fucking clown starts crying" (36). The allusions we recognize, instead of indulging our sense of self-congratulation and reassuring our sense of the breadth of our own knowledge, should immerse us in a wave of humility and uncertainty, since any allusion that we recognize should draw our attention to the very real prospect of the numberless allusions that we are not recognizing and, which, by definition, we are not recognizing that we are not recognizing. The sweep of allusive space that Beatty's work comprehends leaves it all but inevitable that we will encounter something that we know refers to something else without our knowing what that something else is. The establishment of what appears at times to be a private language asserts that Beatty's novel does not succumb to the conventional demands upon African American art.

Beatty's 2015 novel, *The Sellout,* opens with as blatant a gesture as possible toward the sorts of expectations that lead to the kind of double consciousness that Du Bois describes and that Beatty's work rejects. The narrator, who is in the US Supreme Court as the novel begins, is waiting for the court to hear arguments involving the vast legal implications of his having enslaved an older black man and reinstated racial segregation on public conveyances and in the public school system in present-day Los Angeles. As in *Slumberland, The Sellout*'s first words are not just introductory, but revelatory: "This may be hard to believe, coming from a black man, but I've never stolen anything. Never cheated on my taxes or at cards. Never snuck into the movies or failed to give back the extra change to a drugstore cashier indifferent to the ways of mercantilism and minimum-wage expectations. I've never burgled a house. Held up a liquor store. Never boarded a crowded bus or subway car, sat in a seat reserved for the elderly, pulled out my gigantic penis and masturbated to satisfaction with a perverted, yet somehow crestfallen, look on my face" (3). *The Sellout* registers from the beginning the perversely comic potential available to the African American artist at the time that artist is able to see as humorous instead of oppressive the doubly conscious viewing of African American subjectivity.

Beatty's novel meanders its way to a telling apotheosis, in which the narrator's lawyer, Hampton Fiske, enumerates three stages of blackness to the court: "Stage I is the Neophyte Negro. Here the black person exists in a state of preconsciousness" (275). The narrative returns again here to Du Bois. The Neophyte Negro occupies a position that shows "how self-hatred can compel one to value mainstream acceptance over self-respect and morality" (275). If this isn't looking at oneself through the eyes of others, it is difficult to imagine what is. "The distinguishing feature of Stage II blackness is a heightened awareness of race," the court is told. "Here race is still all-consuming, but in a more positive fashion" (276). Hampton Fiske—whose name conjoins the names of two historically black colleges, in its own gesture toward a historical blackness, and conjures a convention-bound mental image at least as reliably as does the name Cutter Pinchbeck III—moves on to Stage III blackness, which he calls "Race Transcendentalism. A collective consciousness that fights oppression and seeks serenity" (276). This is where Fiske's typology really gets interesting: "Examples of Stage III black folks are people like Rosa Parks, Harriet Tubman, Sitting Bull, César Chávez, Ichiro Suzuki" (277). This list puts one in mind of the way Deleuze and Guattari use *blackness* to include John Brown and connote in *blackness* something beyond race to something akin to ethics. While these articulations are resonant and compelling, however, they still succumb to some sense of the explanatory. Each acknowledges—to diminishing degrees, it must be said—the inescapability of race being evaluated by someone who is not black and holds power over the worth of blackness in whatever form it takes.

All of this appears to be in precursory service to the narrator's speculation: "There should be a Stage IV of black identity—Unmitigated Blackness. I'm not sure what Unmitigated Blackness is, but whatever it is, it doesn't sell. On the surface Unmitigated Blackness is a seeming unwillingness to succeed. It's Donald Goines, Chester Himes, Abbey Lincoln, Marcus Garvey, Alfre Woodard, and the serious black actor. It's Tiparillos, chitterlings, and a night in jail. It's the crossover dribble and wearing house shoes outside" (277). As the novel gains momentum in its cataloging of examples, it delivers two quite remarkable statements. The first is "Unmitigated Blackness is simply not giving a fuck" (277).

It's important that Beatty's narrator goes beyond the tripartite presentation of blackness as articulated by his lawyer and suggests a stage that "should be" but does not yet exist. The second statement is "It's the realization that there are no absolutes, except when there are. It's the acceptance of contradiction not being a sin and a crime but a human frailty like split ends and libertarianism" (277). Contradiction militates directly against representativeness or authenticity, especially as either notion might be invoked against the subject whose representativeness or authenticity are being judged.

The premise upon which Unmitigated Blackness is based is that it doesn't sell. In other words, it rejects outright "this sense of always looking at one's self through the eyes of others," to return to Du Bois again. As American capitalism has transformed itself since Du Bois introduced his coinage into the American lexicon, the ability to exchange blackness into something of financial value has also been transformed, but what has remained largely unchanged is the ability of that exchange to benefit white Americans. Unmitigated Blackness works only in the interest of itself, unwilling to succeed, if necessary: "Unmitigated Blackness is coming to the realization that as fucked up and meaningless as it all is, sometimes it's the nihilism that makes life worth living" (277). Celebrating the nihilism that makes life worth living speaks clearly to a complex impulse that is beyond conventional notions of value, exchange, or the ability to impose on or extract value from one's own worth. In fact, it suggests that resisting that imposition is perhaps worth more than life itself.

Beatty's reliance in his narrative on words like *fuck, motherfucker,* and *nigger* suggests an additional irony specific to *The Sellout.* One cannot help but wonder if these linguistic gestures, which dominate the narrative, are an attempt at Unmitigated Blackness on Beatty's part. The fact, then, that his novel won the 2016 Man Booker Prize for Fiction reminds us all too well that, irrespective of the individual's intentions or desires, the impulse toward claiming one's humanity or one's blackness through literally how many or how few fucks one gives may not, in the end, change the market for salable expressions of blackness. But an Unmitigated Blackness would not give a fuck about that either.

As the introductory paragraph of *The Sellout* reminds us, there do appear to be a few consistent principles at the heart of the conventions that have so long influenced images of African Americans within American life. This is not news. Ralph Ellison, in his 1949 essay "The Shadow and the Act," calls the "anti-Negro image" a "ritual object of which Hollywood is not the creator, but the manipulator" (277). Darryl Dickson-Carr, in a thoroughgoing discussion of postsoul satire, refers to Percival Everett's work when he puts a point on the same observation almost seventy years later: "Everett's novels reveal that 'race' and/or 'blackness' stand as . . . markers for an elusive authenticity that writers and publishers are quite willing to exploit at every opportunity, primarily for profit, but also with the secondary effect of reifying 'race' as eternally exploit-able" (272). The eternally exploitable is the perfect commercial product, after all. No matter what shape it takes, it can reliably be sold. It is harrowing to consider how images of blackness satisfy this insatiable commercial desire.

None of this is to suggest that there is a one-to-one association to be mapped onto the relationship between the conventional and the anticonventional, the paranoiac and the schizoid, especially since the focal point of my larger project is actually the asymptotic infinity that exists between any two poles. Conven-tions do not form in a vacuum, of course. This we already know. But it's worth considering how an anticonventional self-presentation might contrast a more conventional one by briefly examining the cover of Fishbone's debut album, *In Your Face,* from 1986.

In Your Face was released only three years before Trey Ellis publishes his essay "The New Black Aesthetic," in which he names the band as part of the "shock troops" who "grew up feeling misunderstood by both the black worlds and the white" (234). The album cover shows the band's founding members: Angelo Moore (lead voice, baritone saxophone, and, incredibly, theremin), John Norwood Fisher (bass and backing vocals), and his brother, Philip "Fish" Fisher (drums and backing vocals). The three young men are posed around a slightly fish-eyed lens that further distorts their already eye-catching appearance and look like they're having a very good time. They look, as Moore says in *Everyday Sunshine,* the 2010 documentary tracing the band's history, like all they want to do is "express themselves."

To compare this album cover to that of another Los Angeles band, N.W.A, whose first full-length album, the now-iconic *Straight Outta Compton,* released a mere two years after *In Your Face,* is to find why the compare and contrast strategy remains the security blanket of many an undergraduate term paper, since this strategy actually serves us quite well here. The similarities to the cover of *In Your Face* are instructive: another group of young black men arrayed in another circle around another camera lens, also looking at the viewer. But the differences are ultimately what matter. Whereas Fishbone are looking *out* at the viewer, a perspective accentuated by a black background, which creates the illusion that they are suspended in midair, N.W.A are most decidedly looking *downward,* since behind them the sky is clearly visible. The viewer of this photograph is to be imagined on the ground, with the members of the band (who refer to themselves as a "gang" in at least one of the songs on the album) looming ominously over the viewer. While it may not be immediately apparent, it eventually becomes clear that the viewer is actually looking up along the barrel of a large handgun being held by Eazy-E (Eric Wright)—on the extreme right of the frame.

One band looks weird, fun, hilarious, the other menacing, violent, and very, very serious. And, of course, there is no mystery in recollecting which group goes on to become the iconic image of black male youth throughout the end of the 1980s and into the 1990s. The juxtaposition of the two album covers suggests a clear preference on the part of the mainstream American marketplace, a preference that persists to this day. As Benjamin Barber has written, "To the world, America offers an incoherent and contradictory but seductive style that is less 'democratic' than physical culture . . . ironically, often dominated by images of black ghetto life—black, however, as in hip and cool, rather than in crime-ridden and squalid, 'baaaad' but not bad" (61). Barber's invocation of blackness as hip and cool is reminiscent of the introductory salvo to *Slumberland,* in which the narrator addresses the long-standing popular image of African Americans as "the once eternally hip, the people who were as right now as Greenwich Mean Time." The lesson, of course, is that it is much more reliably profitable to accede to the conventionalizing, commercializing, and paranoiac pressures of othering—especially when the product is images of African American men—than to follow the much more unpredictable schizoid strategy of attempting to inhabit the infinite space between established categories.[5]

The tensions enacted by the comparison of the two album covers are usefully understood in terms set out by Philip Brian Harper in an article on 1960s and 1970s American television. Harper traces a sharp division in discussions of how African Americans were represented on American television in the 1960s and '70s and helps illuminate the contrast in the two album covers—and perhaps the commercial fates of the two bands—and also continues to be relevant in thinking about the continued commodification of African American men in particular. Harper traces the argument articulated in the 1960s by television critics, which states that "television can have a substantive effect on the social context in which it operates and that, as regards black people specifically, an improvement in their social status can result from their mere depiction in main-stream television programming. Such depictions would thus instantiate what . . . I call 'simulacral realism,' derived from the theorizations of among others, Jean Baudrillard, who has conceived the simulacrum as a representation that usurps the supposed primacy of the 'real' object conventionally understood to serve as its 'original'" ("Extra-Special Effects" 65). The crux of the matter is this: "At the same time, however, many of the critiques issued by the late 1960s and early 1970s implied a demand, not for simulacral realism, but rather for a properly *mimetic* realism—typically referenced in terms of 'relevance' in the pertinent discussions—whereby television would 'reflect' the social reality on which it was implicitly modeled" (70; emphasis in original). Harper then sums up his point: "Paradoxically, therefore, the insistence that television faithfully represent a set of social conditions . . . composing a singular and unitary phe-nomenon known as '*the* black experience' [mimetic realism] runs smack up against a simultaneous demand that it both recognize and help constitute the diversity of African American society [simulacral realism]" (71). *In Your Face* is clearly simulacral, as it suggests the actual limitless variety of African American society, culture, and life by posing three young black men who are about as un-representative (not only of black America, but of most groups of people) as one is likely to meet. The more complex and unsettling implications follow upon the enormous commercial and foundational success of *Straight Outta Compton*, which may be characterized as mimetically realistic—*representin'*, telling it like it is, keepin' it real. But one must ask whether or not that group of young black men is in fact any more representative than are Angelo Moore and the Fisher brothers. When we remember that they are all playing characters within the collectives of their bands, this question of representativeness becomes even more revealing. What we know for sure, though, is that the marketplace of American popular culture has reliably privileged and purchased the ostensibly mimetic over the simulacral, at least where representations of African American men are concerned. It is difficult to rethink our long-established habits of mind, in other words. But factor in economic incentive and reward, and the challenge of rethinking starts to look daunting indeed.

Paradoxically, when we consider the claims for the necessity for mimetic realism that emerge from discussions of 1960s and '70s American television, mimetic realism more reliably gives the people—meaning the American mainstream—what they want. Selling *the* black experience is always more reliably profitable than selling *a* black experience. The fact that N.W.A. have been sold to a whole new generation of white Americans with disposable income, in the form of the 2015 motion picture *Straight Outta Compton,* only reinforces this point, as now the ostensibly mimetic transforms itself into the simulacral, as an image of the band is now for sale in a representation possibly more *real* (whatever that ultimately means) than the initial image of the band in 1988. It's worth considering that here commerce turns the mimetic into the simulacral, while rendering the initially simulacral (Fishbone) mimetic, as the members of Fishbone approximate the actual fate of countless black men who are seen (in one way or another) to be valueless to the American mainstream, while the fates of Ice Cube and Dr. Dre, at least, look like the realization of the American Dream, with Ice Cube making a career as an actor and Dr. Dre selling Beats Audio to Apple Computers for approximately $3 billion.

The schizoid *can* be salable, and black artists can be both conventional and uninteresting even to the mainstream. A particularly compelling figure in this context would be Jimi Hendrix. On the one hand, a transcendent black American artist, who—in a very different cultural moment from our own—combined the prototypically shape-shifting and transformative African American male persona enacted by the members of Fishbone with a blackness and sexuality that existed under erasure at a time punctuated simultaneously by antiwar protests and protestations of peace and love, as well as by the paradoxically conservative dynamics of white kids on college campuses putting daisies down rifle barrels while black and brown kids carried models of those same rifles through the jungles of Southeast Asia because the former group could reliably get deferments while the latter group could not. Jimi Hendrix, who spent some time in the army, attempts to express himself musically, individually, and more anticonventionally blackly over the course of his short career and life, from the time of the success of his debut album, *Are You Experienced?,* in 1967, to his death in September 1970. He replaces Noel Redding and Mitch Mitchell, the two white English sidemen of the Jimi Hendrix Experience with Billy Cox and Buddy Miles, the two African American sidemen of the Band of Gypsies in 1969 and 1970. While this change in roster was complicated by Mitchell's eventual return (Mitchell plays in the large ensemble that performs at Woodstock), Hendrix nevertheless attempts to make the risky transition from the black guitarist in a white rock band to a black guitarist in a black electric blues band. (Picture one or the other as Daniel Barkley, perhaps.) Paul Gilroy, here channeling his inner Hendrix, makes the point like this, and in so doing, introduces an optimistic, although clear-sighted, view of the crosscurrents at play throughout my discussion: "Jimi's trans-ethnic turn is neither a wilful drift away from blackness into exoticism nor a belated programmatic bid to set history straight by invoking some interplanetary Seminole genealogy. The tragic outcome—the castle made of sand—refers us to the enduring presence of alternative possibilities. Another world is possible. Jimi conjures up the prospect of it—a castle in the air—and says that the resources for building that utopia are, unexpectedly and magically, already at hand" ("Bold as Love?" 117). Gilroy's account of Hendrix refuses the binary, embracing not only the contradictory but the unabashedly utopian, in order to make a claim for the "enduring presence of alternative possibilities" and the even more audacious claim that the resources for this utopia are already at hand. This is what the artist does, what the critic can do, and what the citizen may do if encouraged similarly to refuse the seductive traps of the paranoiac binary, and with it, the illusion of definitive resolution.

It's worth invoking one last time what Deleuze and Guattari say by way of introduction to *A Thousand Plateaus*. They point out at least a couple of the reasons why we speak the way we do. We give in to our habits, and we want to speak like everyone else. These useful words encourage some humility as we critique, question, quarrel with, and counsel against the Oedipal forces that dominate so much of our lives. This humility characterizes itself in our simultaneous ability to believe that we know something while not ruling out the prospect that there is something else that we still need to learn, even on subjects about which we've convinced ourselves we know a lot. This provisional knowledge enables us to continue functioning while knowing that our knowledge is never perfect, complete, entire, or impartial. But this knowledge can also provide us with a sense of freedom, releasing us from the pressure of knowing *everything*, while at the same time reinforcing the sense of the infinity of knowledge. This balance characterizes itself in an infinity, since we will always know things and always learn more.

Something of an analogy for the attention achieved by some and the lack of attention (one is tempted to say "obscurity" here) of others may be found in the inclusion of the novelist and essayist Colson Whitehead, who takes up the challenge of representing the usually unrepresented (in this case, some notion of life in the black upper-middle class) in his 2009 bildungsroman, *Sag Harbor*. *Sag Harbor* features the ostensible socioeconomic anomaly of black American families wealthy enough to summer in the Hamptons. Of course, identifying the Cooper family as anomalous because of their ability to use the name of a season as a verb, as only the wealthy do, elides the simple point that most white families cannot afford to *summer* either, making the Coopers anomalous not just among African American families but among American families in general. But it's easy to forget this. The ways in which we continue to be encouraged to think of some people as anomalous and others as simply people—as universal subjects—are captured by Sunera Thobani: "Liberalism claims a universalism that constitutes the enlightenment subject as innocent of all context, history and power. But in its careful delineations of lines of inclusion, it constitutes people of colour as uncivilized and unworthy populations. This universalizing of the Western subject as the human subject while particularizing all Others in the categories of racial and cultural difference is today used to construct the political demands of people of colour as those of 'special' interests" (6).[6]

During one especially heated exchange between two of the adolescent boys at the center of the narrative (Benji Cooper, the novel's fifteen-year-old narrator, and Marcus, one of his friends), Benji stumbles into the difficult relationship between universalism and otherness. Winning or losing this argument hinges on competing essentializing claims of authenticity that can often become the argumentative baseline of the adolescent boy, particularly when feeling threatened. Benji makes what he considers the relatively uncontroversial point that the signature melodic riff from "Planet Rock," the locus classicus of early 1980s rap, by Afrika Bambaataa and the Soul Sonic Force, may first be heard a few years earlier in "Trans-Europe Express," the late 1970s song by the German electronic band Kraftwerk. The argument begins with this group of upper-middle-class African American adolescent boys listening to "Planet Rock" and Benji telling his friends that Afrika "bit" the famous riff that runs through "Planet Rock" off of Kraftwerk. The argument then descends into the sort of adolescent ad hominem chaos that makes many an adult male try to repress the fact of ever having been a teenaged boy, with Marcus laying claim to what he knows to be an unproblematic authenticity by impugning Benji blackness: "'Yeah, right, I forgot you like that white music, you fuckin' Siouxsie and the Banshees–listenin' motherfucker.' He scratched his chest and thought for a moment. 'With your monkey ass'" (62). Marcus's final punctuating flourish—"with your monkey ass"—is itself "bitten" off of an earlier riff in the novel about how verbal putdowns were being constructed by this group of boys in the summer of 1985.

Richard Schur includes a skilled accounting of debates over African American authenticity in his essay "The Crisis of Authenticity in Contemporary African American Literature" and reads this scene, in part, by saying: "Through this exchange and its implicit examination of authenticity in music and language, Whitehead helps the reader understand the complex ways that the rhetoric of authenticity shapes African American post–civil rights era youth. Benji feels compelled to meet dominant constructions—apparently shared by both many African Americans and many whites—about black masculinity even if they do not match his own social conditions and personal history" (248). Schur points to a significant element in Benji's anxiety, which is the question of the authenticity of his own identity, the extent to which he is keeping it real, even though the *real* that he is keeping it has little to do with his real lived experience. But an important mechanism that draws Benji's attention to questions of his identity as a young black man is the marketplace that sells selective, often demeaning, versions of himself back to him. This is a further complication of which Marcus appears unaware, but his not being preoccupied by such questions finds him on surer footing during the argument. Benji's internal conflict should remind us of a similar moment of internal division in another famous young African American male narrator, Ralph Ellison's in *Invisible Man*. When that narrator is fighting in the battle royal scene at the beginning of Ellison's novel, he is momentarily distracted during his final encounter with Tatlock, who, as the narrator surmises, does not have a grandfather's curse to think about. While the narrator is thinking about this disjunction between himself and the other boy, he is knocked out by him, losing the fight.

When Benji provides the above-quoted tidbit from popular music history with the sort of reflection to which retrospective narrators looking back on their fictive childhoods are necessarily given, one aspect of his account is his commercial relationship to rap music, another version of African American authenticity being sold back to these boys, whose anxiety about their elevated financial status makes them ideal targets for such a marketing campaign: "Let the record show that my black T-shirt was in fact a Bauhaus T-shirt, purchased the previous fall down in the Village on the very first of my weekly trips to scavenge for new albums, generally vinyl dispatches from the world of the pale and winnowed, but it was true that I had worn my Siouxsie and the Banshees T-shirt the week before" (63). He goes on to acknowledge, "I didn't buy rap—I heard it all the time, Reggie and Elena [his younger brother and older sister] had all the good stuff, so there was no reason to spend my allowance on it. Rap was a natural resource, might as well pay for sunlight or the very breeze or an early-morning car alarm going off" (63). Brand names are everywhere in *Sag Harbor*. And Benji is nothing if not an avid consumer. In addition to being a different young African American man, Benji appears to be trying to fashion himself as an unusual type of consumer as well: one who—all commercial pressure to the contrary—tries to formulate his own relationship with the marketplace, a marketplace that for him features images of African American artists of whom he is aware but whose products he is already provided with through his siblings' consumerism. And as Benji attempts to resist the conventionalizing consumerist pressures that tell him what he should want to buy, and by extension, who he should want to be, he is also presented in a way that frustrates common consumer expectations of the young African American male who might give voice to this pressure. These expectations find their expression in this scene in Marcus's name-calling.[7]

What's particularly notable about *Sag Harbor* is that all of these effects—regarding anxiety, authenticity, masculinity, and blackness—can be accomplished without either the narrator or implicitly Whitehead raising his voice. Whitehead's aesthetic is introspective, humorous, understated, and, as in the above passages, at times hilariously mock-earnest. This aesthetic is striking in its difference from the voice of the detached observer that one tends to encounter in Everett's work or the more confrontational narrators to which Beatty gives voice. But Whitehead's gaze nevertheless casts a wide-surveying eye that misses nothing when it comes to critiquing the assumptions by which African Americans continue to be talked *about* within the culture they inhabit, rather than speaking within it. Whitehead actually cheats some readers out of the satisfying rage that might be expected from such putatively authentic-sounding voices of African America as Richard Wright, or, more recently, Ishmael Reed, or, on another register, the perhaps equally satisfying catharsis of injustice and suffering nobly endured, as presented in some of Toni Morrison's work.

Reed provides that much more familiar tone in discussing the commercial and critical success of *Precious*, the 2009 film based on Sapphire's 1996 novel, *Push*, which in turn finds a version of itself in *We's Lives in Da Ghetto* in *Erasure*. Reed says, in an article in the *New York Times*:

> Among black men and women, there is widespread revulsion and anger over the Oscar-nominated film about an illiterate, obese black teenager who has two children by her father. The author Jill Nelson wrote: "I don't eat at the table of self-hatred, inferiority or victimization. I haven't bought into notions of rampant black pathology or embraced the overwrought, dishonest and black-people-hating pseudo-analysis too often passing as post-racial cold hard truths." One black radio broadcaster said that he felt under psychological assault for two hours. So did I.
>
> The blacks who are enraged by "Precious" have probably figured out that this film wasn't meant for them. It was the enthusiastic response from white audiences and critics that culminated in the film being nominated for six Oscars by the Academy of Motion Picture Arts and Sciences, an outfit whose 43 governors are all white and whose membership in terms of diversity is about 40 years behind Mississippi.

Reed, writing well before the #OscarSoWhite movement that attempted to draw attention to the composition of the Academy of Motion Picture Arts and Sciences that Reed eviscerates, makes a couple of points that are apposite here. First, he draws attention to the outrageous nature of expectations for black authenticity, as enough filmgoers appear to have seen *Precious* as *typical* or *representative* of African American life, in a manner not unlike those characters lampooned in *Erasure* who saw *Fuck* as *gritty* and *real*. Second, Reed draws a distinction between how blacks and whites might view this film, and by extension, other cultural artifacts like it. Everett, in his essay "Signing to the Blind" from 1991, sees the problem of the paranoiac in more generally national terms: "It is not seeing with 'white' eyes, it is seeing with 'American' eyes, with brainwashed, automatic, comfortable, and 'safe' perceptions of reality" (10). He characterizes this seeing with American eyes as the reason why the expectations of the work of African American writers are convention bound and limited. When he uses the word *automatic,* it is difficult not to hear Deleuze and Guattari's acknowledgment of their concession to *habit* in their introduction to *A Thousand Plateaus.*

It's also worth noting that, in 2009, when Reed's article appears in the *Times,* he remakes Alain Locke's point, as stated in *The New Negro* in 1925, that African Americans are much more often spoken *about* as objects within American culture than they speak for themselves as subjects. Reed's completely valid outrage articulates a frustration that many African Americans have expressed on the subject of how images of African Americans are often represented and sold within mainstream American culture. However, his voicing also finds a somewhat more reliable place within that same mainstream American cultural economy than Benji's might. Reed gives voice to the *angry black man* or *black troublemaker* persona, positions that have unfortunately become tropes almost cliché in their familiarity to many, including those whom it criticizes. His voice becomes less unconventional and more a recognizable part of the already existing American cultural narrative. Reed, in the discovery of yet another trap set by white supremacist capitalist patriarchy, in bell hooks's comprehensive and felicitous phrase, is giving the people what they want, even as he attacks them for wanting it.[8]

Compare Reed's tone with Whitehead's, writing in the same newspaper, in the same week that Barack Obama was elected president of the United States. This is the first paragraph of Whitehead's article: "Over the coming days and weeks, there will be many 'I never thought I'd see the day' pieces, but none of them will be more overflowing with 'I never thought I'd see the day'-ness than this one. I'm black, you see, and I haven't gained a pound since college. I skip breakfast most days, have maybe half a sandwich for lunch, and sometimes I forget to eat dinner. Just slips my mind. Yesterday morning, I woke up to a new world. America had elected a Skinny Black Guy president" ("The Year of Living Postracially").

The expectations as Whitehead knows them to be are on full display from the opening words of his piece, as is his mock-earnest tone, which is why the article is so surprising, published as it was at a time when many African Americans might be safely believed to have been having the "I never thought I'd live to see the day" exchanges that he then deflates.

Or consider Benji's voice, as he addresses concerns similar to those addressed by Reed, about how African Americans are represented within and to the culture in which they live:

> Black boys with beach houses. It could mess with your head sometimes, if you were the susceptible sort. And if it messed with your head, got under your brown skin, there were some typical and well-known remedies. You could embrace the beach part—revel in the luxury, the perception of status, wallow without care in what it meant to be born in America with money, or the appearance of money, as the case may be. No apologies. You could embrace the black part— take some idea you had about what real blackness was, and make theater of it, your 24-7 one-man show. Folks of this type could pick Bootstrapping Striver or Proud Pillar, but the most popular brands were Militant or Street, Militant being the opposite of bourgie capitulation to The Man, and Street being the antidote to Upper Middle Class emasculation. . . . Or you could embrace the contradiction, say, what you call paradox, I call *myself.* In theory. Those inclined to this remedy didn't have many obvious models. (58)

Benji's paradoxical stance is not as recognizable to the economic engine that drives the American economy, white Americans with disposable income, the constituency composing the governors of the Academy of Motion Picture Arts and Sciences, and many of those who flocked to see *Precious,* as Reed's "Militant or Street" stance might be. But Reed's positioning here may stand in for much African American masculine performance, especially as provided through the world of the more hard-edged hip-hop that became known as "gangsta rap." (Think back to the discussion of the image of N.W.A.) The academy membership and *Precious* audience section of the American population might find Reed's voice as palatable for its familiarity as it might find Whitehead's voice for its palliative, nonthreatening tone. It is rarely surprising when the interests of convention, then, line up with those of capital.

Instead of Reed's righteous anger, Whitehead deploys the reductio ad absurdum:

You didn't, for example, walk down Main Street with a watermelon under your arm. Even if you had a pretty good reason. Like you were going to a potluck and each person had to bring an item and your item just happened to be a watermelon, luck of the draw, and you wrote this on a sign so everyone would understand the context, and as you walked down Main Street you held the sign in one hand and the explained watermelon in the other, all casual, perhaps nodding between the watermelon and the sign for extra emphasis if you made eye contact. This would not happen. We were on display. (88)

He adds, though:

For argument's sake, let's say there was a brand of character who was able to say, Forget that. I'm going to walk up and down Main Street with a watermelon under each arm! And one between my legs! Big grin on my face! Peak o' rush hour! Such rebellion was inherently self-conscious, overly determined. It doth protest too much, described an inner conflict as big as that of the watermelon-avoiders. We were all of us stuck whether we wanted to admit it or not. We were people, not performance artists, all appearances to the contrary. (88)

This description of the at least double bind of blackness in America, the distinction between "people" and "performance artists," usefully divides subjects from objects, recognizing at the same time the potential of protesting too much. The anti–double consciousness that I've been describing does not express itself as watermelon avoidance, although it could be attacked for doing just that. An Everett character would carry the watermelon if necessary, without the sign, knowing the others will interpret him as they will. Just think of characters like Robert Hawks in "Alluvial Deposits," who are uninterested in the exaggerated interest whites take in his blackness. Again, it's not about pretending one is not black. It's about trying to be black on one's own terms—to the extent that this objective is possible. Benji's observation "We were on display" brings to mind the shop window. The trap is often that even when we feel we are being our true selves (whoever "we" are), it is easy to lose sight of the fact that we are nonetheless being imbricated within an economy not of our choosing.

Benji makes the above observations to his friend Nick, who carries with him the sort of gigantic portable radio that one still occasionally hears people unthinkingly refer to as "ghetto-blasters." As Benji makes clear, having to lay claim necessarily produces the double bind that entraps both the watermelon avoiders and the watermelon displayers alike. A provisional solution—which is all anyone can expect from dilemmas of identity—is to embrace the conflict, to adopt an anticonventional stance, that of the schizorevolutionary, and then hope for the best. The definitive trap is to attempt to resolve it. The attempt at resolution is just updating double consciousness for a new era. Perhaps, as with the prisoner's dilemma, the most advisable solution is to avoid prisoner's dilemmas.

◆ ◆ ◆

It is as crucial to know that the anticonventional potential of the schizorevolutionary does not come with any guarantees as it is to know that such potential exists in the first place. When we hope for the best, in other words, we are probably obligated to recognize the very real prospect that we will not get *the best* and that whatever we get may take a form that was entirely unpredictable. Fishbone embody what else this schizorevolutionary investment can look like. Even when the result is not the commercial success that perhaps they had hoped for, it remains a vital investment, nonetheless. In addition, it must be said that the way I've described the work of Everett throughout this study, or Beatty's or Whitehead's work in this conclusion, might give the impression that the schizorevolutionary (in spite of the psychoanalytical trace resonant in Deleuze and Guattari's neologism) has things under his (in these cases) control. Fishbone, in terms of performance, but also in terms of the fate of the band over time, dispels this illusion while remaining just as representative of the schizorevolutionary as are Beatty, Everett, or Whitehead, each in his own way.

Whereas Colson Whitehead's approach to embracing the contradictions is humorous while incisive, Everett's is kaleidoscopic, self-referential, and sometimes confusing, and Beatty's more closely approaches images of *militant* or *street*, but with a clear overtone that emphasizes that this is self-presentation for the self and the already sympathetic, Fishbone's may most accurately be approximated as an amalgam of the descriptions of all of these writers. Fishbone want their listeners to know loud and clear that they are up to something different from what American listeners have become accustomed to hearing or expecting when consuming the music of a black band, even if it's not always obvious to the listener what that something is. Their refusal to conform is not mere petulance or avant-gardism for its own sake. Like Everett and Beatty, they are anti–double consciousness artists, looking to make the world look at them through their own eyes rather than looking at themselves through the world's eyes.

Angelo Moore, the band's lead voice, and one of only two members of Fishbone who have been with the band throughout their over-thirty-year career, introduced the band's musical approach at a 2008 concert in Bordeaux, France, by declaring: "We're gonna play a little ska, a little rock, a little funk, a little reggae, a little jazz." The band's musical ancestry, in other words, is almost entirely what is conventionally characterized as *black* music, with rock as the only ostensible outlier, and rock music traces its roots back to the blues and to rhythm and blues, both conventionally identified with African American music. Fishbone, then, plays "black" music; they just don't play it the way they are *supposed* to, the way they are expected to. Put another way, what distinguishes them, and has relegated them to the status of something smaller than a cult band over the same period of time that N.W.A have become a cultural force, appears to have more to do with *how* they sound—as opposed to how they are *supposed* to sound—than what they have to say. "So Many Millions," a song from their 1991 album, *The Reality of My Surroundings,* provides a brief but useful example:

I cannot get over, legitimately, the reality
Of my surroundings
Do not point to the sky
So why should I even try (when there's nuthin' out there to be)
I cannot grow up to be the president
Where only drug dealers own Mercedes Benz.

These lines, which begin the song, might sound like observations performed contemporaneously by N.W.A. What distinguishes Fishbone is *how* they sound while expressing themselves. Moore's introduction to the concert in Bordeaux gestures toward the infinite possibilities—the enduring presence of alternative possibilities—in the continua between any two of the musical genres he lists. To play as the market dictates and expects is the road to the pandering that can easily become by turns watermelon avoiding or displaying, as the market dictates. But this interstitial determination makes the larger point that African Americans are not a Rubik's Cube to be solved by declarations of "newness," or, for that matter, "postness," but as complex and complicated a human subgroup as any other human subgroup. All of this is the case even if this complexity is not reliably salable. In fact, perhaps this complexity defines the lack of salability of some artistic expressions, perhaps even *because* it is not reliably salable. But even as they attempt to assume their own musical provenance, this iconoclastic band still must occasionally claim it out loud. They cannot assume anything about who they are or how they'll be received. They can, however, insist upon being themselves on their own terms, for better and for worse.

The chorus of "So Many Millions" declares the band's ironic critique of the tyranny of convention that has probably contributed to their being so little known after more than thirty years in existence, and to the almost complete turnover in the band's membership over that time—Moore and Norwood Fisher being the only two original members still with the band: "So many millions feel this strong. All these people can't be wrong." The fact that for many Americans the line "I cannot grow up to be the president / Where only drug dealers own Mercedes Benz" would sound the same now as it would have in 1991, speaks volumes about what has and has not changed in America's political and commercial landscape in spite of any one American election or another. Yes, there has now been a black American president, but his legacy consists, at least in part, in the remembered list of legislative disappointments, on the part of his supporters, and the fault of what is—for others—the worsening of race relations in the United States. Of course, this last is also a success, after a fashion, since the population of those who see race issues as worse in America now probably comprises many who are thinking about race issues for the first time in ways that are not only conventional and comfortable to them. I'm not arguing that Obama is a schizorevolutionary, and in fact would not make such an argument. Someone so skillfully aware of how his actions might look to others could not be.

Perhaps this last point captures the nature of Everett's achievement, as well as those of the artists mentioned in this conclusion.

NOTES

PREFACE

1. And, of course, in referencing Hume's commitment to decency, we cannot forget what Kwame Anthony Appiah calls Hume's "notorious footnote, that he was 'apt to suspect' that non-whites were 'naturally inferior to the whites,' devoid of arts and science and 'ingenious manufactures.'" Across time, we must nevertheless evaluate our own understanding of decency. Rana does not mention the notorious footnote in his article.

2. I will have much more to say on this subject in the introduction.

INTRODUCTION

1. It's difficult not to think of books of worship as intended to effect such retraining, but considering how much of human history has been punctuated by fighting over religion, that is a difficult argument to make with a straight face. As will be discussed in chapter 3, Everett's work usually treats religion as a target for mockery, as if to prove this point. However, religion is not exclusively the object of ridicule in his work, which is also worth noting.

2. Everett's work is replete with instances of the anticonventional, if only as relating to moments upon which we might benefit from reflecting, even as we do not. The slash (/) in Barthes's *S/Z* is discussed briefly in *Erasure,* the significance of the hyphen (when it appears) in expressions like *African American,* the idea that the police officer is not a suspect for the crimes under investigation, as occurs in *Assumption,* that the figures of Greek tragedy are white, as is under examination in *For Her Dark Skin* and *Frenzy.* And this is just a sampling.

3. At least what I am attempting here is not as potentially embarrassing as happened when no less a publishing house than Doubleday offered to publish *Erasure* as the inaugural book in a new series titled "Harlem Moon," an idea that would not have been out of place in the novel itself, and about which Everett in several interviews has been amusing (to say the least) at Doubleday's expense.

4. And while the fetish of incomprehensibility is a well-known criticism of post-structuralist thought—a criticism to which I remain sympathetic—the variety within Everett's fiction (including realist narrative from westerns through to postmodernist pyrotechnics) argues against incomprehensibility for its own sake.

5. It seems to me reasonable to believe that Wallace, of all people, as a novelist and as a particular kind of novelist, has insights into the sometimes terrifying implications of entertaining thoughts over which we cannot even pretend to have control, and as a result appears to have insights into the kinds of spaces that I am arguing Everett carves out and creates within.

6. *Everything and More* was first published in 2003, before the ubiquity of Facebook, Snapchat, Instagram, etc. Wallace's point about perpetual distraction has only become more accurate since his first writing.

7. In *What Is Philosophy?*, their last collaborative work, Deleuze and Guattari make a statement that might otherwise sound like it had been made by an Everett character, when they speculate on the nature of philosophical concepts:

> Philosophical concepts are fragmentary wholes that are not aligned with one another so that they fit together, because their edges do not match up. They are not pieces of a jigsaw puzzle but rather the outcome of throws of the dice. They resonate nonetheless, and the philosophy that creates them always introduces a powerful Whole that, while remaining open, is not fragmented: an unlimited One-All, an "Omnitudo" that includes all the concepts on one and the same plane. It is a table, a plateau, or a slice; it is a plane of consistency or, more accurately, the plane of immanence of concepts, the planomenon. (35)

Here, too, they carefully draw out the implications of thinking not only about this distinction between concept and plane but also about the demands of attempting to describe this distinction.

8. And I am not suggesting that a text has only one meaning, nor am I suggesting that any critic would. I am saying that we tend to coalesce around a relatively limited range of readings of a text, and in doing so, we are saying something about how we read that is probably worth our purposeful interrogation.

9. Michel Feith provides another version of the paradoxes and their approach toward a solution, in his discussion of the paradoxes' appearance in *Glyph:*

> The "arrow" paradox states that "[i]f everything when it occupies an equal space is at rest, and if that which is in locomotion is always occupying such a space at any moment, the flying arrow is therefore motionless" (Aristotle 6.9, 239b5). The arrow cannot be moving, since at each snapshot instant it is immobile. The paradox of the "dichotomy," for its part, divides space into segments: "That which is in locomotion must arrive at the half-way stage before it arrives at the goal" (6.9.239b10). If you repeat the dichotomy infinitely, there will always be some space to cover before reaching the goal; therefore, the goal is never reached. In both paradoxes, proof of the impossibility of movement is reached through the infinite division of time or space into discontinuous points. ("Hire-a-Glyph" 315–16)

10. And while Kenneth Warren, in *What Was African American Literature*, has argued for an end to this category, the mere impulse or necessity to make such an argument, not to mention the controversy the assertion created among critics, reaffirms the persistence of the category itself.

11. This is a purely unintended echo of Donald Rumsfeld. As it turns out, locutions about "known knowns" and "known unknowns," not to mention "unknown unknown," things we don't know that we don't know, were actually felicitous.

12. These changes in our perceptions are not unlike the Dunning-Kruger effect, which Cherry Kendra describes as follows: "The Dunning-Kruger effect is a type of cognitive bias in which people believe that they are smarter and more capable than they really are. Essentially, low ability people do not possess the skills needed to recognize their own incompetence. The combination of poor self-awareness and low cognitive ability leads them to overestimate their own capabilities." The reason this phenomenon matters to my discussion is that, as Kendra points out: "The reality is that *everyone* is susceptible to this phenomenon, and in fact, most of us probably experience it with surprising regularity. People who are genuine experts in one area may mistakenly believe that their intelligence and knowledge carry over into other areas in which they are less familiar" (emphasis in original). In other words, we are all subject to failures in what is called metacognition, our ability to evaluate our own cognitive abilities. But this does not mean that we stop holding views or trying to acquire expertise. It does mean that we might be a little more humble about our own abilities and forgiving of the perceived shortcomings of others.

13. The special issues of *Callaloo, Canadian Review of American Studies,* and *African American Review* demonstrate much of the variety in these approaches, as do the critical volumes edited by Anne-Laure Tissut and Claude Maniez, Anne-Laure Tissut and Claude Julien, and Keith Mitchell and Robin G. Vander.

14. I cannot improve on what Derek Maus has already said, in *Jesting in Earnest: Percival Everett and Menippean Satire,* on the subject of Everett bibliography. Maus refers to the "indispensable online bibliography (http://percivaleverettsociety.com/bibliography/) created and fastidiously updated by Joe Weixlmann of Saint Louis University" (11).

CHAPTER ONE

1. Everett makes a point about the importance of self-examination in his work when describing Monk Ellison in *Erasure*. He says in an interview with Sean O'Hagan: "What is most interesting to me about Monk is not his color, but his selfless examination of himself. He does not want to be constrained or reduced by society's demands or expectations. He's alert to that all the time" ("The Books Interview" 32).

2. This aspect of Everett's work is discussed in very usefully articles by James Donahue and Michel Feith in the special issue of *African American Review* (52, no. 1, Spring 2019), coedited by Joe Weixlmann and myself.

3. I have used this remarkable quotation before in my work and return to it again and again in my thinking. See *Visitor: My Life in Canada.*

4. As if to remind us of this minimal qualification for true genius, as Ralph sees it, he returns to this understandable infantile incapacity later: "But still I could not control my waste functions.

Boris did set me on the toilet periodically, but he would wait at the door instead of leaving me alone" (76). However, he also demonstrates the ability to reflect upon whatever *true* genius might be, and quite beautifully, at that:

> Genius, I assume, does not recognize itself, having better things to do. At an age when parents are so quick to attribute genius to any number of pathetically simple accomplishments, I knew that I was no genius. I knew that mere acceleration held in it no truly remarkable merit. I had a headstart, only that, and like any headstart, it would be negated in the middle or at the end. What genius, I guessed then and know now, allows is the start of a new race. Genius means finding a way back to the beginning where the truths are uncorrupted and honest and maybe even pure. (89)

Ralph's genius is, in part, understanding this.

5. And, yes, Sid is labeling, too, when he says this. But as Everett says in "Signing to the Blind," it's not that people are reading with white eyes or black eyes but American eyes. His point about the cognitive problems inherent in living as an American is a specific expression of the more general points about categories and the need to move beyond them or look at the continuum in between them in some way.

6. The name "Ezra Pond," of course, does similar work, by opening up other potential chains of signification that I will leave others to pursue.

7. "The cat tells me I may take this road or that one and that either will get me to a place to which I will be going. The March Hare is that way. The Hatter, the other. My direction matters little They're both mad. And eh cat? He fades back in" (44).

> "How do you know I'm mad?" said Alice.
> "You must be," said the Cat, "or else you wouldn't have come here." (66)
> "Shan't," said the cook. (191)

8. Here, I am using the word "sane" in its expected sense, just to move things along. I am just registering in this note my awareness that I'm doing it.

9. And, of course, the unpunctuated "drip drip drip" reminds us of *The Waste Land*, but also of the potentially infinite matrix of allusions relating to the novel, indeed any novel, some of which we recognize, others we do not, because Zeno really is both right and wrong.

10. And my use of the word *passing* is fraught with further resonance in this context, although Ishmael is not necessarily passing for white so much as passing for "sane," from time to time, when he's out of his house. He is also passing as a woman, as Estelle Gilliam, when he writes the romance novels by which he makes the living that allows him to have a house so private that he can torture a man in his basement without being interrupted or discovered. He may, though, also be passing as a white woman, since he mentioned his being black in conjunction with being a man whose work conventional readers of romance novels probably would not embrace.

11. While there are numerous moments that justify the American foreign policy reading, one in particular can stand in here for the group:

It was stifling hot at Guantanamo. It was always hot there. Marines marched around being marines. Cubans lived their lives on the other side of the impressive fence. Three crew-cut, muscled, narrow-eyed spooks-in-training rested after their cross-country run. One was from Canada, one was from Australia, and the last was an American. The Canadian opened the envelope that held their next training exercise. It said, simply, *Find a deer.*

The Aussie went off into the woods and came back empty handed. He said, "No deer out there, mate."

The Canadian went next and came back with nothing. He agreed that there were no deer in the woods.

The American went into the woods, was gone for a while, and returned with a rabbit.

"What's this all about," asked the Aussie.

"That's not a deer," said the Canadian.

"Yes, it is," said the American. "Ask it." (65–66)

12. It's worth taking note here that this is not a mirror image or a reflection, either of which would involve reversing almost all of the letters, with the exception of o, 1, and w. This is a transposition, where the letters are rearranged and presented in reverse order, suggesting the difficulties in working with the somewhat relentlessly inelastic medium of words.

13. In his 2005 interview with Mills, Julien, and Tissut, Everett shows how easy it is for critics to be drawn into the traps that he sets, sometimes completely inadvertently. The exchange also demonstrates the division of labor between critics and artists: "With my latest novel, *American Desert,* I knew I wanted to write a novel. I mean I felt something was brewing inside me. I was driving back to my ranch in the desert and noticed an exit sign to Theodore Street. That name struck me. I pulled off and the novel fell into place with Theodore Street for its main character. I cannot say why but I do not question such things. I just did as I was told: went home and started working." Claude Julien acknowledges, in response to this revelation: "So, that's where the name Theodore Street comes from! I had built up an onomastic game opposing this character's first name, 'Gift of God' in Greek, to the banality of his last name, 'Street.' It appears I was in a blind alley." Everett replies, simply: "That's fun. That's what literature can do for you" ("An Interview" 81). It is difficult not to see as fortuitous the homonymy of *onomastic* and *onanistic,* especially as relates to the critic's role in this division of labor. I'm just glad that on this occasion it wasn't me.

14. *Ted* here might remind some readers of *Tod,* the name of the character who dies at the hands of the police in *Invisible Man,* Tod Clifton. That *Tod* means *death* in German adds further resonance to that character's name, and to this one's. In Everett's novel, we get both the visual reference to Clifton's first name and the aural resonance of Ted's name rhyming with his physical state and the German sense of the other name.

15. Put another way, in *The Water Cure* the convention of identifying the body is inadequate to its emotional resonance. In *American Desert,* the expression is inadequate for almost pedantically empirical reasons.

16. In a sense, the desire for a Christian allegory is short-circuited by *American Desert,* in Big Daddy's church, which features numerous mute men all named *Jesus,* with numerals attached. It

is, for instance, Jesus 23 who helps Ted later in the novel. The effect here seems to be: "How's this for a Christian allegory?" Another moment when we are made to feel the butt of a joke.

CHAPTER TWO

1. In his interview with me, Everett discussed these expectations on the part of readers and publishers, in response to my suggestion that a difference between being exotic and merely out of place is that the exotic can be commodified and sold, whereas the merely out of place cannot: "Exactly, which is why the easy road for American publishing has been to publish novels about black farmers or inner-city, you know. . . . And slaves. Because these are pictures that are easily commodified. But if it's the black middle class, and it's not so different from someone else, then what's exotic about that?" ("Uncategorizable," 124).

2. There are several excellent critical discussions of *Erasure*. Margaret Russett's article "Race under 'Erasure' for Percival Everett, 'A Piece of Fiction'"; Judith Roof's "Everett's Hypernarrator"; and Marc Amfreville's "*Erasure* and *The Water Cure*: A Possible Suture?" warrant particular attention, as each draws out a different but complementary aspect of the narrative. Roof focuses on the nature of the narrator, while Russett attends especially to the novel's structure and lack of a resolution. Amfreville focuses on the role that trauma plays, which is particularly significant since trauma is, by definition, unresolved, and so helps consolidate some of Russett's observations.

3. Of course, it remains possible that the Frenchmen are also black, although that seems less likely. There may also be an upper limit to how many departures from preference a bigot can process at any one time. Who's to say?

4. Barkley grows up in South Carolina; he plays the guitar, not to mention being at least financially comfortable. He also goes to Brown, as Everett did. Everett also contributed to discussion about the Confederate flag's place in South Carolina political life, as I discuss briefly in the preface to this book.

5. Think back to the difference between who is present and who is absent in Ishmael's basement as well.

6. I was fortunate enough to see "Erased de Kooning Drawing" in May 2016 at the San Francisco Museum of Modern Art. It carried with it a whole additional experience when I returned to the gallery in May 2018 to look at the erased drawing again, only to find out that it had been part of a special exhibit when I had seen it the first time, and it was no longer in the SFMOMA. I found myself, at that moment, thinking about the weird experience of being disappointed about not being able to see a work of art that is already not there, because it was no longer there. It's difficult not to think about the significance of absence at a moment like that.

7. I've mentioned this passage already in chapter 1 as well. It serves a different function here.

8. The political significance of colors is another of those symbols that is worth thinking about and learning from. For instance, in moving from Canada (where I was born) to the United States, I had to relearn these associations, since the Conservative Party's color is blue in Canada, and the Liberal Party's color is red. (There is also a New Democratic Party—which is social democratic—

whose color is orange.) After five years of living in the United States, I am only beginning to not have to consciously reverse the colors in conversation or when reading or listening to the news. Like any symbol, there is nothing inherent about them. We just too often interact with them as if there is.

9. It is valuable to keep the resonance of the split personality in the back of the mind, though, since imagining the in-between nature of the schizoid in the sense that Deleuze and Guattari mean the term is aided by thinking in terms of a splitting of consciousness, as well as of the space between categories (in the sense of Zeno's paradox).

10. It might well be asked why I turn to texts written in the late 1960s and early 1970s for a vocabulary of revolution. My answer is threefold: (1) it is not too much to say that these writers articulate a crucial outlook relating to the kinds of psychic, emotional, and by extension, political and social restrictions that continue to entrap us as a species, particularly when it comes to the demands of thinking differently about positions in which we have become entrenched; (2) the myriad and ever-changing problems of these entrapments continue to beguile us and find new forms of expression almost daily, without suggesting any novelty in their entrapping nature; and (3) Everett's writing reliably produces characters who embody the particular schizorevolutionary potential that Deleuze and Guattari theorize.

11. Like *schizophrenic*, Deleuze and Guattari use *nomadic* in a way that is related to but different from its more standard usage. But both connotations apply to many of Everett's characters, as they appear peripatetic, if not nomadic, and have little holding them to a particular place, just as they free themselves from being held to standard ways of approaching the world around them. It's also worth recognizing how the traces of the more familiar meanings, which persist in their usages of *schizophrenic* and *nomad*, serve as further challenges for the kind of rethinking that they, in their way, and Everett in his, impose on the reader. If they had chosen wholly other words, these traces would not pose these additional challenges.

12. This is the group of people who live forever but never stop aging. Their lives are an eternal misery, instead of the wealth of endless discovery, vitality, fascination, and opportunity that Gulliver initially imagines.

13. But here it is worth thinking about the way third person works in *American Desert*, as a distanced first person. This may be a way to think of all third-person narration. Very little is straightforward, with Everett or in general.

CHAPTER THREE

1. Everett has often cited Samuel Butler's *The Way of All Flesh* as one of his favorite novels, and its versions of religion must account in part for his preference. One particular example of this concordance of attitude occurs when the narrator considers the role of the clergyman:

> A clergyman, again, can hardly ever allow himself to look facts fairly in the face. It is his profession to support one side; it is impossible, therefore, for him to make an unbiased examination of the other.

We forget that every clergyman with a living or a curacy is as much a paid advocate as the barrister who is trying to persuade a jury to acquit a prisoner. We should listen to him with the same suspense of judgment, the same full consideration of the arguments of the opposing counsel, as a judge does when he is trying a case. Unless we know these, and can state them in a way that our opponents would admit to be a fair representation of the views, we have no right to claim that we have formed an opinion at all. The misfortune is that by the law of the land one side only can be heard. (118)

It is more than a little telling that the clergyman is on the side of the defense in this formulation and not the prosecution, although the prosecution has a higher burden of proof.

2. Rorty, in *Contingency, Irony, and Solidarity,* defines the notion of the *final vocabulary* in the following terms:

All human beings carry about a set of words which they employ to justify their actions, their beliefs, and their lives. These are the words in which we formulate praise of our friends and contempt for our enemies, our long-term projects, our deepest self-doubts and our highest hopes. They are the words in which we tell, sometimes prospectively and sometimes retrospectively, the story of our lives. I shall call these words a person's "final vocabulary."

It is "final" in the sense that if doubt is cast on the worth of these words, their user has no noncircular argumentative recourse. Those words are as far as he can go with language; beyond them there is only helpless passivity or a resort to force. A small part of a final vocabulary is made up of thin, flexible, and ubiquitous terms such as "true," "good," "right" and "beautiful." The larger part contains thicker, more rigid, and more parochial terms, for example, "Christ," "England," "professional standards," "decency," "kindness," "the Revolution," "the Church," "progressive," "rigorous," "creative." The more parochial terms do most of the work. (73)

John Livesey's parochial terms probably include *loyalty* and *family,* among other words. I have used Rorty's definition in my work before as well as in my teaching, and continue to find it generative. However, in thinking about the notion of the final vocabulary in the context of my work on this book, and the places that Everett's work tends to take me, as well as the challenges his work issues to me, I have found myself stumbling upon something that Rorty overlooks or omits. Simply, but significantly, my use of *family* will inevitably differ from someone else's use of the same word. This means that while I might be able to assemble my sense of someone else's final vocabulary, I cannot really know what the terms in their vocabulary mean to them. I can only know what I think those terms mean to me. This realization does not mean that the final vocabulary of any one individual is more or less authentic (whatever that might mean) than that of someone else, but it does mean that I am always only approximating someone else's vocabulary. Once again, we rarely if ever benefit from thinking in terms of the definite and learn more from observing the spaces in between the definite categories.

3. It's worth adding here that *Percival Everett by Virgil Russell* provides an additional prayer, this one combining the attitude toward religion that usually expresses itself in prayers and the kind of play with the conventions of language that would be right at home in *The Water Cure:* "How farther

art this in headland, hellhole, be the same. Die keen drum dumb, die kill beat drum, dawn dearth ass with ill den even. Rive dust gist weigh dour gaily dead, sand relieve just tour dress patches, alas we relieve clothes due dress patch relent gust, kin leave rust snot unto our nation, cut shiver lust from Melville. Core dine in this thief dome and the sour and the gory, endeavor, endeavor. End it how you like" (130). The coup de grâce here is the editorial comment that follows this version of "The Lord's Prayer": "I was never much with prayers, but all superstitions have their place" (130).

4. This is the first appearance by Warren Fragua in Everett's fiction; he appears later as a "ghostly echo," as Ogden Walker's sidekick in *Assumption.*

5. This sequence cannot help but also remind us of the imagined encounter between Ishmael and the police officer in *The Water Cure.* There, too, a black man is caught dead to rights doing something illegal and is also allowed to continue on his way. Maybe Everett is a fantasy writer!

6. In his review of *So Much Blue,* Paul Devlin notes this treatment of art through the treatment of the art world: "A giant mystery canvas in Pace's detached studio is the subject of speculation, in his family and in the art world at large (which is not subjected to as much satirical attack as might be expected from Everett)." Devlin can't be blamed for anticipating that even if art is off limits for satire, the art world would be fair game.

7. I know I'm not alone in seeing a little of a young version of myself in the young Monk's posturing.

8. It is a little uncomfortable to recognize in Pace's comment about himself here a resonance of what Ogden Walker says about people being most interesting when they're dead.

9. Joe Weixlmann rightly points out, however, that "Everett's narrator shows himself throughout the novel to be a troubled soul and admitted liar, both of which characteristics cast a heavy shadow of doubt over the veracity of the radical personal transformation Kevin claims to have occurred in the book's final paragraphs. Thus, the final words of the novel, as evocative as they are, and the painting which is so powerful that it elicits Linda's stunned, repeated response, should not be misconstrued as a final word on the relationship, or the story" (40). So, Kevin's ostensible admission still comes across as another calculated lie. The novel's resolution (an expression I persist in using in spite of its inadequacy) is actually all the more mesmerizing for this last inconsistency.

CHAPTER FOUR

Portions of this chapter first appeared as "Talking about Race, Exposing the Desire for the Post-Racial, and Percival Everett's *Assumption*" in *Lectures du Monde Anglophone* 1 (March 2015).

1. Claude Julien, in his introduction to the first essay collection published on Everett's work, resulting from a gathering of scholars in Tours, France, describes Everett as "a prolific African-American writer who refuses to confine his art to racial protest because it gags imagination" (9). This evaluation usefully implies an additional question: Whose imagination? I would argue that as often as not, art about race (not all of which is racial protest) gags the imagination of viewers, readers, listeners, and audiences who are bound up in conventional thinking about race.

2. As it turns out, though, the authors collected in the series are not all African American, which may be an example of another moment of what anticonventional thinking can look like. This is, after all, also the publisher of *The Jefferson Bible,* Everett's take on Thomas Jefferson's take on the King James Bible.

3. King writes there, quite famously,

> I have almost reached the regrettable conclusion that the Negro's great stumbling block in his stride toward freedom is not the White Citizen's Counciler or the Ku Klux Klanner, but the white moderate, who is more devoted to "order" than to justice; who prefers a negative peace which is the absence of tension to a positive peace which is the presence of justice; who constantly says, "I agree with you in the goal you seek, but I cannot agree with your methods of direct action"; who paternalistically believes he can set the timetable for another man's freedom; who lives by a mythical concept of time and who constantly advises the Negro to wait for a "more convenient season." Shallow understanding from people of good will is more frustrating than absolute misunderstanding from people of ill will. Lukewarm acceptance is much more bewildering than outright rejection. (2:599–600)

4. In an interview with Edward Champion, Everett says: "Some figures just present themselves as too alluring to ignore. I mean, how could I go through my life and not at some point address Strom Thurmond? (Laughs.)" ("The Bat Segundo Show" 167).

5. See the preface to this book on Everett's relationship to South Carolina. He also published the essay "Why I'm from Texas" in *Callaloo* in 2001, further complicating his relationship with South Carolina.

6. David Frum, in the *Atlantic,* suggested something eerily similar, drawing a distinction between thinking and feeling that would comfortably accommodate the distinction between thinking and believing that Thurmond is characterized as making in the novel. Frum is explaining the illiberal impulse that he sees accounting for the election of November 8, 2016:

> The story ends, then, in a great irony. Integral to the liberal project, again in the broad sense of the word *liberal,* is confidence in the power of reason. Words and arguments can overbear ignorance and prejudice. Over the long term, words and arguments can even overcome oppression and violence. That's why liberals in the broad sense are so uniquely horrified by official lying: How can reason prevail unless words connect to reality? How can we argue against people who will spread fictions, if serviceable to them, without a qualm?
>
> Illiberals and anti-liberals, on the other hand, appreciate the dark energy of human irrationality—not merely as a fact of our nature to be negotiated, but as a potent political resource. People do not think; they feel. They do not believe what is true; they regard as true that which they wish to believe. A lie that affirms us will gain more credence than a truth that challenges us. That's the foundational insight on which Trump built his business career. It's the insight on which Trump's supporters built first their campaign for president and now their presidency itself.

7. See the conclusion of chapter 3.

8. There is, however, something a little satisfying in a "rough" neighborhood excluding a black person, since *rough neighborhood* has become a conventional euphemism for black neighborhood. Richard Rothstein discusses such euphemisms—such as "inner city" instead of "ghetto"—in his book *The Color of Law.*

9. In an interview with Alice Mills and Jack Lanco, Everett says: "But the most segregated city in the entire United States is not in the South: that's Chicago, Illinois; and the only place in the whole United States where I have ever been called a 'nigger' is Cambridge, Massachusetts. I grew up where the Civil War started but no one ever called me a 'nigger' there, though I know my father was" ("The South" 92). This moment in *Wounded* is one of those moments when we are tempted to conflate Everett and one of his characters, but this is an impulse that it is better to keep at bay.

10. Ta-Nehisi Coates's article "The Case for Reparations," for instance, presents a thorough-going account of the continuity of racism through measures like housing and lending policies, which continue to account for race-based disparities in wealth. And, as Paul Gilroy reminds us, racism causes race, not the other way round. He moots the circumstance under which traditionally oppressive understandings of race persist and concludes: "'Race' would then become an eternal cause of racism rather than what it is for me—its complex, unstable product. I should probably emphasize at this point that neither race nor racism are the exclusive historical property of the minorities who are their primary victims" (*After Empire* 16).

11. It's also worth adding that the search for this citation reinforced for me the fiction of completeness or mastery upon which so much of scholarship must be based, and which I mentioned at the beginning of this book.

In thinking that I remembered this story, I was sure that Wallace had begun his Kenyon address talking about swimming fish, but had forgotten that the story also appears in *Infinite Jest,* a novel that I have read, taught, and listened to as an audiobook twice. I was driving in my car on my way to the office during the period when I was coincidentally finishing edits on the manuscript for *Approximate Gestures,* when I realized that I was listening to the passage in Wallace's novel that I cite here. While it is true that I could have researched scholarship on Wallace's novel, and would probably have stumbled upon the fish passage from *Infinite Jest* there, I could not help but marvel for a moment at what the odds might be of the coincidence of my happening upon this brief passage tucked into the middle of a very long book that I happened to be listening to at that moment, so that I could then authoritatively cite the passage in my own scholarship. (I cannot help but think back to Wallace's own speculation about the Principle of Induction—which I discuss in the Introduction to *Approximate Gestures*—and how we might go insane were we to ponder every little thing we do, encounter, or consider over the course of an average day.)

Perhaps this coincidence is no more interesting than the phenomenon that we experience when we buy a Volkswagen, for instance, and then start noticing how many other Volkswagens there are on the road, but I think the coincidence is, nevertheless, noteworthy. Not unlike the passage I quote in the preface of this book in which Everett makes his statement about the confederate flag and minefield signs, I continue to be amazed at the relationship between these two perceptual ideas. One: that we continue to adhere to a belief in our own mastery, as scholars. Two: that anyone continues to believe that they can with certainty know everything there is to know about another group of people, usually a group about whom they know very little, as bigots do. After all, bigotry is about imposing one's own mastery—in one way or another—over someone else.

Either impulse towards mastery might be productively held at bay by a simple acknowledgment and enactment of the value of humility. Recognizing the size and scope of that idea, which is not the purpose of this book—as such—I relegate this important notion to a probably inadequate footnote. Nevertheless, it is worth noting.

12. Again, this is Farouq's point in *Open City,* in the epigraph to chapter 1.

13. Eduardo Bonilla-Silva has seized upon perhaps the most felicitous expression of this postintentional impulse for which Perry argues, when evaluating racism and racist acts, in the title of his widely discussed book *Racism without Racists: Color-Blind Racism and the Persistence of Racial Inequality in America.*

14. Nor have they been destroyed by the election of another, less exceptional, one.

15. Commenting on Gilroy's observations about how race estranges blacks and whites, and "amputate[s] their common humanity," Sharon Holland writes: "Gilroy's visceral insights is a testament to the fact that we cannot get away from our interpretation of the primary work of race at the junction of black and white; the estrangement that Gilroy alludes to is odd, given that relations between the two are and have been so intimately articulated" (7).

16. The Oedipal nature of this piece of evidence in confirming Ogden's identity just highlights again how thoroughgoing Oedipus is as a governing metaphor. *Wounded* carries a similarly Oedipal anxiety, as David, the son of John Hunt's college friend, reflects on his father's prejudices: "He hates me. That's logic. Right?" (70).

17. My intention here is not to be glib, or even overly critical, but merely to draw out to their conclusions the implications inherent in suggesting that race is irrelevant to the "My American Cousin" section of *Assumption.*

18. I think Derrida would say that these people think about (t)race so that they no longer have to think about (t)race.

CONCLUSIONS

1. Houston Baker, while criticizing what he sees as the many shortcomings of *Erasure,* nevertheless corroborates Everett's and Sollors's evaluations of how difference-based expectations determine the worth of nonmajority (however defined) artists. Speaking to an "almost completely white audience" in South Carolina, Baker found that "to a person, they hated *Erasure*'s main storyline of family dissolution, skipped or glossed the sidebars from Barthes to *Virtue* [sic] *et Armis,* did not know what to make of Kenya Dunston, but . . . adored, and could quote almost by the paragraph, *My Pafology/FUCK*" (141). In other words, this audience were getting what they were expecting (hoping for?) from the ghetto novel but appear to have resented Everett's forgetting of his place as a black artist. The icing on the cake here, of course, is that this event took place in South Carolina, the state where Everett grew up and which he has disavowed in print more than once.

2. See chapter 1.

3. As with Everett, Beatty also provides the occasional multileveled, multilingual joke. As Ulla Haselstein pointed out at a talk I gave on Beatty's work at the John F. Kennedy Institute for North American Studies in Berlin, *schwa*, in addition to the phonetic application Beatty's novel provides, contains traces of several German words that only enhance our interpretations of *Slumberland*. *Schwa* is the beginning of the German word for *swan*, a bird identifiable for its size and its whiteness. *Schwa* is also most of the German word for black, *Schwarze*, which carries within it a more derogatory intonation, approaching *nigger*. *Schwa* also carries within it the trace of the German slang word for phallus, *Schwantz*. The collocation of words connoting whiteness, blackness, and the phallus, all relating to the discovery of an almost completely anonymous African American male jazz musician is the kind of chain of signification that is impossible to forget once one has seen it.

4. DJ Darky, in turn, is translated as Schallplattenunterhalter Dunkelmann, which Sowell describes as "an approximation of my nom de musique, DJ Darky. The bartender explained to me that in German, Dunkelmann means 'obscurant' or, more literally, 'dark man,' and that Schallplattenunterhalter was an East German term for 'disk jockey.' East Germany being a place where the global predominance of English had yet to suck the fun out of the language's tongue-twisting archaism" (*Slumberland* 43). This old-fashioned German transliteration would hold special pleasure for someone with a phonographic memory.

5. I'm not arguing that the members of Fishbone are devotees of Deleuze and Guattari (although I won't argue that they're not, either), but the coincidence that their 1993 album, *Give a Monkey a Brain, and He'll Swear He's the Center of the Universe,* has a song titled "Drunk Skitzo" is worth at least mentioning.

6. Obviously, this version of liberalism, probably more closely approaching neoliberalism, is not what I meant and identified with in my introduction. I include this version of liberalism here as a further indicator (concession, really) of the unresolved nature of just about anything we determine to talk about.

7. Even though only fifteen years of age, Benji's socioeconomic status is reminiscent of Daniel Barkley's, Ishmael Kidder's, and Not Sidney Poitier's, all African American men whose horizons for self-expression and self-possession are broader in part because of financial independence.

8. Reed's positioning by the culture here, as he is published in the *New York Times*, cannot help but signal a similar dynamic in Beatty's *The Sellout* being awarded the Man Booker Prize for Fiction.

BIBLIOGRAPHY

Amfreville, Marc. "*Erasure* and *The Water Cure*: A Possible Suture." In "The Art of Percival Everett—Rewriting a Black American Narrative," edited by Anthony Stewart. Special issue, *Canadian Review of American Studies* 43, no.2 (Summer 2013): 180–88.

Appiah, Kwame Anthony. "The Dialectics of Enlightenment." *New York Review of Books*, May 9, 2019, https://www.nybooks.com/articles/2019/05/09/irrationality-dialectics-enlightenment/.

Baker, Houston A., Jr. *I Don't Hate the South: Reflections on Faulkner, Family, and the South.* New York: Oxford, 2007.

Baldwin, James. "James Baldwin: The Art of Fiction no. 78." Interview by Jordan Elgrably. *Paris Review* 91 (1984). https://www.theparisreview.org/interviews/2994/james-baldwin-the-art-of-fiction-no-78-james-baldwin.

Barber, Benjamin. *Jihad vs. McWorld: How Globalism and Tribalism Are Reshaping the World.* New York: Ballantine, 1995.

Bauer, Sylvie. "The Music of Words in *Zulus*." In *Percival Everett Transatlantic Readings*, edited by Claire Maniez and Anne-Laure Tissut, 153–72. Paris: Éditions Le Manuscrit, 2007.

Beatty, Paul. *Slumberland.* New York: Bloomsbury, 2008.

———. *The Sellout.* New York: Farrar, 2015.

Bhabha, Homi K. *The Location of Culture.* London: Routledge, 1994.

Bonilla-Silva, Eduardo. *Racism without Racists: Color-Blind Racism and the Persistence of Racial Inequality in America.* New York: Rowman and Littlefield, 2003.

Butler, Samuel. *The Way of All Flesh.* New York: Modern Library, 1998.

Cannon, Uzzie. "A Bird of a Different Feather: Blues, Jazz, and the Difficult Journey to the Self in Percival Everett's Suder." In *Perspectives on Percival Everett*, edited by Keith B. Mitchell and Robin G. Vander, 94–112. Jackson: UP of Mississippi, 2013.

Caruth, Cathy. *Unclaimed Experience: Trauma, Narrative, and History.* Baltimore: Johns Hopkins UP, 1996.

Cassuto, Leonard. "Human Objectification and the Racial Grotesque." In *The Inhuman Race: The Racial Grotesque in American Literature*, 1–29. New York: Columbia UP, 1997.

"Chapter Fourteen: The Ceiling." Episode of *The Wilderness*, a podcast by Crooked Media. https://crooked.com/podcast/chapter-14-the-ceiling/.

Cherry, Kendra. "What Is the Dunning-Kruger Effect?" Verywellmind.com, https://www.verywellmind.com/an-overview-of-the-dunning-kruger-effect-4160740.

Coates, Ta-Nehisi. "The Case for Reparations." *Atlantic*, June 2014, https://www.theatlantic.com/magazine/archive/2014/06/the-case-for-reparations/361631/.

Cole, Teju. *Open City*. New York: Random House, 2011.

Deleuze, Gilles. *Difference and Repetition*. Translated by Paul Patton. 1968. Reprint, New York: Columbia UP, 1994.

Deleuze, Gilles, and Félix Guattari. *Anti-Oedipus: Capitalism and Schizophrenia*. Translated by Robert Hurley, Mark Seem, and Helen R. Lane, introduction by Mark Seem. New York: Penguin, 2009.

———. *A Thousand Plateaus: Capitalism and Schizophrenia*. Translated and with a foreword by Brian Massumi. Minneapolis: U of Minnesota P, 1987.

———. *What Is Philosophy?* Translated by Hugh Tomlinson and Graham Burchell. New York: Columbia University Press, 1994.

Derrida, Jacques. "Différance." 1968. In *Critical Theory since 1965*, edited by Hazard Adams and Leroy Searle, 120–36. Tallahassee: Florida State UP, 1986.

Devlin, Paul. "Writer of Color." *Nation*, June 26, 2017, https://www.thenation.com/article/percival-everett-abstract-art/.

Dickson-Carr, Darryl. "Afterword: From Pilloried to Post-Soul: The Future of African American Satire." In *Post-Soul Satire: Black Identity after Civil Rights*, edited by Derek C. Maus and James J. Donahue, 269–80. Jackson: UP of Mississippi, 2014.

Donahue, James. "Voicing His Objections: Narrative Voice as Racial Critique in Percival Everett's *God's Country*." In "So Much Percival Everett," edited by Joe Weixlmann and Anthony Stewart. Special issue, *African American Review* 52 no. 1 (Spring 2019): 75–86.

Du Bois, W. E. B. "From *The Souls of Black Folk*." In *The Norton Anthology of African American Literature*, 3rd ed., edited by Henry Louis Gates Jr. and Valerie A. Smith, 1:687–760. New York: Norton, 2014.

Ellis, Trey. "The New Black Aesthetic." *Callaloo* 38 (1989): 233–43.

Ellison, Ralph. *Invisible Man*. 1952. 2nd Vintage International ed. New York: Vintage, 1995.

———. "The Shadow and the Act." In *Shadow and Act*. 1946. Reprint, New York: Vintage, 1995, 273–81.

Everett, Percival. "Alluvial Deposits." In *Damned If I Do*, 39–60. St. Paul: Graywolf, 2004.

———. *American Desert*. New York: Hyperion, 2004.

———. "The Appropriation of Cultures." In *Damned If I Do*, 91–104. St. Paul: Graywolf, 2004.

———. *Assumption.* St. Paul: Graywolf, 2011.

———. "*The Bat Segundo Show #295* (Percival Everett)." Interview by Edward Champion. In Weixlmann, *Conversations with Percival Everett,* 165–76.

———. *The Body of Martin Aguilera.* Camano Island, WA: Owl Creek, 1997.

———. "The Books Interview: Percival Everett." By Sean O'Hagan. In Weixlmann, *Conversations with Percival Everett,* 32–34.

———. *Cutting Lisa.* Baton Rouge: Louisiana State UP, 1986.

———. *Erasure.* New York: Hyperion, 2001.

———. "The Fix." In *Damned If I Do,* 3–24. St. Paul: Graywolf, 2004.

———. *Frenzy.* St. Paul: Graywolf, 1997.

———. *Glyph.* St. Paul: Graywolf, 1999.

———. *I Am Not Sidney Poitier.* St. Paul: Graywolf, 2009.

———. *Infinite Jest.* New York: Little, Brown, 1996.

———. "An Interview: May 3rd, 2005." By Alice Mills, Claude Julien, and Anne-Laure Tissut. In Weixlmann, *Conversations with Percival Everett,* 78–89.

———. "Interview with Percival Everett." By Barbara DeMarco-Barrett and Marrie Stone. In Weixlmann, *Conversations with Percival Everett,* 148–53.

———. "Percival Everett." Interview by Rone Shavers. In Weixlmann, *Conversations with Percival Everett,* 57–70.

———. *Percival Everett by Virgil Russell.* St. Paul: Graywolf, 2013.

———. *Re: F (Gesture).* Los Angeles: Red Hen, 2006.

———. "Signing to the Blind." *Callaloo* 14 (Winter 1991): 9–11.

———. *So Much Blue.* St. Paul: Graywolf, 2017.

———. "The South." Interview by Alice Mills and Jack Lanco. In Weixlmann, *Conversations with Percival Everett,* 90–92.

———. *Suder.* Baton Rouge: Louisiana State UP, 1999.

———. "Uncategorizable Is Still a Category: An Interview with Percival Everett." By Anthony Stewart. In Weixlmann, *Conversations with Percival Everett,* 119–47.

———. "Warm and Nicely Buried." In *Damned If I Do,* 105–28. St. Paul: Graywolf, 2004.

———. *The Water Cure.* St. Paul: Graywolf, 2007.

———. *Watershed.* Boston: Beacon, 1996.

———. "Why I'm from Texas." *Callaloo* 24 no. 1 (2001): 62–63.

———. *Wounded.* St. Paul: Graywolf, 2005.

"Everett, Percival." *South Carolina Encyclopedia.* http://www.scencyclopedia.org/sce /ecms/e/page/7/.

Everett, Percival, and James Kincaid. *A History of the African-American People [Proposed] by Strom Thurmond, as Told to Percival Everett & James Kincaid.* New York: Akashic Books, 2004.

Everyday Sunshine: The Story of Fishbone. Directed by Lev Anderson and Chris Metzler, performances by Fishbone. Grindstone Media, 2010.

Feith, Michel. "Hire-a-Glyph: Hermetics and Hermeneutics in Percival Everett's *Glyph.*" *Canadian Review of American Studies* 43, no. 2 (Summer 2013): 301–19.

———. "Philosophy Embedded in Space: Rethinking the Frontier in Percival Everett's Western Novels." In "So Much Percival Everett," edited by Joe Weixlmann and Anthony Stewart. Special issue, *African American Review* 52 no. 1 (Spring 2019): 87–99.

Felski, Rita. Introduction to *The Limits of Critique,* 1–13. Chicago: U of Chicago P, 2015.

Fishbone. "Introduction to 'Unyielding Conditioning.'" *Live in Bordeaux.* San Francisco: Controlled Substance Sound Lab, 2009.

———. *In Your Face.* Album art by John Scarpati, photographer, Sunset Sound Factory, 1986.

———. So Many Millions." *The Reality of My Surroundings.* New York: Columbia, 1991.

Frum, David. "The Real Lesson of My Debate with Steve Bannon." *Atlantic,* November 4, 2018, https://www.theatlantic.com/ideas/archive/2018/11/bannon-frum-munk-debate -what-really-happened/574867/.

Gilroy, Paul. *After Empire: Melancholia or Convivial Culture?* New York: Routledge, 2004.

———. "Bold as Love? Jimi's Afrocyberdelia and the Challenge of the Not-Yet." *Critical Quarterly* 46, no. 4 (December 7, 2004): 112–25.

Gladwell, Malcolm. "Late Bloomers: Why Do We Equate Genius with Precocity?" *New Yorker,* October 20, 2008, https://www.newyorker.com/magazine/2008/10/20/late -bloomers-malcolm-gladwell.

Harper, Philip Brian. *Abstractionist Aesthetics: Artistic Form and Social Critique in African American Culture.* New York: New York UP, 2015.

———. "Extra-Special Effects: Televisual Representation and the Claims of 'the Black Experience.'" In *Living Color: Race and Television in the United States,* edited by Sasha Torres, 62–81. Durham, NC: Duke UP, 1998.

Hoban, Russell. Afterword to *Riddley Walker,* expanded ed., 223–27. Bloomington: Indiana UP, 1998.

Holland, Eugene W. "Social Production and the External Critique of Oedipus." In *Deleuze and Guattari's "Anti-Oedipus": Introduction to Schizoanalysis,* 58–89. New York: Routledge, 1999.

Holland, Sharon. *The Erotic Life of Racism.* Durham, NC: Duke UP, 2012.

Hooks, bell. *Black Looks: Race and Representation.* New York: Routledge, 1992.

Julien, Claude. "Introduction: Reading Percival Everett: European Perspectives." In *Reading Percival Everett: European Perspectives,* edited by Claude Julien and Anne-Laure Tissut, 9–20. Tours: Presses Universitaires François-Rabelais, 2007.

Julien, Claude, and Anne-Laure Tissut, eds. Reading *Percival Everett: European Perspectives*. Tours: PU François Rabelais, 2007.

Kincaid, James, ed. "Percival Everett: A Special Section." Callaloo: *A Journal of African Diaspora Arts and Letters* 28, no. 2 (Spring 2005).

King, Martin Luther, Jr. "Letter from Birmingham Jail." In *The Norton Anthology of African American Literature,* 3rd ed., edited by Henry Louis Gates Jr. and Valerie A. Smith, 2:594–607. New York: Norton, 2014.

Lear, Jonathan. "A Note on Zeno's Arrow." *Phronesis* 26, no. 2 (1981): 91–104.

Maniez, Claire, and Anne-Laure Tissut, eds. *Percival Everett Transatlantic Readings.* Paris: Éditions Le Manuscrit, 2007.

Márquez, Gabriel García. "A Very Old Man with Enormous Wings." In *Collected Stories,* 203–10. New York: Harper and Row, 1984.

Maus, Derek C. *Jesting in Earnest: Percival Everett and Menippean Satire.* Columbia: U of South Carolina P, 2019.

Miller, Gregory Leon. "Identity Crisis." *Los Angeles Review of Books.* January 23, 2012, https://www.lareviewofbooks.org/article/identity-crisis/.

Mitchell, Keith B., and Robin Vander, eds. Perspectives on Percival Everett. Jackson: UP of Mississippi, 2013.

Morton, Seth. "Locating the Experimental Novel in *Erasure* and *The Water Cure.*" In "The Art of Percival Everett—Rewriting a Black American Narrative," edited by Anthony Stewart. Special issue, *Canadian Review of American Studies:* 43, no. 2 (Summer 2013): 189–201.

N.W.A. *Straight Outta Compton.* Album art by Ithaka Darin Pappas, photographer. Audio Achievements, 1988.

Obama, Barack. *Barack Obama: Words That Inspired a Nation; Essential Speeches, 2002 to the Inauguration.* Foreword by Victor Dorff. New York: Fall River Press, 2009.

O'Brien, Flann. *At Swim-Two-Birds.* 1939. Reprint, New York: Penguin, 1967.

Perry, Adele. "Graduating Photos: Race, Colonization, and the University of Manitoba." In *Too Asian? Racism, Privilege, and Post-Secondary Education,* edited by R. J. Gilmour, Davina Bhandar, Jeet Heer, and Michael C. K. Ma, 55–66. Toronto: Between the Lines, 2012.

Perry, Imani. *More Beautiful and More Terrible: The Embrace and Transcendence of Racial Inequality in the United States.* New York: New York UP, 2011.

Rana, Zat. "David Hume: Why You're Probably Wrong about Everything You Know." *Medium,* September 26, 2018, https://medium.com/personal-growth/david-hume-why-youre-probably-wrong-about-everything-you-know-62fb4caa2b21.

Reed, Ishmael. "Fade to White." *New York Times,* February 10, 2010, http://www.nytimes.com/2010/02/05/opinion/05reed.html?_r=0.

Roof, Judith. "Mr. Everett Anthologizes." In *Percival Everett Transatlantic Readings,* edited by Claire Maniez and Anne-Laure Tissut, 35–47. Paris: Éditions Le Manuscrit, 2007.

———. "Everett's Hypernarrator." In "The Art of Percival Everett—Rewriting a Black American Narrative," edited by Anthony Stewart. Special issue, *Canadian Review of American Studies* 43, no. 2 (Summer 2013): 202–15.

Rorty, Richard. *Contingency, Irony, and Solidarity.* Cambridge: Cambridge UP, 1989.

Rothstein, Richard. *The Color of Law: A Forgotten History of How Our Government Segregated America.* New York: Liveright, 2017.

Russett, Margaret. "Race under Erasure: For Percival Everett, 'A Piece of Fiction.'" In Percival Everett: A Special Section," edited by James Kincaid. *A Journal of African Diaspora Arts and Letters* 28, no. 2 (Spring 2005): 358–68.

Sacks, Sam. "A Protean Chronicler of Racial Puzzles." *Wall Street Journal,* October 29, 2011, https://www.wsj.com/articles/SB10001424052970203687504576654802353 219090.

Schneider, David. *The Psychology of Stereotyping.* New York: Guilford, 2004.

Schur, Richard. "The Crisis of Authenticity in Contemporary African American Literature." In *Contemporary African American Literature: The Living Canon,* edited by Lovalerie King and Shirley Moody-Turner, 235–54. Bloomington: Indiana UP, 2013.

Smith, Daniel W. "Deleuze and the Question of Desire: Towards an Immanent Theory of Ethics." In *Essays on Deleuze,* 175–88. Edinburgh: Edinburgh University Press, 2012.

Sollors, Werner. "What Could a New Anthology of American Literature Look Like?" *American Studies: Questions, Problems, Provocations,* February 13, 2012, https://sunny americas.wordpress.com/2012/02/13/what-could-a-new-anthology-of-american -literature-look-like/.

Stewart, Anthony. "About Percival Everett: A Profile by Anthony Stewart." *Ploughshares* 40, nos. 2 and 3 (Fall 2014): 188–193.

———, ed. "The Art of Percival Everett—Rewriting a Black American Narrative." Special issue, *Canadian Review of American Studies* 43, no. 2 (Summer 2013).

———. "Giving the People What They Want: The African American Exception as Racial Cliché in Percival Everett's *Erasure.*" In *American Exceptionalisms from Winthrop to Winfrey,* edited by Sylvia Söderlind and James Taylor Carson, 167–90. New York: SUNY Press, 2011.

———. "Setting One's House in Order: Theoretical Blackness in Percival Everett's Fiction." In "The Art of Percival Everett—Rewriting a Black American Narrative," edited by Anthony Stewart. Special issue, *Canadian Review of American Studies* 43, no. 3 (Summer 2013): 216–24.

———. *Visitor: My Life in Canada.* Halifax: Fernwood, 2014.

———. *You Must Be a Basketball Player: Rethinking Integration in the University.* Halifax: Fernwood, 2009.

Stout, Martha. *The Sociopath Next Door.* New York: Crown, 2005.

Sundquist, Eric. "'We Dreamed a Dream': Ralph Ellison, Martin Luther King, Jr., and Barack Obama." *Daedalus* 140, no. 1 (Winter 2011): 108–24.

Thobani, Sunera. "No Academic Exercise: The Assault on Anti-Racist Feminism in the Age of Terror." *R.A.C.E.link,* (Spring 2008) 3–8, http://coms.concordia.ca/pdf/RACElink -2008.pdf.

Tissut, Anne Laure. "Percival Everett's *The Water Cure:* A Blind Read." *Exposure/Over- exposure* 17 (2014), https://journals.openedition.org/sillagescritiques/3496.

Toscano, Alberto. "The Colored Thickness of a Problem." Preface to *The Signature of the World, Or, What Is Deleuze and Guattari's Philosophy?,* by Éric Alliez, ix–xxv. Translated by Eliot Ross Albert and Alberto Toscano. New York: Continuum, 2004.

Vanderbilt, Tom. *Traffic: Why We Drive the Way We Do (and What It Says About Us).* New York: Vintage, 2008.

Vonnegut, Kurt. *Breakfast of Champions.* 1973. New York: Dial, 2002.

Wallace, David Foster. *Consider the Lobster and Other Essays.* New York: Little, Brown, 2006.

———. *Everything and More: A Compact History of Infinity.* New York: Atlas Book, 2003.

———. *This Is Water: Some Thoughts, Delivered on a Significant Occasion, about Living a Compassionate Life.* New York: Little, Brown, 2009.

Weixlmann, Joe. "Bibliography." https://percivaleverettsociety.com/bibliography/.

———, ed. *Conversations with Percival Everett.* Jackson: UP of Mississippi, 2013.

———. "Revealing the Artistry of Percival Everett's *So Much Blue.*" In "So Much Percival Everett," edited by Joe Weixlmann and Anthony Stewart. Special issue, *African American Review* 52, no. 1 (Spring 2019): 27–46.

Weixlmann, Joe, and Anthony Stewart, eds. "So Much Percival Everett." Special issue, *African American Review* 52, no. 1 (Spring 2019).

Whitehead, Colson. *Sag Harbor.* New York: Doubleday, 2009.

———. "The Year of Living Postracially." *New York Times,* November 3, 2009, http://www .nytimes.com/2009/11/04/opinion/04whitehead.html?_r=0.

INDEX

abstract thinking, 10–11, 12

aesthetics, 44, 46; aesthetic judgments, 48, 191

Africa Bambaataa and the Soul Sonic Force, 206

African Americans, 23, 100, 167, 202–3; African American artists, 23, 176, 190, 208; African American authenticity, 207–8, 209–10; African American literature, 38, 219n13; African American men, 202–3, 211, 229n7; African American music, 214–15; African American writers, 100, 159–60, 171, 175, 192; chronology of African American culture, 196–97; conventions that influence our images of African Americans, 200–201; frustrations of concerning how African Americans are perceived in American culture, 210–11; self-consciousness of, 193

Akashic Urban Surreal series, 162, 226n2

Alliez, Eric, 35

"Alluvial Deposits" (Everett), Robert Hawks in, 186, 212

American Desert (Everett), 17, 32–33, 94, 139, 221n13, 223n13; attention to the basics of Theodore Street's condition in, 87–88; Big Daddy in, 89; the breach between life and death in, 33–34; the Christ analogy in, 87, 221–22n16; conclusion of, 92; distancing and change of the narrative point of view in, 81–82; Emily Street in, 85, 86; Gloria Street in, 85; juxtaposition of the meta-physical and the mundane in, 87; Larville Staige's funeral eulogy of Theodore Street in, 136–37; the line between high and low comedy in, 89; metaphysical aspects of, 92–93; Mr. Ash in, 84; Mr. Graves in, 85; nature of irony in, 82; questions of categories in, 86–87; surreal and slapstick nature of the headless Theodore Street in, 82–83; Theodore Street in, 17, 33, 81–82, 92–93, 136; Theodore Street's acceptance of his modified state of being in, 88–89; Theodore Street's resurrection in, 84–86; Theodore Street's unconventional relationship with life and death in, 83–84

anticonvention, 6, 54, 107, 217n2; distinction between unconventional and anti-conventional, 47

anti-double consciousness, 46–47, 55, 61, 160–61, 192, 212, 214

Anti-Oedipus (Deleuze and Guattari), 9, 123, 140, 156; on religion, 128–29

"Appropriation of Cultures, The" (Everett), 103; Daniel Barkley in, 103–4, 112, 205, 222n4; Daniel Barkley's anger in, 106; Daniel Barkley's "condition" in, 104–5; Daniel Barkley's discovery in, 106; Daniel Barkley's rendition of "Dixie" in, 105–6; frat boys in, 105; and the gesture of "taking" in, 107; Sarah in, 106–7

Are You Experienced? (1967), 204

Erasure (Everett) *(continued)*
189; Thelonious "Monk" Ellison in, 43–44, 73, 96–97, 101–2, 142, 183, 191; Monk Ellison's motivation for writing his parody of a ghetto novel in, 146–47; Monk Ellison's self-observation (self-reflection) in, 102–3, 130, 219n1; the question of what is and what is not art in, 107, 108–10; *We's Live in Da Ghetto* in, 96, 101, 107, 146, 209. *See also* "Erased de Kooning Drawing" (Rauschenberg, 1953)

Everett, Percival, 38–39, 43–44, 227n9; challenges presented by his work, 47, 123, 179; as a character in his own novels, 99; examples of quintessential Everett sentences, 143; identity of as an African American artist, 7–8, 23, 159; kaleidoscopic nature of his work, 22, 29–30, 34, 38, 128, 132, 134, 151, 154, 159, 213; multifarious body of his work, 26–27; placing of his characters in extreme circumstances by, 159–60; work of as fighting against the reading process itself, 100; on writing novels, 36

Everett, Percival, themes concerning religion in his work, 130, 217n1, 224–25n3; art and religion, 32–33, 144, 151; latent seriousness concerning religion in his work, 132–33, 136–37

Everett, Percival, themes of in his work, 12–13, 79; the American West, 192; anti-double consciousness posture of as motivation for his characters, 46–47, 55, 61, 160–61, 192, 212, 214; and the challenges presented to his readers, 7, 8–9, 14, 25–26, 36, 75, 143; categories and oppositions of categories, 61–62; the idea of the schizorevolutionary as invaluable to his work, 25; identification of a character as black by how others view him, 172–73; importance of the inconclusive, 65; and the infinite middle, 69, 72, 76; and the infinite space between categories,

77, 95–96, 127–28, 153–54, 158, 160; and the issue of race, 26, 175–78; on the meaning of everything, 34–35; prominence of didactic central characters in his novels, 30–31, 90, 92, 97; representations of race in his work, 158–161, 187; on retaining our habits of mind, 5–6; schizophrenic nature of his characters, 117–18; tensions presented between different conventions, 8; water, 134–35. *See also* Everett, Percival, themes concerning religion in his work

Everyday Sunshine (2010), 201
Everything and More: A Compact History of Infinity (Wallace), 10–11, 218n6

Feith, Michel, 218n9
Felski, Rita, 16, 35
feminism, 26
Finnegans Wake (Joyce): discussion of in *Erasure*, 145–46; reliance of on convention, 167
Fishbone, 201, 204, 213–15, 229n5; as playing "black" music, 214
Fisher, John Norwood, 201, 215
Fisher, Philip "Fish," 201
"Fix, The" (Everett), 14–20, 86, 103; and Christian allegory, 16–17; conclusion of, 28; Douglas Langley in, 14, 15, 16, 17–19; the idea of fixing people in, 19–20; the implications of fixity in, 22, 28; and limitlessness. 21–22; repeated use of the word "fix" in, 18; Sherman Olney in, 14–15, 22, 27–28; Sherman Olney's humility in, 15–16; Sherman Olney's response to Douglas Langley's questioning in, 16–18; Sherman Olney's revival of a dead woman in, 18–19; singularity in both surnames of Douglas Langley and Sherman Olney, 22
fixity, 22, 28, 159; Bhabha's description of, 19–20
For Her Dark Skin (Everett), 114
Foucault, Michel, 178

Frenzy (Everett), 127; Dionysos in, 132; Vlepo in, 132

genius, and precocity, 54

Gilroy, Paul, 181–83, 227n10; on the distinction between the paranoic and the schizophrenic, 182; on Jimi Hendrix, 205

"Giving the People What They Want" (Stewart), 59–60

Glyph (Everett), 43, 61, 62, 75–76, 78–79, 86, 94, 114, 120, 143; anticonventional nature of Ralph Townsend in, 54; infinite possibilities explained in, 89–90; juxtaposition of with *Suder*, 54–55; paradoxes in, 21, 218n9; Ralph Townsend in, 30, 31, 32, 67, 75, 191; Ralph Townsend as either baby or genius in, 53–54, 219–20n4; Ralph Townsend and paradox in, 53; Ralph Townsend's potential versus actual infinities in, 52–53; self-consciousness of Ralph Townsend in, 54; testing of Ralph Townsend's IQ in, 53; trope of codes and codebreaking in, 76–77; trope of lines in, 90–91

Grand Canyon, Inc. (Everett), 135; Rhino Tanner in, 166

grotesque, the, analysis of, 91

Guattari, Félix, 9–10, 35, 36, 90, 114, 132, 154–55, 210; on blackness, 25; on the definition of schizoanalysis, 26–27; on doing things purely out of habit, 191, 205; and the idea of the schizorevolutionary, 24–25, 118–20, 167–68; identification of family, capitalism, and sex as limiting Oedipal forces, 172; on the interrelationship between habit and power, 23–24; and the nomadic, 23, 25, 27, 119, 223n11; preference of for nonstandard languages, 155–56; on religion, 128; on schizoid investment, 183; on the schizophrenic and social coding, 117–18; use of blackness by, 199

habits, 98–100, 121, 123, 191; habits of mind that enable moral exclusion, 4–5; retention of, 5–6

Half an Inch of Water (Everett), 134

Harper, Philip Brian, 202–3

Hendrix, Jimi, 204–5

hermeneutics, of suspicion, 16, 35

History of the African-American People [Proposed] by Strom Thurmond, as Told to Percival Everett & James Kincaid (Everett and Kincaid), 99, 226n6; author's note concerning, 161–62; Clarence Thomas scene in, 168–69; Edgefield lunch scene in, 163–64; James Kincaid in, 163–64, 167, 171; Percival Everett in, 162, 163, 167, 171, 184; Strom Thurmond as a fascinating character in, 164–65; Strom Thurmond as an in-between figure in, 171–72; Strom Thurmond as a white whale figure in, 163; Strom Thurmond's death in, 170; Strom Thurmond's lecture on the difference between thoughts and beliefs in, 165–68; Strom Thurmond's reconstruction of his past in, 162–63; Strom Thurmond's reflection on the Battle of the Bulge in, 169–70

Hoban, Russell, 100

hooks, bell, 45

Hughes, Langston, 46

I Am Not Sidney Poitier (Everett), 1, 99, 111–12, 184; allusion to *Moby Dick* in, 116; manner in which convention expresses itself in, 114–15; Not Sidney's opinion of Maggie's family in, 116–17; Not Sidney's reflections on his name in, 112–13; Portia Poitier in, 112; reliance of jokes on convention as a subtext in, 114; response of Maggie's father to Not Sidney's name, 115–16; Ted Turner in, 112; tension in created by what a character is not doing and what is perhaps actually happening, 6–7; wealth of Not Sidney in, 112

George W. Bush's foreign policy, 70, 220–21n11; harrowing quality of the narrative in, 62–63; inadequacy of language presented in, 64–65; and the infinite, 74–75; and the infinite middle, 72; intellectual and emotional role of language in, 78–79; Ishmael Kidder in, 6, 12–13, 21, 62, 65, 67, 96, 110–11, 112, 123, 134, 225n5; Ishmael Kidder and schizorevolutionary potential in, 172, 187; Ishmael Kidder's anguish at the loss of Lane in, 152; Ishmael Kidder's declaration to his captive in, 72; Ishmael Kidder's obsession with identity in, 73–74; Ishmael Kidder's pseudonym (Estelle Gilliam) in, 73, 111, 220n10; Ishmael Kidder's purchase of mirrors and the status of reflection in, 66–69, 221n12; Lane in, 62, 63, 65; poetic typography of, 74–76, 79; primary leitmotifs of, 63, 65–66; questions concerning the breed of dog at the scene where Lane's body is found, 63, 68–69, 70; questions and inconclusive answers in the conclusion of, 70–71; as a revenge fantasy, 79–81; Sally in, 110

Watershed (Everett), 32, 139, 186; James Reskin in, 134; James Reskin's quoting of scripture verses in, 132–36; James Reskin's saying of grace to resolve his own anxieties in, 131–32; Karen Reskin in, 131, 134; Robert Hawks in, 131, 134, 135

Way of All Flesh, The (Butler), 223–24n1

Weixlmann, Joe, 225n9

"What Could a New Anthology of American Literature Look Like?" (Sollors), 189–90

What Is Philosophy? (Deleuze and Guattari), 218n7

What Was African American Literature (Warren), 218–19n10

White Boy Shuffle, The (Beatty), 192

Whitehead, Colson, 192, 206, 213; aesthetic of, 208; on the double-bind of blackness in America, 212–13

Wounded (Everett), 120, 227n9; issues of race and racial difference in, 173–75; John in, 173, 174; Robert in, 173, 174–75

Wright, Jeremiah, 181

Wright, Richard, 208

Zeno, 13, 51; and the paradox of being both right and wrong, 21, 28, 30, 52–53, 123, 145, 156, 166–67, 182–83, 220n9

Zulus (Everett), 79

www.ingramcontent.com/pod-product-compliance
Lightning Source LLC
Chambersburg PA
CBHW030301100426
42812CB00002B/522